Flavor It Greek!

A Celebration of Food, Faith and Family

Published by the members of
Philoptochos Society of Holy Trinity Greek Orthodox Church
Portland, Oregon

COOKBOOK AWARDS

Oxmoor House National Award, "America's Best Recipes"

National Tabasco Award, Regional Winner

1st Place National Philoptochos Fundraising Project of the Year

Included in "Best of the Best from Oregon:
Selected Recipes from Oregon's Favorite Cookbooks"

©1999 Philoptochos Society of Holy Trinity Greek Orthodox Church

3131 N.E. Glisan Street, Portland, Oregon 97232
(503) 234-0468   Fax (503) 236-8379   http://www.flavoritgreek.com

First Printing: October, 1999 5,000 copies
Second Printing: January, 2005 3,500 copies
Printed in U.S.A. All rights reserved

Library of Congress Catalog Card Number 99-90810
ISBN 0-9673935-0-7

Flavor It Greek!
A Celebration of Food, Faith and Family

is dedicated to

∼ our families who brought our food and
faith to Portland, Oregon;

∼ our parish priests who have guided us
through these many generations;

∼ our parishioners, community leaders and
Philoptochos members who preserved
our families and traditions;

∼ the greater Portland community for
supporting many Holy Trinity programs
and the annual Greek Festival.

For embracing our celebration of food, faith and family,
this is our gift to you.

Cookbook Chairs

Paula D. Diamond
Karen Henkhaus

Spriritual Guidance

Father James Retelas
Father Demetri Tsigas

Philoptochos Presidents

Georgia Liapes
Georgia Vareldzis

The Cookbook Committee

Ellen Belesiu
Mari Lou P. Diamond
Yianna Doherty
Anastasia Gianopoulos
Antigone Koukoumanos
Miriam Lendaris
Georgia Liapes

Mary Maletis
Katharine Melcher
Eleni Nicholson
Antoinette Papailiou
Pearl Pavlos
Lisa Psihogios
Helen Stratikos
Georgia Vareldzis

Production

Jack and Katherine Lockie

Art Director

Mari Lou P. Diamond

Editors

Demetra Ariston
Maria Boyer
Karen Henkhaus
Helen Stratikos

Design and Layout

Presvytera Eleni Tsigas
Christy Sutton

Illustrators

Frank and Victoria Colburn

Writers

Maria Boyer
Paula D. Diamond
Thomas Doulis

Legal Advisors

Greg Kavounas
Thomas J. Lekas

Printed by

Dynagraphics, Inc. Portland, Oregon USA

FLAVOR IT GREEK !

～A Word about Portland's Greek Community

*I*n the early 1900s, the first Greeks to arrive in Oregon came as bachelors to pay off family debts and earn dowry money for their sisters. According to the Census Report of 1910, they made up a migratory population of unmarried males numbering 200 in Portland in the summers, when most of the workers were out in the lumber camps or on railroad gangs, and 700 in the winters, when weather put an end to their work. That year they numbered 3,555 in Oregon and were scattered wherever their work had taken them. A few of the earliest immigrants were fishermen who settled in villages like Clifton that no longer exist along the Columbia River.

In 1907, Holy Trinity Greek Orthodox Church of Oregon was established. Fishing communities like Clifton and Astoria, whose fleets sailed as far north as Alaska, dedicated the entire catch for certain days to the church. Coffeehouses assessed their patrons. Section chiefs rode the hand-cars from section to section and from station to station to solicit money from the many Greeks working at various locations along the railroad. Workers in lumber camps, farms, and sawmills were not surprised when roving collectors stopped at their work sites, even during storms, and asked for their support.

A fine photograph exists of the ground-breaking ceremony that shows a large crowd, among which there are only two women. The deed of sale for a lot at Southeast 17th and Taggart Street is dated July 22, 1907; building commenced in the spring of 1908 and the church was completed in 1910.

A few of the early Greek immigrants to the United States married American women, but most married girls from their own or nearby villages. The Portland Greeks seem to be unique in that many married "picture brides," brought over by brothers, since the ratio of Greek men to Greek women was, to put it mildly, favorable. Besides, the distance between Portland and Greece is formidable, and, if the men owned their own businesses, which many did by this time, they hesitated to leave them in someone else's trust for the half year it would take to attend to everything.

Sometimes, when a marriage was agreed upon between partners who were separated by thousands of miles, the man made his decision on the basis of a photograph and comments made about the girl by her fellow villagers.

Obviously, the men who once considered themselves "birds of passage" had changed their minds about returning. With the arrival of the picture brides and sisters after the Great War, feast days began to be celebrated and fasts were observed in earnest. By that time, many Greeks had begun their own businesses, initially restaurants and taverns, but later branching out into other service industries. Although there were some professional men at the beginning, it was left for the subsequent generations to enter the fields of education, medicine, law and the sciences.

With the end of the Second World War and the return of the men and women from the armed forces, the community elders decided that a new church was necessary and purchased property on Northeast Glisan Street. The present Holy Trinity was completed in 1952, dedicated on September 7 of that year and consecrated on July 29, 1956. At that time, its "parish" was identified as "Oregon and Southern Washington." The Greek Community has since expanded to include two more churches, St. George's Greek Orthodox Church in Eugene and St. John the Baptist on the west side of Portland. The community includes third and fourth generations. Many are products of interfaith marriages and a remarkable number are converts from other faiths.

Almost all parishioners, regardless of their ethnic origins, work for the annual Greek Festival, founded in 1952 as the church bazaar. Holy Trinity was the first parish in the nation to establish a Greek Festival. A sizable proportion of the Festival proceeds goes to support local, national, and international philanthropic objectives.

~ *Thomas Doulis*
Community Historian
Emeritus Professor, Portland State University

~A Word about Philoptochos

*P*hiloptochos, established in 1931 by the late Patriarch Athenagoras I, means "Friend of the Poor" and is the philanthropic arm of the Archdiocese of the Greek Orthodox Church in America. Philoptochos is a non-profit, tax exempt organization which has earned the distinction of being the second largest philanthropic organization in the United States.

There are nine metropolises which comprise the national Philoptochos organization. The Holy Trinity Philoptochos is a part of the San Francisco Metropolis. On this level, Philoptochos serves as the liaison between the national organization and local chapters. Philoptochos is volunteer-driven and initiates or supports many church activities and charitable projects.

The Portland chapter is uniquely organized into a "circle" concept in order to enhance membership participation. Members may join any one of six smaller, more intimate circles. Monthly meetings promote fellowship and spiritual sharing through service projects and chapter activities. The full membership meets bi-annually to review and approve all Philoptochos programs.

The Philoptochos Society of Holy Trinity Greek Orthodox Church has been involved in philanthropic projects for over fifty years. One of the main on-going fundraising activities of the organization is the operation of Philo House, a volunteer-staffed thrift shop established in 1979. Proceeds support welfare and activities for senior citizens.

In 1995, the Holy Trinity Philoptochos initiated Kids 'N' Cancer: Camp Agape. This annual week-long camp, operating out of Camp Angelos on the Sandy River, provides children with cancer and their families a time to be together with meals, lodging and activities free of cost; all they have to do is enjoy each other.

Other current activities sponsored by the Portland, Oregon Chapter include providing support to the National Children's Cardiac Fund, The Salvation Army, Project Mexico, Ionian Village (a spiritual camp in Greece), the Hellenic College/Holy Cross Seminary, local Greek and Sunday School programs, the annual Greek Festival and annual academic scholarships to community youth.

The Philoptochos Society of Holy Trinity Greek Orthodox Church in Portland, Oregon embodies the principles of a Christian ministry while offering support, assistance and encouragement to all in need.

⁓Foreword

*O*ur world has been wonderfully seasoned and flavored by generations of food, faith and family – an undeniable and cherished reality of our Greek heritage.

What makes a certain place extraordinary? Since the beginning of time, mealtime has been the universal activity that transcends all languages and ethnic backgrounds. In Greek households, much of the closeness within our families is due to our culinary traditions. The combination of sights, sounds, smells and feelings surrounding meal preparation and presentation often transcends the common to the extraordinary. The "ethos" created by parents and relatives preparing a special dish with loving care and strong hands is stored in our memories as a "warm and fuzzy" place to visit often.

As we began the exciting task of creating a cookbook to record and preserve our Greek cooking traditions in Portland, Oregon, we quickly realized how food, faith and family are intertwined and fundamental to who we are as a community. Some of us were born here and are first generation Greeks; others are immigrants from the mainland or Greek islands; many of us came into the Greek community through marriage or by personal choice. Regardless of our backgrounds, light conversations among Greeks lead to discussions of our children or relatives, a food event, a restaurant or a meal and inevitably something to do with church – food, faith and family.

This cookbook has been a labor of love whose vision was born out of the desire to "capture" the essence of Greek cooking as we know it in the Portland area. Our mission was to record recipes, many of which originated with our ancestors. This legacy of treasured cooking traditions is our gift to our friends and family and generations to come – complete with personal notes from the recipe contributors.

The challenge for the cookbook committee was to translate family recipes that included ingredients listed as "a pinch" of this or "a wine-glass-full" of that. The process lasted twenty-four months during which time recipes were collected, edited, translated to English and reviewed again by the contributor. The results are a compilation of the common and uncommon appetizers, authentic main courses, delicious side dishes, robust vegetables and an enormous selection of exceptional sweets.

The Mediterranean diet found in the recipes of **Flavor It Greek!** wins praises for its abundant use of fruits and vegetables, fish, beans and olive oil. Cooks who flavor it Greek will discover an earlier generation's surprisingly simple recipes, rich in taste and made with the fresh ingredients of the season. Other recipes have varying degrees of complexity. Some require plenty of preparation time and may be pre-assembled. Don't be afraid to use your hands and fingers when preparing the breads and sweets. You will discover the art of Greek cooking and a "contentment to the soul" shared by many who love to cook.

Flavor It Greek! A Celebration of Food, Faith and Family also includes a section on Faith and Tradition. The vast majority of Greek people are of the Orthodox Christian Faith. Not only does Orthodoxy provide a powerful spiritual base, it has specific food traditions associated with the faith that enrich our liturgical lives such as the preparation of Prosphoro (bread used for Holy Communion), Artoklassia (bread blessed and shared with the parishioners) and the preparation of Koliva (boiled wheat prepared and shared in remembrance of a departed loved one). Look for ☦ indicating lenten dishes (food prepared without dairy or meat products and, in the case of a "strict" fast, without oil).

Try a traditional recipe for mayiritsa, a soup of "lamb innards", prepared to break the fast in the wee hours of Easter morning after the midnight church service. Learn about the traditional way to color Easter eggs. Read the Vassilopita recipes and discover how to be assured a year of good luck.

Welcome to our world – The world of Greek cooking in Portland, Oregon. **Flavor It Greek!**

Table of Contents

Mezethes

Contents

~ DIPS & SPREADS ~

~ HOT & COLD MEZETHES ~

ΤΖατΖίκι

Yogurt Garlic Dip
Tzatziki

1 (32-ounce) container plain yogurt
2 medium-sized cucumbers
1 head of garlic, or less, to taste
4 tablespoons extra virgin olive oil
3 tablespoons wine vinegar or lemon juice
1 teaspoon fresh or dried dill weed
Salt and pepper to taste
Fresh mint leaves, parsley sprigs and olives for garnish

Place yogurt in a large square of double cheesecloth or coffee
filter. Tie the cheesecloth at the top and let any excess liquid
drain. (Will take approximately 4 hours).

Peel cucumbers; remove seeds with a spoon. Grate, then
squeeze to drain excess liquid. Peel and mince garlic. In a
medium-sized bowl combine olive oil, vinegar, dill, salt and
pepper. Add cucumber, garlic and yogurt. Mix all ingredients
well. Refrigerate until ready to use. Serve in a bowl and garnish
with fresh mint, parsley and olives.

Note: Tzatziki is a fantastic dip for peppers, celery, broccoli,
crackers and even cucumbers. Also, it is the traditional sauce
for souvlakia and gyros. Keep refrigerated.

~Alexander
Theoharis

Serves: 6 to 8

One of the reasons my younger sister, Jaclyn,
and I like going to my father's village is to enjoy a
unique dip that my Yiayia Katerina makes.
Yiayia lives in the small village of Vournikas on the
island of Lefkas. She has her own sheep and makes
her yogurt from its milk. Yes, it's rich in calories, but
very tasty. Yiayia doesn't make any claim for the
health benefits, but Aunt Eleni says it's a refreshing
sauce and recommends it to the health-conscious.

Fish Roe Dip ☦
Taramosalata

1/2 cup fish roe
2 slices French bread, 3/4 inch thickness
1/4 cup lemon juice
2/3 cup olive oil, divided

Put 1/2 cup of roe in bowl of electric mixer. Take 2 slices of French bread and remove top crusts. Soak bread under tap and squeeze out water. Put the bread into the bowl with roe and beat at medium speed for 3 minutes. Pour in 1/3 of the oil and beat for 2 minutes at medium speed. Pour in 1/2 of the lemon juice and continue beating for 2 more minutes. Pour in 1/3 of the remaining olive oil and beat an additional 2 minutes. Pour in remaining lemon juice and beat 3 to 4 minutes until you have a firm but creamy consistency.

~Catherine
Lingas

Note: Fresh or bottled lemon juice may be used. The amount may vary according to desired tartness. The secret is the consistency of the bread - not too squishy, not too firm. Recipe can be used as a dip or spread on crackers or bread.

Yield: 1 1/2 cups of dip.

This recipe came from a cookbook I had in Kansas, which I have since lost, so I just kept it in my head for 30 years. It is the first time I've written it down.

Ταραμοσαλάτα

Fish Roe Dip ☦
Taramosalata

4 tablespoons fish roe (tarama)
6 slices bread, soaked in water and squeezed
Juice of 2 lemons
1/2 cup olive oil

In a mixer, combine roe and bread. Gradually beat in oil
and lemon juice until mixture appears smooth and creamy.

This may be used as a dip with potato chips or crackers,
or served with sliced French bread.

~Constantine
Deleganes

Αγκιναροσαλάτα

Artichoke Dip
Aginarosalata

2 (14-ounce) cans artichokes, drained and chopped
1 cup light mayonnaise
1 cup Parmesan cheese
Juice of 1 lemon
Garlic powder to taste
Parmesan cheese for topping

In a bowl, combine artichokes, mayonnaise, cheese, lemon
juice and garlic powder. Mix well and put in baking dish. Add
Parmesan on top and bake in a preheated 350 degree oven
25 to 30 minutes.

~ Helen
M. Lampus

Serve with crackers or breads.

Garlic Dip ☦
Skorthalia

5 cups dried French bread, crusts removed
1/2 cup garlic cloves, peeled and halved
1/3 cup white vinegar
1/2 teaspoon salt
1 1/2 cups vegetable oil

Soak bread in water. Squeeze excess water from bread and set aside. Put garlic, vinegar, salt and oil in a food processor. Blend until garlic is well chopped. Add bread and mix until smooth. Chill before serving. Serve with carrot sticks, fried eggplant and fried zucchini.

~Georgia
Belesiu

Note: Will keep in the refrigerator for 2 weeks. Can be frozen.

Yield: 5 cups.

"This recipe was given to me by my mother, Antonia Mahairas."

Σκορδαλιά με Ψωμί

Garlic Dip with a Bread Base ☦
Skorthalia me Psomi

6 to 7 slices dry bread, crusts removed
5 to 6 garlic cloves
2/3 cup olive oil
1/4 cup vinegar
Pinch of salt

~Maria
Garifalakis

Soak the bread in water, then squeeze the water out. Place all the ingredients in a blender or food processor and gradually blend just until smooth. Take care not to over mix to prevent oil from separating.

Eggplant Salad
Melitzanosalata

1 large eggplant
1 green onion
2 to 3 sprigs parsley, trim stems
Salt and pepper to taste
1/3 to 1/2 cup olive oil
2 tablespoons red wine vinegar, or adjust to taste
1 heaping tablespoon mayonnaise

Wash eggplant and pierce skin several times with a fork. Place
in a baking dish and bake in a preheated 350 degree oven about
1 hour and 15 minutes, or until skin looks dry and wrinkled.
(Turn over once in baking dish while baking.) Let cool.

Peel eggplant; remove seeds and put in food processor. Add
green onion, parsley and sprinkle with salt and pepper. Process
until onion and parsley are in very small pieces. Add the olive
oil and vinegar, adjusting the amounts for taste, and process.
Add mayonnaise and process until blended. Refrigerate
overnight for best flavor. Serve with freshly baked bread   ~Anna Stratis
as an appetizer or with a meal.

*This recipe was given to me by my
mother-in-law, Frantzeska Stratis, who
lives on the island of Andros in Greece.
It has become a favorite in our family.
It differs from other versions of
melitzanosalata as it does not
contain any garlic.*

Eggplant Salad
Melitzanosalata

5 large eggplants
2 cups plus 1/2 cup olive oil
2 garlic cloves, peeled
1 cup feta cheese
1 teaspoon salt
1 teaspoon ground pepper
1/4 teaspoon oregano
1 medium red onion, finely chopped
1 teaspoon fresh mint leaves, finely chopped

Line two 11x13 inch baking pans with parchment paper.

Wash the eggplant and slice lengthwise. Dip each piece
in olive oil. Place in a single layer in the prepared pans.
Bake about 1 hour in a preheated 375 degree oven.

In a blender or food processor combine the garlic, feta
cheese, salt, pepper, oregano, and 1/2 cup olive oil. Blend
until creamy.

Allow the cooked eggplants to cool slightly, then cut them
into very small pieces. Place in a large bowl and toss with
~ Anastasia   the above mixture. Add the red onion and mint and mix
Kondilis   well. Serve chilled.

Serves: 10

Feta Cheese Spread
Htipiti

4 ounces feta cheese, crumbled
1 tablespoon olive oil
1 teaspoon lemon juice
1 garlic clove
1/4 cup green onions, chopped
3 ounces sun-dried tomatoes
1/4 cup bottled roasted red peppers

Combine all ingredients in food processor. Blend well.
Serve with pita bread, crackers or crusty bread.

Serves: 10

~Paula
Dudunake
Diamond

*An easy, "new" Greek recipe, that makes
the perfect appetizer for any gathering.*

Hummus ☦

Houmous

1 (15-ounce) can garbanzo beans, reserve juice
1 1/4 tablespoons tahini
1/4 cup fresh lemon juice
1 large garlic clove
1/2 teaspoon salt
1 tablespoon olive oil

Heat beans over medium heat until they come to a boil.
Reserve juice. Put beans and next 4 ingredients in a food
processor or blender. Slowly add juice from beans (not all the
juice). Blend until creamy and very smooth. Place in a bowl
or a platter. Drizzle with olive oil. Serve with vegetables, pita
bread or crackers.

~Catherine
Diamond Owen

Hint: Taste to make sure there is enough garlic, lemon juice and
salt after ingredients are blended.

Yield: 1 1/2 cups.

My parents, Violet and Nicholas Diamond,
always served this dip when they entertained.
Hummus has now become very popular
in restaurants and stores.

Flaming Fried Cheese
Saganaki

4 to 5 ounces kefalotiri cheese
4 teaspoons olive oil
2 to 3 teaspoons Metaxa brandy
Freshly squeezed lemon juice

Cut kefalotiri cheese into thick slices. Heat olive oil or butter in frying pan. Fry cheese: brown slightly on one side and turn over to other side and brown (cheese should be soft when toothpick is inserted in the center). Remove from pan and place on heated plate. Flame it with brandy. Put out flame with fresh-squeezed lemon. Enjoy!

Serves: 4

~Demetri's
Mediterranean
Restaurant

Χταπόδι Ξυγδάτο

Octopus in Vinegar ✝
Htapothi Ksithato

Octopus, cut tentacles and remove ink sac
Olive oil to taste
Vinegar to taste

In a sauté pan, over medium-high heat, place octopus and cook until juices are absorbed. When almost dry, add some olive oil and continue to cook. Add vinegar and cook for another 10 minutes. When done, cut into bite-sized pieces.

Serves: 6 to 8

~Thanasi
Kosmas

Mussels with Ouzo ☦

Mithia me Ouzo

2 pounds mussels
3 garlic cloves, sliced
1 medium onion, chopped
3 tablespoons fresh parsley, chopped
1/2 cup olive oil
1/2 cup ouzo
Salt and pepper to taste

Wash mussels thoroughly. In a saucepan sauté garlic, onion and parsley in olive oil until onions are translucent. Add mussels and ouzo to the pan with the onion mixture and season with salt and pepper. Cover tightly. Bring to a boil and cook for 10 minutes.

~Voula
Bakouros Serve hot as an appetizer with toast, sourdough or French bread.

Marinated Shrimp ☦

Marinade:
2 garlic cloves, minced
1 tablespoon ground cumin
1 tablespoon ground coriander
1 teaspoon cardamom
1/2 to 1 teaspoon cayenne pepper
1 teaspoon pepper
4 scallions, minced (tops only)
1/4 cup fresh parsley, finely chopped
1 teaspoon salt
1 tablespoon lemon zest
1 cup olive oil
1 teaspoon fresh ginger, grated

3 pounds cooked medium shrimp
Lemon wedges
Fresh parsley sprigs

~Connie
Prekeges In a medium bowl, combine all ingredients for marinade. Rinse shrimp (leave shells on). Add to marinade. Chill for at least 4 hours. Garnish with lemon wedges and parsley sprigs.

Boiled Octopus ☦
Htapothi Vrasto

3 pounds octopus

Dressing:
3/4 cup olive oil
3 garlic cloves, chopped
4 to 5 tablespoons vinegar
4 tablespoons fresh parsley, chopped
Salt and pepper to taste

With a knife slit open the head of the octopus. Remove the ink sac and all of the internal organs. Remove the teeth from the bottom end and remove the eyes. Wash and clean the octopus making sure no sand remains.

Place octopus in a pot to boil. Do not add water or salt (the octopus will release its own juices). Cover and boil for one hour or until tender. If needed, add a small amount of water before octopus is done cooking. Drain octopus and allow to cool. Then cut the entire octopus into bite-sized pieces. Place octopus into a salad bowl and toss with remaining ingredients.

~Angeliki
Anasis

Serves: 12 to 15

Boiled octopus is usually served at room temperature as an appetizer.

Μανιτάρια Γεμιστά

Stuffed Mushrooms
Manitaria Yemista

1 tablespoon salt
1 tablespoon lemon juice
30 large mushrooms
1 tablespoon butter
1 tablespoon olive oil
2 tablespoons green onion, finely chopped
2 tablespoons white wine
Salt and pepper to taste
1 tablespoon fresh dill, chopped
2 tablespoons heavy cream
1 cup feta crumbled or kasseri cheese grated,
   or a combination of both
Parmesan cheese for topping

In a medium saucepan bring water with salt and lemon juice
to a boil. Blanch mushrooms. Drain and remove stems. Brush
mushrooms with melted butter. Place them top down in a
baking dish and set aside while preparing filling.

In a small skillet sauté onion lightly in olive oil. Add wine, salt
and pepper and allow to simmer gently until most of the liquid
has evaporated. Remove from heat; add dill, cream and cheese.
Mix well.

~Maria
Garifalakis

Stuff mushroom caps with mixture and sprinkle with Parmesan
cheese. Bake in a preheated 350 degree oven 10 minutes.

Zucchini Fritters
Kolokithokeftethes

2 pounds zucchini squash, grated
3 tablespoons olive oil
4 tablespoons onion, chopped
1 cup kefalotiri or mozzarella cheese, grated
1 cup dry breadcrumbs
2 eggs
2 tablespoons parsley, finely chopped
2 tablespoons fresh mint leaves, finely chopped
Salt and pepper to taste
Flour, for dusting
Oil, for frying

In a medium saucepan, boil grated zucchini in a small amount of water until tender. Place in a colander or sieve and drain excess water well. In a skillet over moderate heat, sauté the onion in the oil. Place the well-drained zucchini in a large bowl and purée with the back of a wooden spoon. Add the onion, cheese, breadcrumbs, eggs, parsley, mint, salt and pepper. Combine well. If mixture is not firm enough to form patties, add more breadcrumbs.

Let mixture set up a little in the refrigerator, then form into small patties. Dust with flour and fry in a generous amount of cooking oil until browned on both sides.

~Maria
Garifalakis

Eggplant and Feta Appetizers
Mezethes me Melitzana ke Feta

1 baguette-sized loaf French bread
1 eggplant
1 (6-ounce) jar roasted sweet red pepper-and-olive pesto
1/2 cup olive oil
1/2 pound feta cheese

Slice eggplant into 1/4-inch thick slices. Using a pastry brush, brush each side of eggplant with olive oil and broil until lightly browned. Slice bread into 1/2-inch slices. Broil until toasted on both sides.

With a knife, spread one side of each slice of bread with red pepper-and-olive pesto. Place a slice of the eggplant on each. At this point, you may refrigerate and reheat later. Before serving, thinly slice feta and place one slice on top of eggplant. Serve immediately.

~Diane
Kondos

Serves: 4 to 6

Kasseri Melt
Kasseropita

3 teaspoons lemon juice
1 flour tortilla
1 teaspoon oregano
1/2 cup kasseri cheese, grated
1/4 cup green pepper, diced

Rub lemon juice on tortilla. Sprinkle with oregano. Add 1/2 of the grated cheese and all of the green pepper. Fold tortilla in half and use remaining cheese on top. Place in microwave oven for 30 seconds or until cheese has melted. Slice into sections and serve.

~Constantine
N. Deleganes

Μελιτζάνες Τηγανιτές με Φέτα

Fried Eggplant Sandwiches
Melitzanes Tiganites me Feta

3 small eggplants, about 1/2 pound total weight, peeled and
   cut crosswise into slices 1/2-inch thick
Olive oil
Salt and freshly ground pepper to taste
6 ounces kasseri or Monterey Jack cheese, grated
6 ounces feta cheese, crumbled
3 eggs
2 tablespoons fresh flat-leafed (Italian) parsley, chopped
1 tablespoon fresh dill, chopped
1 cup flour
1 1/2 cups fine dried bread crumbs
Vegetable oil for deep frying

Place the eggplant slices on oiled baking sheets, then brush each
slice with olive oil. Sprinkle to taste with salt and pepper and
bake in a preheated 400 degree oven until almost cooked
through, about 15 minutes. Let cool.

In a bowl, combine the cheeses, one egg, parsley and dill. Place
a heaping spoonful of filling on half of each eggplant slice. Top
with second slice about the same size and press together. Put
the flour and bread crumbs in separate shallow bowls. Break the
remaining 2 eggs into another shallow bowl and beat lightly. Dip
the eggplant sandwiches first in the flour, then in the egg and
finally in the bread crumbs, coating evenly. Place on a rack or a
baking sheet lined with parchment paper. Let stand 1 hour. (Or
refrigerate overnight, but bring the eggplant sandwiches to room
temperature before frying.)

Pour oil into a deep sauté pan to a depth of 3 inches and heat to
375 degrees, or until a bit of bread dropped into the oil begins to
color within moments. When the oil is ready, slip in the sandwiches,
a few at a time, for about 2 minutes. Using a slotted spoon, lift
out the sandwiches and let them rest for 1 minute to melt the
cheese, then return them to the oil, top side down to fry until
golden, about 2 minutes longer. Using a slotted spoon remove
to paper towels to drain briefly and repeat with the remaining
sandwiches. Arrange on a warmed serving platter. Cut in half
and serve at once.

~Diane
Kondos

Serves: 4 to 6

*I serve these as an appetizer when I entertain
and my guests love them!*

Γαρίδες Γιουβέτσι

Shrimp with Feta Cheese
Garithes Youvetsi

1 1/2 pounds large shrimp or prawns, peeled and deveined
Salt and freshly ground pepper to taste plus 2 teaspoons pepper
1/2 cup olive oil, divided
1 yellow onion, chopped
1 bunch green onions, including tender green tops, minced
2 cloves garlic, finely minced
1 tablespoon dried oregano
3 tablespoons fresh basil, chopped or dill (optional)
4 fresh tomatoes, peeled, seeded and chopped or
   1 (14 1/2-ounce) can stewed tomatoes, drained
1 teaspoon honey or sugar
1/2 cup dry white wine
1/2 pound feta cheese, crumbled
5 tablespoons fresh flat-leaf (Italian) parsley, chopped

Sprinkle shrimp with salt and pepper. In a large sauté pan over high heat, warm 1/4 cup of the oil and sear shrimp quickly on both sides. Remove from the pan and set aside. May be done ahead and refrigerated.

In the same pan, over medium heat, place the remaining 1/4 cup oil and sauté the yellow onion until tender and translucent, 8 to 10 minutes. Add the green onions, garlic, oregano and the basil or dill, and cook 5 minutes longer. Add the tomatoes, honey or sugar and wine and simmer briskly to thicken the mixture, 8 to 10 minutes. Season with the 2 teaspoons pepper; do not add much salt as the feta will be salty.

Meanwhile, preheat oven to 400 degrees. Divide half of the tomato sauce among 4 ramekins. Divide the shrimp evenly among the ramekins. Spoon the remaining tomato sauce over each shrimp and top each portion with an equal amount of the cheese. Bake in a preheated 400 degree oven until the shrimp is cooked and the cheese melts, about 10 minutes. Serve hot, sprinkled with parsley.

~Diane
Kondos

Alternate method: cook the tomato sauce as directed. Return the seared shrimp to the tomato sauce; sprinkle the feta on top. Cover and simmer until the cheese melts, about 7 minutes.

Serves: 4 to 6

*I like to serve this dish as a starter –
just perfect to perk up everyone's taste buds.*

FLAVOR IT GREEK !

Cheese Triangles
Tiropites

1 (8-ounce) package cream cheese
1 pound cottage cheese
1 pound feta cheese
3 eggs

1 pound phyllo dough
2 cups (4 sticks) butter, melted

Combine cream cheese, cottage cheese and the feta. Add the eggs and mix well.

Cut phyllo sheets into long strips 3 inches wide. Place a damp towel over phyllo sheets to protect them from drying. Work with one strip at a time, brushing each with melted butter. Place 1 teaspoon of the cheese mixture near the bottom edge of each strip. Fold the corner up and to the left to form a triangle. Continue to fold the strip upward at right angles until you reach the end and have formed a small triangle. Continue this method until all the ingredients are used.

Place triangles on baking sheets and brush each with butter. Bake in a preheated 375 degree oven for 15 to 20 minutes until golden brown. Serve at once.

Note: These triangles may be prepared ahead of time, sealed and frozen. Bake when desired without defrosting.

~Virginia
Rozos

Yield: 40 pieces.

Spinach Pie "Fiesta"
Spanakopita Fiesta

3 (10-ounce) packages frozen chopped spinach
1/2 pound feta cheese, crumbled
1/2 pound small curd cottage cheese
1 bunch green onions, chopped
1 tablespoon dried mint
1/2 cup minced parsley
5 eggs, slightly beaten
Salt and pepper to taste
1 cup (2 sticks) butter, melted
1 package 12 flour tortillas

Drain frozen spinach well, pat dry and chop again. In a large bowl, mix together feta cheese, cottage cheese, green onions, mint, parsley, eggs, salt and pepper.

Butter one tortilla at a time. Spread mixture over half of the tortilla. Tightly roll and pinch ends to secure filling. Place folded side down on a greased baking sheet large enough to hold all the tortilla rolls without crowding. Butter tops generously with the melted butter and bake at 350 degrees for approximately 1 hour. Cool slightly before cutting into bite-size pieces, about 3/4 to 1 inch in diameter. Serve warm or at room temperature.

~ Katy
Vokos

Note: To serve as a side dish, cut rolls into thirds.

Yield: 60 pieces.

The idea for this appetizer came from my Koumbara and friend, Gloria Papadimos.

Meat Rolls
Kreatopitakia

1/4 cup (1/2 stick) unsalted butter
1 pound lean ground beef or lamb, or 1/2 pound of each
1 medium onion, peeled and grated
1/2 cup pine nuts
1 teaspoon salt
1/4 teaspoon ground black pepper
1/2 teaspoon ground allspice
1 egg, beaten
1/2 cup sherry or white wine
1 cup Parmesan cheese, grated
2 tablespoons tomato paste

1 pound phyllo dough
1 pound unsalted butter, melted and clarified

In a large skillet melt 1/2 stick butter. Sauté the meat, onion and pine nuts, about 5 minutes. Add remaining ingredients, except phyllo and remaining butter. Stir over moderate heat 10 to 15 minutes, until most of the liquid is absorbed.

Cut phyllo sheets in quarters, lengthwise. Using one sheet at a time, brush each layer generously with butter. Place a spoonful of the meat filling at one end about 1/2-inch from the end. Fold sides in and roll up, jelly roll fashion, to the other end. Brush surface with butter and place on ungreased baking sheet (can be frozen at this point). Bake in a preheated 375 degree oven for 20 to 25 minutes.

Note: If baking frozen, heat oven to 350 degrees and bake slightly longer until nicely browned.

~Georgia Vareldzis

Yield: 70 to 90 pieces.

These rolls make wonderful hot hors d'oeuvres. Work with a pound of phyllo dough at a time and freeze them in layers in a plastic container with waxed paper between each layer. They can be baked frozen in large batches or a few at a time as needed.

Spinach Balls
Spanakokeftethes

3 (10-ounce) packages frozen chopped spinach
3 eggs
3 tablespoons butter
1 large onion, minced
1 cup kasseri cheese, grated
1/2 cup feta cheese, crumbled
1/2 cup fresh dill, minced
Salt and pepper to taste
1/2 pound kasseri cheese, cut into 1/2-inch cubes
1 cup bread crumbs
Olive oil for frying

Defrost and drain the frozen spinach in a colander. When completely defrosted, squeeze out all excess water. Mix all ingredients together except bread crumbs, oil and the cubes of kasseri cheese.

~Evangelos
Fasilis
Take one tablespoon of the spinach mixture and pat it flat. Place a cube of kasseri cheese in the middle and form into a ball. Roll in bread crumbs and deep fry in hot oil until golden brown. Drain on paper towels. Serve warm or cold.

Yield: approximately 24 balls.

Grapevine Leaves Stuffed with Rice ✝
Dolmathes Yialadzi

1 (16-ounce) jar grape leaves
2 cups long-grain rice
1 cup fresh parsley, finely chopped
1 tablespoon fresh dill, finely chopped or 3/4 teaspoon, dried
1 large onion, finely chopped
5 garlic cloves, finely chopped
Salt and freshly ground pepper to taste

1/4 cup extra virgin olive oil
1/4 cup lemon juice
3 cups warm water

Juice of 1 lemon
Lemon slices and parsley for garnish, if desired

Drain the grape leaves in a colander. Cut off the stems and wash in cold water to remove the brine taste. Set aside to drain. In a bowl combine the rice, parsley, dill, onion, garlic, salt and pepper.

On a working surface, place a grape leaf with the veins up; cut stems. Spoon a heaping tablespoon of the filling into the center. First fold the left side and then the right side over the filling and roll tightly to form a cylinder. If the leaf is very small, place another small leaf overlapping the first one to form a larger area to contain the filling and to secure it better when folded. Arrange dolmathes tightly in a baking dish in rows and layers.

Heat the olive oil, lemon juice and water and bring to a boil in a saucepan. Pour over the dolmathes. Cover the top of the dolmathes with grape leaves. Then cover the dish with its cover or aluminum foil and place on the lower rack of the oven. Bake in a preheated 375 degree oven for approximately 45 minutes or until the rice is tender. Remove from the oven and drain excess water. Transfer the dolmathes to a serving platter. Squeeze the juice of 1 lemon over them and garnish with slices of lemon and parsley. Serve hot or cold.

Note: To serve cold, uncover and let stand for 10 minutes. Then cover and put in the refrigerator. When cooled, cover with plastic wrap to keep the leaves from drying.

~ George
Papas

Yield: 60

Zesty Feta Cheese Appetizer
Mezes me Feta Pikantikos

1 block feta cheese, about 3 x 3 x 1¹/2-inches,
    rinsed and left in block form
1 to 2 garlic cloves, minced, for each block of cheese
¹/2 teaspoon dried oregano (approximately)
    per block of cheese
¹/4 teaspoon dried red pepper flakes (approximately)
    per block of cheese
12 Black peppercorns (approximately) per block of cheese
Olive oil to cover

Rinse the feta cheese and place on a serving plate. Then, in
the order listed, sprinkle the spices over the cheese. Be sure
to allow some of the spices to spill over onto the plate. Pour
enough olive oil over to cover, but not saturate. The oil will be
absorbed by the cheese over time and may be refreshed after
a day, if necessary.

This appetizer lasts for at least a week with the flavors becoming
more intense as time passes. The marinade is also delicious
~Rhonda   over black and green olives and makes a lovely compliment
Gadinas   to the cheese.

Serves: 6 to 8 people per block of cheese.

*This appetizer is so delicious and looks terrific
when served with a sliced baguette or plain crackers.
Best of all, it could not be easier to prepare.
Allow a couple of hours for the flavors to
blend before serving.*

Breads

Contents

Greek Corn Bread
Bobota

2 cups yellow cornmeal
3 cups flour
1 cup sugar
5 teaspoons baking powder
1 cup vegetable oil
1 cup milk
1 1/2 cups cold water

Cinnamon and sugar mixed together for topping

Sift all the dry ingredients together into a large mixing bowl.
Pour in the oil and milk. Stir by hand and then begin adding
the water gradually. The mixture should become the consistency
of a "semi-liquid." Pour the batter into a greased 9 x 13 inch
baking pan. Sprinkle cinnamon sugar mixture lightly over the
top. Bake for 35 minutes in a preheated 350 degree oven.

Serve with honey for a delicious morning treat. To reheat,
pieces can be placed in the microwave for 10 to 15 seconds.

~Georgia
Liapes

Optional: Add 1/4 cup nuts and/or 1/4 cup raisins to the mixture
prior to baking.

*This was a favorite recipe from my father's
home town of Nestani and has been
a special recipe in
our family.*

Georgia's Bread
Psomi tis Yeoryias

2 cups milk
2 cups water
1/2 cup (1 stick) butter
1/2 cup (1 stick) margarine
1 cup sugar
1 1/2 teaspoon salt
3 eggs, slightly beaten
1/4 pound yeast cake (from bakery)
4 1/4 pounds all purpose flour
1 egg, beaten, for top
Sesame seeds

In a large pan over very low heat combine first six ingredients.
Melt, blending all ingredients at 90 to 100 degrees (use a candy
thermometer). Add the eggs, then add the yeast cake; crumble
and dissolve.

In a separate bowl measure the flour. Slowly add the liquid
mixture until well blended. Knead at least 15 minutes. Cover
with heavy towels and allow to rise to twice its size. (Be sure
you put the bowl covered with towels in a warm spot.) Punch
down and let rise again.

Put 1 to 1 1/4 pounds of dough in each greased loaf pan (makes
about 8 pans) and let rise again. Brush tops with beaten egg
and sprinkle with sesame seeds. Bake 30 to 35 minutes in a
preheated 350 degree oven.

~Georgia
Maletis Miller

Yield: 8 pans.

*My mother's recipe,
a favorite of mine.*

Yiayia's Skillet Pies
Tiganopites tis Yiayias

3 cups flour
4 tablespoons vegetable oil
1 egg, beaten
3/4 cup water (medium to hot)
1/4 teaspoon salt
1 quart vegetable oil
2 cups Parmesan cheese, grated
Feta cheese, crumbled (optional)

Place flour in a large mixing bowl. Add oil, egg, water and salt
and mix together. Knead well until mixture can be formed into
a ball without crumbling. Divide dough into pieces (size depends
on how big you want each tiganopita. An 8 inch diameter and
1/8 inch thickness is average). With a rolling pin, roll out each
piece as if making a pie crust. Dust with flour to facilitate
rolling. Place each tiganopita on a clean, floured surface until
all the dough has been rolled into pites.

Using a large skillet, cover the bottom with enough oil so that
each pita floats while frying. Fry each pita separately until
lightly browned on each side, turning only once. Remove from
the oil with a fork and place on a platter. Sprinkle generously
with grated Parmesan cheese. Stack each one on top of the
other until all pites have been fried. To serve, fold each pita
in half twice or enjoy open face as is. Add feta if desired.

~Mari Lou
Psihogios
Diamond

Serves: 8

*This recipe comes from my Yiayia Thomas who
brought it with her from Samos, Greece.
We love these especially in the summer
served with a fresh salad.
They look like a soft taco, only crunchier.*

Ψωμί της Γιαγιάς

Yiayia's Bread
Psomi tis Yiayias

1 quart milk (use 1 percent milk)
1 cup sugar
1/2 cup (1 stick) butter
3 tablespoons vegetable shortening
3 packages rapid-rise yeast
9 cups flour
5 large eggs
1 tablespoon vanilla flavoring
1 tablespoon anise flavoring (or more to taste)

Glaze: (optional)
1 egg yolk, beaten
1/2 can (about 3 ounces) evaporated canned milk
Sesame seeds

In a saucepan over medium heat, combine milk, sugar, butter and vegetable shortening until warm, then set aside. Combine yeast and flour in a large bowl (all the ingredients will end up in this bowl to rise before baking). Add milk mixture and the rest of the ingredients to this bowl. Knead dough and allow to rise for 1 hour. Knead again and allow to rise for another hour. Divide dough and place into 5 or 6 loaf pans or 3 (8-inch) round cake pans. Let the bread rise again in the pans for at least another 45 minutes.

If desired, prepare glaze by combining 1 beaten egg yolk, the evaporated milk and brush on top of bread with a pastry brush. Sprinkle with sesame seeds. Bake in a preheated 350 degree oven until golden brown, about 30 to 35 minutes (baking time will vary, depending on the oven).

Jo Anne Mouskondis Finicle

Yield: 5 to 6 bread pan loaves or 3 (8-inch) round pan loaves.

Bread ☦

Psomi

4 cups lukewarm water
2¹/₂ tablespoons yeast
1¹/₂ to 2 tablespoons salt
¹/₂ to ³/₄ cup olive oil
¹/₄ teaspoon sugar

4 to 5 pounds flour (approximately)

In a bowl dissolve yeast in 2 cups water. Add enough flour to make a batter that is the consistency of pancake batter. Cover and let rise in a warm place 30 to 60 minutes. Put some flour into a pan and form a well in the center. Gradually add yeast mixture and the 4 cups lukewarm water along with the salt and sugar. Mix well and add enough flour to make a sponge-like dough while adding oil to hands to prevent dough from sticking. Knead about 15 minutes. Cover and let rise in a warm place 1 to 2 hours. Punch down. Place in 4 or 5 buttered loaf pans, cover and let rise again. Bake in a preheated 375 degree oven for about 15 to 20 minutes.

Variation: Pitted olives may be added to dough.

~Dina
Lazarithis

Sweet Bread
Gliko Psomi

1 cup (2 sticks) butter, room temperature
5 pounds flour
3 cakes yeast
5 cups sugar
2 teaspoons salt
7 eggs, beaten
1 quart milk, warmed

1 egg yolk, beaten and diluted with milk for top
Sesame seeds

In a bowl blend by hand the butter into the flour. Thoroughly mix yeast into flour mixture, then add sugar, salt and eggs. Slowly pour the milk into the dough and knead well. Cover; set in a warm place to rise overnight.

Knead again, then form into an 8 inch round pan. Cover and allow it to rise once again. Brush the top of the bread with the egg yolk mixture. Sprinkle sesame seeds lightly over the loaves. Bake in a preheated 300 degree oven for one hour.

~Evanthia
Liapes

Yield: 5 loaves.

This is the bread recipe that
I prepared for the pastry booth in
the early years of the church bazaar.

Fried Yeast Rolls
Tiganopsoma

2 cups milk, lukewarm
1 teaspoon sugar
1/2 teaspoon salt
2 packages yeast, rapid rise
3 1/2 cups flour
1 cup canola oil

Honey
Cinnamon

In a saucepan, heat milk to warm; add yeast, salt and sugar. Pour into a bowl. Gradually add flour, stirring with a wooden spoon. The dough should be slightly sticky. Knead for five minutes with the spoon. Cover and leave overnight.

Next morning, pour oil in frying pan. Heat oil until it sizzles. Take a handful of dough in floured hand and flatten on a floured board. Cut in pieces. Stretch pieces in your hand and carefully drop into the hot oil. As soon as dough bubbles and is lightly browned, turn over and cook for same amount of time. Drain on paper towels.

Serve with hot honey and cinnamon.

—Anastasia Dussin (submitted by Mary Maletis, Mrs. Dussin's Goddaughter)

I fondly remember this recipe, for this was the recipe my nouna always made for me whenever I visited her.

Village Bread †
Horiatiko Psomi

2 packages yeast
6 cups unbleached flour
1 teaspoon salt
2 cups warm water
1 tablespoon oil

Sesame seeds (optional)

In a large, wide bowl, mix the yeast and the flour. Dissolve the salt in a cup of water. Add liquid to bowl. Begin to knead mixture with knuckles, working to mix the flour and water completely. Knead until all the dry spots on the surface of the dough disappear and all the dough sticking to the bowl is worked in. Add a slight sprinkling of flour to the bowl only when it starts to stick again as you work. When the dough appears to have achieved a uniform texture, check it by slicing into it with a sharp knife to expose the inside. There should be no holes. The dough will be stiff and dense.

Soften the dough by working in more warm water, about 2 tablespoons at a time, up to about 1/4 cup. Knead briefly. Add the oil to the bottom of the bowl. Knead this in also.

When the dough is soft, pliant and responsive, turn it out onto a lightly floured surface and knead with the heel of the hand, folding and turning the dough for as long as you like. The surface will start to look a little bubbly.

~ *Georgia Katchis (as recorded by her daughter Maria K. Boyer)*

Spray or lightly grease two loaf pans. Sprinkle them lightly with sesame seeds. Divide dough in half. Shape each into an oval to fit the length of the pans. Place them in the pans and press out to fill out the bottom of the pans. Cover loosely with plastic wrap. Cover with blankets on a bed (or other warm place) and let rise. The best rise is achieved when the top of the loaf seems to be tearing away from the bottom. Only one rise is necessary. Bake in a preheated 300 degree oven about one hour or until a golden brown color is achieved and a hollow sound is produced when the surface is tapped.

Yield: 2 loaves.

Soups
&
Salads

Contents

∼ SOUPS ∼

∼ SALADS ∼

Σούπα Καρότου με Άνηθο

Carrot Soup with Dill
Soupa Karotou me Anitho

2 tablespoons butter
2 onions, thinly sliced
2 pounds carrots, peeled and sliced
6½ cups or more chicken stock
2 tablespoons rice
2 tablespoons fresh dill, chopped
Salt and pepper to taste

Melt the butter in a large, heavy duty saucepan over medium-high heat. Add onions and sauté about 5 minutes until translucent. Stir in carrots. Add the chicken stock and rice. Bring to a boil. Reduce heat and simmer on low uncovered until vegetables are tender (about 35 minutes). Cool slightly.

Working in batches, purée soup in blender or processor. Return to saucepan. Stir in more stock, if desired. Simmer again. Stir in dill. Season with salt and pepper and serve immediately.

~Betty
Phoutrides

Egg-Lemon Soup
Soupa Avgolemono

1 whole chicken
12 cups water
1 small onion, sliced
1 cup rice
3 egg yolks
Juice of 2 lemons, freshly squeezed
2 teaspoons salt

Wash the chicken well. Put chicken, onion and water in stock pot and bring to a boil. Cook for 1 1/2 hours over medium heat or until chicken is done. Remove chicken. (Keep warm if adding to the soup or refrigerate for another time.)

Strain broth into another stock pot. There should be around 8 cups of broth. If not, supplement with water. Bring to a boil and add rice. Cook over medium-low heat (still boiling) until rice is done.

~ Georgia
Belesin

In a medium bowl, beat the egg yolks with 2 tablespoons water with a wire whisk. Add lemon juice, beating constantly. Gradually add some of the broth to the egg-lemon mixture. Remove pot with the broth and rice from heat source and whisk eggs into broth until well mixed. Return to stove and bring to a boil, stirring constantly. Add chicken pieces to the soup, if desired.

A favorite of my grandchildren
Nick, Athan, Thomas
and Matthew.

Σούπα Αυγολέμονο Γρήγορη

Fast Track Egg-Lemon Soup
Soupa Avgolemono Grigori

1 can chicken rice soup
2 eggs, separated
Juice of 1 lemon
Salt and pepper taste

In a saucepan, heat the soup over low or medium heat. In a bowl, beat egg whites until very stiff. Pour stock from chicken rice soup into stiff egg whites while still beating. Blend or stir in yolks and lemon juice and continue to beat. Return this combination to soup pot and warm. Do not use high heat or let boil, as mixture will curdle. Season with salt and pepper.

Serves: 2 to 3

~Konstantina Goritsan. From Konstantina's Kitchen to Sophie Sly's Kitchen

A saying: "No fuss, no muss, no bother." A recipe when you're out of time and you feel like hot soup!

Σούπα με Μανιτάρια και Κριθάρι

Mushroom Barley Soup ☦
Soupa me Manitaria ke Krithari

3/4 cup barley
8 cups water
2 tablespoons oil
1 cup onions, chopped
2 garlic cloves, minced
1 pound mushrooms, sliced
1/4 cup sherry
1/4 cup "lite" soy sauce
1 teaspoon salt
1 teaspoon pepper

Cook barley in water 45 minutes. In a sauté pan, cook onions and garlic in 2 tablespoons oil until tender. Add mushrooms. Add this mixture to the barley along with the sherry and soy sauce. Simmer another 20 minutes covered over low heat. Taste to correct the seasoning.

~Georgia Maletis Miller

A CELEBRATION OF FOOD, FAITH & FAMILY

Lentil Soup ☦
Fakes Soupa

4 tablespoons olive oil
1 carrot, chopped
1 stalk celery, diced
2 garlic cloves, crushed
1 onion, chopped
1 1/2 cups lentils, washed
5 cups water
1/2 cup tomato sauce
Dash of red wine vinegar
1 teaspoon salt
1/4 teaspoon pepper

Mari Lou
Psihogios
Diamond

Sauté carrots, celery, garlic and onions in oil in a large pot. Add remaining ingredients. Bring to a boil. Reduce heat and simmer for approximately 1 hour.

Serves: 4

A Diamond family favorite.

Φακές Σούπα

Cook's Lentil Soup ☦
Fakes Soupa

2 large onions
1/4 cup olive oil
4 garlic cloves, minced
6 ribs celery, chopped
3 carrots, chopped
1 teaspoon pepper
1/2 teaspoon thyme
2 bay leaves
2 1/2 quarts water (may substitute any broth
    for part or all of the water)
3 cups diced tomatoes
2 cups lentils, washed
1/2 cup dry sherry (optional)
Salt to taste, after cooking
1 teaspoon curry (optional), after cooking

In a large stockpot, over medium-high heat, sauté onion in oil
until tender. Add garlic, celery, and carrots. Reduce heat and
continue cooking about 10 minutes. Add all other ingredients.
Bring to a boil, reduce heat and simmer about 1 1/2 to 2 hours
until lentils are cooked. May be served with rice.

~Diane Cook

Serves: 8

*A new twist to an old favorite,
from a café in Mt. Shasta, California!
When I started making this lentil soup,
I put an end to my husband Bob saying,
"lentils again"?*

Φασουλάδα του Παππού Δήμα

Papou Demas' Bean Soup ☦
Fassoulatha tou Papou Thima

2 cups small white beans
1 teaspoon baking soda
1 onion, chopped
4 carrots, chopped
2 stalks celery, chopped
1 garlic clove, chopped
3 tablespoons olive oil
Salt and pepper to taste
1 (3-ounce) can tomato sauce
Oregano to taste

Soak beans overnight in water and baking soda. Make sure water covers beans by about 2 inches. In a stockpot, cook onion, carrots, celery and garlic in olive oil for 15 minutes. Add salt and pepper. Drain beans and add to sautéed vegetables. Braise for 15 minutes. Add tomato sauce and stir. Add 3 cups hot water. Bring to boil, then simmer for 1 hour. Add small amount of oregano. Simmer 15 minutes or longer until beans are tender.

~Recorded by Aristides Phoutrides

Serves: 8

Ψαρόσουπα

Fish Soup ☦
Psarosoupa

9 cups water
2 small onions, sliced
10 small potatoes, peeled and cut in half
5 small carrots, cut into 2 inch pieces
2 celery stalks, cut into 2 inch pieces
1/4 cup olive oil
Salt and pepper to taste
3 pounds white fish or codfish
1/2 cup fresh lemon juice
Fresh parsley, chopped

In a medium size stockpot combine water, vegetables, oil, salt and pepper. Cook until vegetables are half done. Add fish and cook until done. Add lemon juice. Sprinkle with chopped parsley before serving.

~Georgia Belesin

Serves: 6

White Bean Soup ✝
Fassolatha

1 pound navy beans
2 tablespoons oil
1 medium onion, chopped
1 cup celery, sliced
1 cup carrots, sliced
2 to 3 bay leaves
1 pinch dried rosemary
1 teaspoon flour (optional)
1/3 cup lemon juice

Clean and wash beans. Put into a stockpot and add enough water to cover the beans completely. Boil for about 5 minutes. Drain water and cover beans with fresh water (about 11 cups). Add oil, onions, bay leaves, rosemary, celery and carrots. Cook over medium heat for about 1 hour or until the beans are soft. Add lemon juice and flour. Salt and pepper to taste.

~Roula
Tsirimiagos

Note: The flour and lemon juice is for creamier texture and lemony taste.

My mother's favorite recipe.

Greek Lima Bean Soup
Fassolatha

1 pound dry lima beans
1 large onion, chopped
Several garlic cloves, chopped
Olive oil
1 (6-ounce) can tomato sauce
2 bay leaves
Salt and pepper to taste
1 meaty hambone

Pick over beans for rocks. Wash the beans and soak them in
water overnight, drain and reserve the water. In a large stockpot
braise the onion and garlic in olive oil until brown. Stir in beans,
tomato sauce, bay leaves, salt and pepper. Add the reserved
water to cover the beans. Add hambone. Cover and simmer
on medium heat until tender. For a thicker casserole, remove
lid the last half hour of cooking. Remove hambone. Cut ham
into chunks and add to beans.

Note: For vegetarian version omit hambone. Can be prepared
in a crockpot for slow cooking method (10 hours on low).

Serves: 8

~Kathryn
Leventis
Molesa

Christina Economus brought this recipe
to America in 1908 from
Vlahorafti, Greece, near Tripoli.
This recipe of my grandmother's has been
handed down for many generations.

Armenian Ravioli Soup
Manti

6 cups flour
1 teaspoon salt
3 eggs, slightly beaten
3 tablespoons vegetable shortening
1 1/2 cups boiling water

Filling:
2 pounds lean ground beef
1 large onion, grated
1/2 bunch fresh parsley, chopped (optional)
Salt and pepper to taste

1 cup vegetable shortening, melted and kept warm

Broth:
8 to 10 cups chicken broth
Yogurt (condiment)
Sumac powder (condiment)
Garlic powder (condiment)

In a bowl, combine ground beef, onion and parsley. Add salt and pepper to taste; cover and refrigerate until ready to use.

In a large mixing bowl, place the flour and make a well in the center. Add eggs, water, melted vegetable shortening and salt. Mix together with a fork. Knead the dough and form into a ball. If the dough is sticky, work in some more flour. The dough is ready when the texture is smooth and shiny and has an elastic consistency. Divide the dough into 4 balls; cover and set aside for half an hour.

Place one of the balls onto a floured surface and begin by flattening with the palm of your hand. With a long and narrow rolling pin, roll out until dough is about 1/8 inch thin round. If at any time the dough is sticky, sprinkle flour with a shaker and continue to roll.

With a sharp knife, cut the dough into 2-inch squares, by first cutting vertically and then horizontally.

To prepare the ravioli (small bow ties that resemble boats), place a dab of the filling on each 1 1/2 inch square and pinch corners together, shaping like a bow tie or canoe. Do not overfill and work quickly as the dough will dry out. This stage is more successful when several people are working side by side. If necessary, dip hands in flour to seal ends.

In a very well greased round baking pan with a 2-inch lip, place ravioli close together touching one another, open side up to form a beautiful circular pattern. When all the balls of dough are complete and placed in a baking pan, pour melted vegetable shortening over the top (covering the ravioli completely but not soaking in shortening). Bake in a preheated 375 degree oven until golden brown and crispy. (At this point you can freeze the ravioli in an air-tight container for future use.)

To prepare broth, in a large stockpot, bring the chicken broth to a boil. Add the mantis and cook for approximately five minutes. Serve hot in a wide mouthed soup bowl. Serve with a dollop of yogurt, sumac powder and garlic powder to taste.

~Arminé Megurian, submitted by Karen Henkhaus

Serves: 10 to 12

This is a very old Armenian recipe which is familiar to many Greeks whose background is from the Asia Minor region. If you haven't tasted this soup before, you may be tempted to experiment. Traditionally prepared for a family gathering.

Λαχανοσαλάτα

Cabbage Salad ☦
Lahanosalata

1/2 head cabbage, shredded
2 garlic cloves, thinly sliced
1/2 cup olive oil
1/4 cup fresh lemon juice or vinegar
Salt and pepper to taste

Place shredded cabbage in a serving bowl. Add garlic. Mix together the olive oil and lemon juice or vinegar and pour over cabbage. Add salt and pepper. Mix well and serve.

~Antoinette
Belesiu Papailiou

Note: For another version, you may add 1/2 cup crumbled feta cheese and 1 tablespoon fresh, finely chopped oregano.

Serves: 6

Χωριάτικη Σαλάτα

Greek Village Salad
Horiatiki Salata

3 fresh tomatoes, cut into chunks
2 cucumbers, cut into chunks
1/2 red onion, sliced
1/4 pound feta cheese (cut into size of small sugar cubes)
1/4 pound Kalamata olives
1/2 cup extra-virgin olive oil (Greek)
1/2 cup red wine vinegar
Oregano
Pepper

~Demetri's
Mediterranean
Restaurant

Combine ingredients. Sprinkle with fresh oregano and dash of black pepper.

Serves: 4 to 6

Beet Salad ✟
Padzaria Salata

2 pounds small beets, remove greens and roots
1/2 cup olive oil
1/4 cup vinegar
2 garlic cloves, thinly sliced
Salt to taste

Rinse beets well to remove sand. In a large pot over medium-high heat cover beets with water and bring to a boil. Cover and reduce heat and simmer until tender. In a colander drain beets and rinse under cold water. While rinsing peel beets by rubbing skin off.

Slice beets and put into a bowl. Add olive oil, vinegar, garlic and salt. Gently toss and serve at room temperature.

Note: May be prepared in advance and refrigerated.

Serves: 6

~Antoinette
Belesin Papailiou

Μελιτζανοσαλάτα

Eggplant Salad ☦
Melitzanosalata

3 large eggplants
2 garlic cloves, chopped
2 to 3 tablespons fresh parsley, chopped
Salt and pepper to taste
1/3 cup olive oil
Lemon juice to taste

Wash the eggplants and make lengthwise incisions 1 1/2 inches apart and 1 1/2 to 2 inches deep leaving at least 1/2 inch on both ends uncut. Sprinkle salt into the cuts and place in a pan. Bake at 350 degrees until soft.

~ Angeliki
Anasis

Cool and cut eggplants into pieces. Place in a salad bowl. Add chopped garlic, parsley, salt, pepper, oil and lemon to taste.

Serves: 4 to 5

Πατατοσαλάτα

Greek Potato Salad ☦
Patatosalata

2 pounds small potatoes
1 bunch green onions, chopped
2 garlic cloves, chopped
2 tablespoons fresh parsley, chopped
1 tablespoon fresh dill, chopped
1/2 cup olive oil
2 tablespoons white vinegar
Salt and pepper to taste

Boil potatoes in their skins in a stock pot until tender. Cool. Remove the skins and cut the potatoes into small cubes. Add

~ Georgia
Belesin

onions, garlic, parsley, dill, oil, vinegar, salt and pepper. Toss gently. Serve at room temperature.

Village Salad
Horiatiki Salata

2 large tomatoes, cut in wedges
1 green pepper, cut into rings
1 cucumber, sliced
1 red onion, sliced into rings

Dressing:
1/4 cup olive oil
1 1/2 tablespoons red wine vinegar
1 teaspoon oregano, dried
Salt and pepper to taste

1/4 pound feta cheese, cut in squares or crumbled
1/2 cup Kalamata olives
Oregano to taste

Place ingredients in a bowl. Make dressing by whisking together the olive oil, red wine vinegar, oregano, salt and pepper. Pour dressing over salad.

Garnish with the feta cheese, olives and sprinkle with more oregano.

Serves: 4

~Helen
Kallimanis
Buhler

A classic Greek summer salad.

Village Salad
Horiatiki Salata

4 large tomatoes
2 medium cucumbers
1/4 cup feta cheese, crumbled
1/2 cup Kalamata olives
1 large sweet yellow onion
3 leaves fresh mint

Dressing:
1/2 cup olive oil
1/4 cup red wine vinegar
Pinch each of Greek oregano and parsley (fresh or dried)
1 garlic clove, crushed
1/2 teaspoon salt
Pinch of pepper

~Chryssi
Diamond

Chop all vegetables. Place in bowl. Mix dressing, pour over vegetables and combine.

Serves: 4

My favorite summer salad made with fresh tomatoes from our garden that I help water.

Μαρουλοσαλάτα

Romaine Lettuce Salad
Maroulosalata

1 large head romaine lettuce
4 green onions, chopped
2 tablespoons fresh dill, chopped (optional)
4 to 5 tablespoons olive oil
2 to 3 tablespoons freshly squeezed lemon juice
Salt and pepper to taste

Wash the lettuce well and drain. Cut the leaves fine with a sharp knife in very thin strips. Place the lettuce in a bowl. Chop the green onions and the fresh dill, and add them to the lettuce. Just before serving, toss the salad with the olive oil, lemon juice, salt and pepper.

Note: Vinegar may be substituted for the fresh lemon juice.

~Petroula
Konkoumanos

Serves: 3 to 4

Πατάτες και Μελιτζάνες Σαλάτα

Potato and Eggplant Salad ☦
Patates ke Melitzanes Salata

2 eggplants
4 large potatoes
2 garlic cloves, chopped
2 to 3 green onions, chopped
Olive oil
Freshly squeezed lemon juice to taste
Fresh parsley, chopped
Oregano to taste
Salt and pepper to taste

Olives and parsley sprigs for garnish

Wash eggplants. Cut incisions lengthwise 1 1/2 inches apart and 1 1/2 to 2 inches deep, leaving at least 1/2 inch on both ends uncut. Sprinkle salt in the cuts and place in a baking pan.

Wash and scrub the potatoes. Pierce each potato with a fork 3 to 4 times and place into the same pan with the eggplants. Bake in a preheated 350 degree oven until soft.

~Angeliki Anasis

Remove cooked eggplants and potatoes. Cut into pieces and place in a salad bowl. Add all the other ingredients and toss lightly. Garnish with olives and parsley sprigs.

Serves: 4 to 6

Vegetable Dishes

Contents

Κολοκυθοκεφτέδες

Zucchini Patties
Kolokithokeftethes

2 to 3 medium zucchini, grated
1/4 cup fresh parsley, finely chopped
1/4 cup fresh mint, chopped or 1 teaspoon dried
1/2 teaspoon garlic powder
3 green onions, chopped
1 cup feta cheese, grated
1 cup cheddar cheese, grated
1/4 cup Parmesan or Romano cheese, grated,
   or a combination of both
1 cup flour
3 eggs, beaten
Salt and pepper

Vegetable oil

In a bowl, combine the above ingredients except oil. Heat oil in a large skillet and drop squash mixture by spoonfuls into hot oil. As they fry, shape them into round patties with a spoon. Brown to a golden brown on each side and remove with a slotted spoon.

~Helen
Carandanis
Stratikos

Serves: 4

This recipe was created by my mother, Despina Carandanis. I embellished it a little and entered it in a James Beard cooking contest in the 1970's and to my surprise it won an "honorable mention" award! These patties are delicious hot or cold and are a wonderful picnic item. I used to bring them to the annual Greek picnic, and everyone loved them.

Zucchini with Potatoes ☦
Kolokithakia me Patates

4 thin zucchini, sliced in 1/4 inch circles
5 medium potatoes, cut in half and
    sliced in 1/4 inch half circles
2 cups baby carrots, sliced in 4 long strips
1/2 cup fresh mint, chopped
1/2 cup fresh parsley, chopped
1 medium red onion, chopped
1 cup olive oil
Juice of 1/2 lemon
1 (28-ounce) can crushed tomatoes
2 1/2 cups water
Salt and pepper to taste

Antigone
Koukoumanos

Combine all ingredients in a medium size baking pan. Cover with foil. Bake in a preheated 400 degree oven about 1 3/4 hours. Uncover and bake an additional 30 minutes or until slightly browned, and most of the water has been absorbed.

Serves: 6 to 8

Zucchini Pita
Kolokithopita Kritiki

10 medium zucchini
Salt to taste
Oil (for greasing the pan)
Flour (for dredging)
1 cup fresh mint, chopped
Pepper to taste
1 1/2 cups feta crumbled, or Parmesan cheese, grated

Slice zucchini lengthwise and place in a colander. Sprinkle with salt and toss. Place in refrigerator for a few hours or overnight. The salt draws excess water out of the zucchini.

Lightly oil a 9 x 12 inch baking pan. Roll zucchini slices in flour and place a layer of floured zucchini in the pan. Sprinkle with mint, pepper and crumbled feta or Parmesan cheese. Repeat with layers of zucchini, mint and cheese until pan is filled. Cut into serving size pieces before baking. Drizzle top with olive oil and cheese. Bake in a preheated 375 to 400 degree oven until tender.

~Martha
Athanasakis

Yield: 16 to 20 dozen.

*This recipe is from my beloved
mother-in-law, Eugenia Athanasakis.
In her loving memory.*

Zucchini Fritters
Kolokithokeftethes

1 1/2 pounds zucchini
3 tablespoons fresh parsley, minced
3 slices bread, soaked in water
   (or 1 cup seasoned bread crumbs)
3 tablespoons sharp cheese, grated
2 eggs beaten
1 onion, minced or grated
Salt and pepper to taste

Flour
Butter or oil (olive, vegetable, corn or canola)
   or butter and oil combined

Scrape zucchini lightly to remove most of the green part. Grate and sprinkle with salt. Let stand in colander about 30 minutes. Squeeze out water. Mix with parsley, bread, cheese, eggs and onion. Season with salt and pepper. Shape approximately 1 tablespoon of the mixture into a ball. Roll in flour and shape into flat round fritters. Heat the oil in a large skillet over medium-high heat. Cook the fritters until golden brown on both sides.

Note: Canned pumpkin or 2 (10-ounce) packages frozen chopped spinach (well squeezed of excess water) may be substituted for zucchini. Oregano may be added or substituted for parsley.

~Theodora
Vlachos

Serves: 5 to 6

Stewed Okra ☦

Bamyes

1 1/2 pounds okra, fresh or frozen
3/4 cup vinegar
1/2 cup olive oil, divided
2 medium onions, sliced
3 to 4 garlic cloves, sliced
Salt and pepper to taste
2 cups tomatoes, chopped
1/2 cup water
2 tablespoons fresh parsley, chopped
1 bay leaf
1 tablespoon sugar

Wash and carefully trim okra, not too close to the pod. Sprinkle
well with vinegar and let stand for 1/2 hour.

In a heavy pot, prepare the sauce by sautéing the onions and
garlic in 1/4 cup olive oil over medium-high heat. Add salt and
pepper to taste. Add the tomatoes, water, parsley, bay leaf and
sugar, then simmer a little longer. Rinse the okra and drain well.

Place remaining oil in a frying pan. Add okra and sauté for a
few minutes. Remove from heat. Add okra to sauce and simmer
until tender.

Alternate method: place 1/2 of sauce in a casserole. Add okra
and pour over remaining sauce.

Cover and bake in a preheated 375 degree oven until done,
about 40 minutes.

*~Angeliki
Anasis*

Serves: 5 to 6

Μπάμιες Λαδερές

Okra in Olive Oil ☦
Bamyes Latheres

2 (16-ounce) bags frozen okra
1/4 cup vinegar
1 to 1 1/2 teaspoons salt

3/4 cup olive oil
2 medium onions, finely chopped
2 garlic cloves, finely chopped,
    or 1 teaspoon garlic powder
1 (8-ounce) can tomato sauce,
    or 1 (16-ounce) can diced tomatoes
2 cups water
1/2 teaspoon salt
Pepper to taste
Italian seasoning to taste
2 tablespoons fresh parsley, chopped

Thaw the okra and spread them in a large glass baking dish. Sprinkle with the vinegar and salt. Set aside for 1 to 2 hours (if the weather is sunny, they may be set in the sun).

Heat the oil in a heavy pot and add the onion and garlic, and sauté lightly. Add the tomato, water, salt, pepper, and Italian seasoning. Allow to cook for 5 minutes.

Rinse the okra in a colander. Place them in the pot so they are submerged in the tomato mixture, adding a little water, if necessary. Add the parsley on top. Cover and simmer on low heat 30 to 45 minutes. Shake the pot from time to time to prevent sticking and scorching. Do not stir with a spoon or the okra will fall apart.

~Chrysiis
Rigas

Serves: 8

Αγκινάρες με Κουκιά

Beans and Artichokes ✝
Aginares me Koukia

1 pound dried broad, haricot or other large white beans
6 medium or 12 miniature artichokes
1 1/2 cups oil
5 small spring onions, cut into fine slices
1 small bunch fresh dill, finely chopped
4 to 5 cups water, as needed
Juice of 4 lemons
Salt and pepper to taste
4 to 5 cups water as needed

Soak beans in water overnight.

Take each artichoke and break off the tough outer leaves. Slice
off the stem and trim the base. Snip off the leaves. Using a
spoon or scoop, scrape out the choke. Rub with lemon juice
and allow the hearts to stand in water so they don't discolor.
If using miniature artichokes, wash, remove outer leaves and
use whole.

In a large saucepan, heat onions and oil until softened. Add
the dill, water, lemon juice, then add the beans and artichokes.
Salt and pepper the ingredients and bring to a boil. Reduce
heat, cover and cook over low to moderate heat for about
3 1/2 to 4 hours or until beans and artichokes are tender.

~Christine
Rulli

Serves: 6 as a main course.

Stewed Green Beans ☦
Fassolakia

2 large onions, sliced
4 garlic cloves, sliced
1/3 cup olive oil
2 pounds fresh green beans, ends trimmed
3 fresh tomatoes, chopped
    or 1 (16-ounce) can chopped tomatoes
Salt and pepper to taste
1/2 cup tomato sauce
1 tablespoon sugar
1/2 cup fresh parsley, chopped
1 bay leaf
1/2 cup water

Place onions, garlic, and oil in a large saucepan and sauté 3 to 5 minutes until onion is translucent. Add beans and mix with onions. Simmer 5 minutes. Add the tomatoes, salt and pepper, and stir. Add tomato sauce, sugar, parsley, bay leaf and water. Cover saucepan and simmer 45 minutes or until beans are tender.

~Angeliki
Anasis

Serves: 8

Stewed Fava Beans ☦
Koukia

3 cups cooked fava beans, fresh, dried or canned
1/2 cup olive oil
2 medium yellow onions, peeled and chopped fine
2 garlic cloves, peeled and minced fine
2 ribs celery with leaves, chopped
1 (15-ounce) can tomato sauce
1/2 cup water and 1/2 cup white wine, or 1 cup water
Salt and pepper to taste

Prepare the beans: For fresh beans, shell and blanch in
boiling water for 15 seconds. Rinse under cold water and
slip off the skins. Cook in boiling water until tender, about
10 or 15 minutes. Drain and set aside.
- For canned beans, drain and rinse
- For dried beans, soak overnight in cold water and remove
  the skins. Cook as for fresh.

In a 10-inch sauté pan or 6-quart stockpot, heat olive oil and
sauté onions, garlic and celery over medium heat until the
onion becomes translucent, about 5 to 7 minutes.

Add tomato sauce and liquid and simmer for 10 to 15 minutes.
Add the fava beans and continue to simmer another 5 to 10
minutes. Season to taste.

Hint: Do not substitute vegetable oil for the olive oil, as the olive
oil enhances the flavor of this dish.

~Georgia
Vareldzis

Serves: 4 to 6

*Fava beans are found fresh in some specialty
produce markets, especially those catering to Italian or
Mediterranean customers. They can also be purchased canned.
Usually the fresh ones are available in warmer seasons.
They belong to the family of "shell beans" because they must be
shelled (like fresh peas) to remove the beans from the pod.
They are also known as "broad beans" or "horse beans".
Greeks call them "koukia." They are also available dried.*

Green Beans ☦
Fassolakia

1 cup olive oil
1 green onion, chopped or sliced
3 garlic cloves, minced
2 large tomatoes, chopped
   or 1 (12-ounce) can diced tomatoes
1 pound fresh string beans (cut off tips and rinse well)
10 ounces water
1 teaspoon dill, fresh or dried

In frying pan, heat 1 cup of olive oil. Sauté onion and garlic. Add tomatoes. Cook for 10 minutes over medium heat. In a saucepan, boil water and add fresh green beans. Add fresh dill. Cook covered over medium heat for 25 minutes. When beans are done, combine with the tomato sauce.

~Demetri's
Mediterranean
Restaurant

Serves: 6 to 8

Lima Beans in Tomato Sauce ☦
Yigandes Yiahni

1²/₃ cup dried large lima beans
1 medium onion, sliced thin
1 tablespoon oil
1 garlic clove, minced
1¹/₂ cups crushed tomatoes, fresh or canned
¹/₂ teaspoon oregano, crushed
Pepper to taste

Rinse beans well. Soak beans overnight in 6 cups of water. The next day, without changing the water, bring to a boil. Simmer until beans are just tender (about 45 minutes). Meanwhile, sauté onion in the oil until lightly browned. Add minced garlic and crushed tomatoes. Simmer 15 minutes. Add cooked beans, oregano and pepper, and cook for an additional 20 minutes.

~Diane
Jonganatos
Cook

Just add a salad and crusty bread and enjoy!

Yiayia Pauline's Green Beans ✟
Fassolakia tis Yiayias Polixenis

1 medium onion, grated
2 garlic cloves, grated
2 tablespoons olive oil
2 pounds fresh green beans, trimmed
1/2 teaspoon salt
1 teaspoon sugar
1/4 teaspoon pepper
1 tablespoon tomato paste
    or 1 small (8-ounce) can tomato sauce
Boiling water
1/2 teaspoon cinnamon
Tomatoes (optional)

Place the onion and garlic into a large saucepan with the olive oil and sauté until brown. Add the green beans, salt, sugar and pepper. Stir in the tomato paste or tomato sauce and cook for 5 minutes. Add enough boiling water to cover the beans. Cook until the beans are soft, adding enough boiling water to keep from burning. Add the cinnamon.

Hint: In season, add ripe, chopped tomatoes.

~Bessie Lekas

Serves: 4

In her younger years, my mother would always make this dish with fresh green beans and tomatoes from her garden. They were so good that a friend of mine who was an overnight guest asked to have them for breakfast!

Vegetable Casserole ✟
Briami

Eggplant, cut in slices or chunks
Carrots, cut in slices
Celery, cut in slices
Leek, cut in 1-inch slices
Okra, whole
Potatoes, peeled and sliced
Fresh green beans, halved or whole
Peas, fresh or frozen
Cauliflower florets
Yellow zucchini squash, sliced

Sauce:
1 (15-ounce) can stewed tomatoes
3 garlic cloves, chopped
1 large onion, cut into wedges and thinly sliced
1/2 cup tomato sauce
1/2 to 1 cup olive oil
1 teaspoon basil, dried or 3 sprigs fresh
1/4 teaspoons thyme, dried or fresh
1/4 teaspoons mint, dried or fresh
1/4 to 1/2 cup fresh parsley
1/2 teaspoons oregano, dried or fresh
Salt and pepper to taste
1/2 cup white wine (optional)
1 to 2 cups water or chicken stock

A wide choice of vegetables may be used in this dish in any quantity. For the sauce vary the amount of ingredients to be proportionate to the amount of vegetables.

Arrange the vegetables in a baking pan or dish. Pour sauce plus 1 cup water or chicken stock over the vegetables and stir. Cover and bake in preheated 375 degree oven for 35 to 40 minutes. Stir periodically and add more water if necessary. Uncover and bake 15 minutes longer until vegetables are fork tender. Serve warm with French bread and cheese.

~Eleni
Nicholson

*My family used this dish as a main or a side dish.
Tasty hot or cold . . . makes a great summer dish.*

Vegetable Casserole ✝
Briami

3 zucchini, cut into 1-inch rounds
5 large potatoes, cut into 1-inch rounds
1 eggplant, cut into 1 inch-rounds
1 medium onion, chopped
4 garlic cloves, chopped
1/4 cup fresh dill, chopped
1/4 cup fresh mint, chopped
1/4 cup fresh parsley, chopped
1 (14-ounce) can diced tomatoes
1/2 (8-ounce) can tomato sauce
1 cup olive oil
1 teaspoon Italian herbs
Salt and pepper to taste

Sprinkle eggplant with salt. Let stand for 15 minutes, then rinse. Mix all ingredients and place in a large baking pan. Bake in a preheated 400 degree oven for about 1 1/2 hours or until all vegetables are tender. Check frequently and add water if vegetables seem dry. (Liquid should be absorbed when done.)

Note: You may add okra to this dish.

Serves: 6 to 8

~ Georgia
Belesin

Μπριάμι

Vegetable Casserole ✝
Briami

1/2 cup olive oil
1 large sweet onion, sliced
5 garlic cloves, minced
2 large carrots, sliced
2 zucchini, sliced
2 Chinese eggplants, sliced
1 green pepper, sliced
1 red pepper, sliced
3 large potatoes, sliced
1 pound green beans, trim ends
1 large (15-ounce) can red tomatoes
1/2 cup wine
5 fresh basil leaves, chopped
Salt and pepper to taste

Pour 1/4 cup oil into a large roasting pan. Place sliced onion
and garlic in bottom of pan. Layer the rest of the fresh
vegetables, leaving the string beans on top. Cut the tomatoes
and lay them over the string beans. Pour 1/2 cup wine over the
top and then the remaining 1/4 cup of olive oil. Salt and pepper
to taste and sprinkle with the chopped basil. Cover with foil.
Bake in a preheated 375 degree oven for 1 hour. Remove the
foil and stir the vegetables. Bake uncovered about 20 to
30 minutes longer. Check periodically to prevent vegetables
from overcooking and burning.

~Katharine
Antonis
Melcher

Serve in the baking dish or transfer to a deep platter.

Serves: 5 to 6

*This is a family briami recipe that
I have modernized a little bit.*

Fresh Beets ✝
Padzaria Freska

5 large fresh beets, with greens if desired
1/2 cup olive oil
1/4 cup balsamic vinegar, or more to taste
Salt and pepper to taste
Dash of sugar
1/2 cup red onion, sliced and slivered
3 to 4 tablespoons fresh parsley, chopped

Boil fresh beets until tender along with the greens. Drain; run
cold water over beets, and peel. Cut into small pieces and place
in a bowl.

Add the olive oil, vinegar, salt and pepper until desired taste is
reached. Add a dash of sugar to taste. Fold in the onion. Cover
and refrigerate to marinate.

~Mary
Radtke

Before serving, add chopped parsley.

Serves: 6 to 8

This delicious vegetable dish can be
served warm or cold.
It can be made a day ahead.

Αγκινάρες αλά Πολίτα

Artichokes à la Polita ☦
Aginares ala Polita

10 artichokes, preferably small-sized
15 small boiling onions, peeled and left whole
1 teaspoon salt
Juice of 1/2 lemon (about 1 1/2 tablespoons)

Waxed paper (cut to fit diameter of a large pot)
1/2 cup olive oil
1 cup onion, finely chopped
3 cups water
Juice of one lemon
2 teaspoons fresh dill weed, chopped
Salt and pepper to taste

Sauce:
1/4 cup olive oil
2 heaping tablespoons flour
Liquid from the cooked artichokes and onions
Juice of 1 1/2 lemons
1/2 teaspoon salt
Dash pepper

Remove all the tough outer leaves from the artichokes. Cut off the tougher leaves remaining at the top. Cut off most of the stem, leaving about 1/2 inch. Peel away the outer skin of this remaining portion of the stem. Scoop out the fibrous choke of the artichoke with a teaspoon and discard. If the artichokes are large, they can be sliced in half lengthwise. To prevent artichokes from discoloring, put them into a large bowl of cold water to which salt and lemon juice has been added. Also, add the whole onions to this water.

In a large cooking pot, heat the olive oil and sauté the chopped onion until translucent. Add 3 cups water, the juice of 1 lemon, the dill and the salt and pepper. Bring to a boil and allow to simmer. Remove the artichokes and onions from the bowl of water and add them to the simmering pot. Cover the vegetables with the trimmed waxed paper. Poke a few holes in it with a fork to allow steam to escape. Simmer over medium heat for about half an hour. Remove the waxed paper and poke into the base of the artichokes with a knife to check for tenderness. If the artichokes are not done, continue simmering until tender.

Transfer the artichokes to a platter and place them upside down (with the stems pointing up). Position a whole onion on top of each artichoke. Scatter the remaining onions on the plate to complete the garnish and pour the sauce over, covering all the vegetables.

To prepare the sauce: Strain the liquid in which the vegetables were cooked and set aside. In a saucepan, heat the oil and stir in the flour. Allow it to cook slowly a few minutes until smooth. Slowly add the strained pot liquid, stirring constantly. Add the lemon juice, salt and pepper and allow the sauce to simmer until it is thick enough to cover the artichokes and onions.

~Chrysiis
Rigas

Serves: 10

Αγκινάρες Φρέσκες

Fresh Artichokes ✝
Aginares Freskes

4 artichokes
1 large onion, chopped
3/4 cup olive oil
Juice of 1 to 1 1/2 lemons
Salt and pepper to taste
2 sprigs fresh dill, chopped

Strip the petals off the artichokes down to the hearts. Cut out the choke. Cut the stems in pieces. Cut artichoke hearts into 1/2 or 1/4 inch pieces. Soak in water to keep them from discoloring.

In a skillet, sauté the onion in olive oil until translucent. Do not brown. Place the cut-up artichoke hearts and stems in a layer on top of the onion, adding water and additional olive oil to the pan. Top with lemon juice, salt and pepper to taste and fresh dill for a wonderful flavor. Simmer over medium-low heat until very tender, up to 2 hours.

~Mary
Radtke

Serves: 4

Αγκινάρες και Πατάτες Αυγολέμονο

Artichokes and Potatoes
in Egg-Lemon Sauce
Aginares ke Patates Avgolemono

6 large artichokes
1 cup olive oil
2 to 3 spring onions
1/3 cup fresh dill, finely chopped
3 large potatoes, peeled and quartered
2 cups water
Salt and pepper to taste

Egg-Lemon Sauce (Avgolemono):
2 eggs
Juice of 2 to 3 lemons
Freshly ground pepper

Prepare the artichokes by removing all their tough outer leaves.
Cut the ends of the tender leaves and scoop out the choke with
a spoon. Place the cleaned artichoke hearts in a bowl of water
(add a little lemon juice to prevent them from turning brown).
Allow artichokes to stand for a few minutes, then cut them in
quarters. In a pot, heat the olive oil and sauté the onions and the
dill very lightly. Add potatoes and brown them 1 to 2 minutes,
then add the water. When the potatoes are half cooked, add the
artichokes and a little more water, about one cup. Add the salt
and pepper, and simmer until all the water is absorbed,
approximately 45 minutes.

To make the egg-lemon sauce, beat eggs lightly in a bowl. Add
the juice of 2 lemons, a little at a time, beating continuously.
Gradually add a few tablespoons of the liquid from the pot in
which the artichokes are cooking, and keep beating. Pour the

*Petroula
Koukoumanos*

mixture in the pot over the artichokes and potatoes, stirring
lightly. Serve garnished with freshly ground pepper.

Serves: 4

Σπανάκι με Αγκινάρες

Spinach and Artichokes ☦
Spanaki me Aginares

2 cups water
Juice of 2 lemons

3 to 5 medium artichokes
2 bunches fresh spinach
1/4 cup olive oil or to taste
1 small onion, chopped
Salt and pepper to taste
1/2 teaspoon oregano, dried or 6 fresh sprigs

In a bowl, combine water with the lemon juice and set aside.

To prepare artichokes, cut off all but 1 inch of the artichoke stems. Remove tough outer leaves and chop the tops off the artichokes to remove sharp points. Cut each into 4 pieces and scrape out the choke with a spoon. Submerge trimmed artichokes into lemon water to prevent them from turning brown.

Wash spinach thoroughly. In a saucepan over medium-high heat, sauté onion in olive oil until translucent. Add spinach and artichokes. Cover and cook over low heat until tender. Add seasonings. Serve warm.

Note: 1 1/2 cups sweet peas and/or 1 bunch asparagus may be substituted for artichokes, if desired.

~Amalia
Gianopoulos

Serves: 4 to 6

*This is a Sunday afternoon
favorite with our family.*

Sautéed Spinach with Feta Cheese
Spanaki Tiganito me Feta

2 pounds fresh spinach
1/2 cup finely chopped onion or
   1 cup chopped green onions
1/2 cup olive oil
1/3 cup water*
Salt and freshly ground pepper to taste
3 tablespoons (1-ounce) feta cheese, crumbled
Dill, fresh or dried, to taste

Wash the spinach thoroughly in cold water. Remove discolored
leaves and trim off the roots and any tough stems. Cut the
spinach into halves or thirds. Combine all the ingredients in
a 4-quart saucepan or 6-quart pot. Cook carefully for about
5 minutes on medium-high heat, turning the spinach with a
fork until it begins to wilt to about half of its volume. Stir the
spinach as needed and cook for another 12 to 15 minutes, less
if the spinach is young and tender. Remove the spinach from
the pan and put into a serving dish. Mix in half the crumbled
feta cheese. Top with the remaining feta cheese and sprinkle
lightly with dill. Serve with Greek country bread.

*If the spinach does not have sufficient water clinging to the
leaves, add 1/3 cup water with the ingredients so as not to
scorch the spinach.

*Fotini
Rumpakis &
Maria
Rumpakis
Hanches

Alternatives: The feta and dill may be omitted for a recipe that
is similar, yet still tasty and nutritious. Leftover spinach may be
used to make a delicious frittata or omelet.

Serves: 4 to 5

*This recipe is based on a delicious sautéed spinach recipe given
to me by my mother, Fotini Rumpakis who was born
in 1910 on the island of Karpathos. It was passed down
to her from her mother and grandmother. I have
added feta cheese and dill to give it a different twist.
My family enjoys both recipes.*

Mediterranean Vegetable Platter ☦
Lahanika Thiafora

1 pound fresh green beans, snapped into 2-inch lengths
2 tomatoes, sliced
1 medium red onion, sliced
1 cup canned artichoke hearts, halved
1 1/2 cups fresh mushrooms, sliced
1 (2.2-ounce) can sliced black olives, drained

Dressing:
1/2 cup red wine vinegar
3 tablespoons olive oil
2 cloves garlic, minced
1 teaspoon fresh basil leaves, chopped
1/2 teaspoon oregano leaves
Pepper to taste

1 tablespoon feta cheese

In a pot of boiling water, blanch green beans 4 to 5 minutes.
Drain. Plunge in cold water, and drain again. Layer vegetables
on platter, beginning with the sliced tomatoes, then the onions,
artichokes, mushrooms, olives, and lastly the beans. In a small
bowl, whisk together the vinegar, oil, garlic and herbs. Add
pepper to taste. Pour dressing over top and chill for 4 hours.
Baste several times with dressing which has run to sides of
platter. Top with crumbled cheese at serving time.

~Joy Neitling

Yield: 10 cups.

*This is a low fat, heart-healthy dish.
It is nice because it can be
made in advance.*

Ιμάμ Μπαϊλντί

Stuffed Eggplant ☦
Imam Baildi

2 small long eggplants
2 onions, chopped
2 garlic cloves, minced
2 large tomatoes, peeled and chopped
2 tablespoons fresh parsley, chopped
1 teaspoon pepper
4 teaspoons olive oil

Split eggplants in half lengthwise. With a spoon, scoop out
the inner pulp of each eggplant leaving a shell about ¼ inch
or slightly thicker. Chop the pulp and set aside.

Heat the oil in a skillet, and add the onion and garlic, and sauté
until translucent, stirring often. Add the eggplant pulp along
with tomatoes, parsley and pepper. Continue cooking 20
minutes. Spoon equal amounts of the mixture into the
eggplant shells. Place the eggplant halves in a baking pan
in which ½ inch of water has been added. Bake uncovered
in a preheated 350 degree oven for 30 minutes.

~Diane
Jouganatos
Cook

Serves: 4

Pan-fried Eggplant ✟
Melitzanes Tiganites

4 Japanese or Italian eggplants
   or 2 medium regular eggplants
2 cups unbleached white flour
1 teaspoon granulated garlic
1 teaspoon granulated onion
Salt and freshly ground pepper to taste
2 cups olive or vegetable oil, for frying

Wash the eggplant under cold running water. With a sharp knife, cut stems off, then cut into 1/4 inch slices, lengthwise.

To blanch, add ample water in a large saucepan and bring to a rolling boil. Add the eggplant slices in the boiling water for only 4 minutes. Remove to paper towels to drain.

In a bowl, combine the flour, garlic, onion, salt and pepper and dredge the eggplant in the seasoned flour.

Heat the oil in a large sauté pan over medium-high heat. Add a few slices of the eggplant to cover the bottom of the pan. Fry until golden brown and crispy, approximately 6 minutes on each side. Remove to drain on a plate lined with paper towels. Repeat until all the slices are fried, adding oil as needed.

~George
Papas

Serves: 14

From the book, "Papas' Art of Traditional Greek Cooking" This dish can be served hot or cold with scorthalia, and is a perfect complement to grilled or broiled lamb.

Easy Skillet Eggplant Lasagna
Lazania me Melitzana sto Tigani

1 (1 pound) eggplant, cut into 8 (1/2-inch) slices
1 egg, slightly beaten
1/2 cup seasoned dry bread crumbs
2 tablespoons vegetable oil
1 (14-ounce) jar spaghetti sauce
1 cup mozzarella cheese, shredded

Dip eggplant slices in egg, then in seasoned breadcrumbs.
Heat oil in nonstick skillet over medium heat. Fry eggplant
in oil 2 to 4 minutes turning once until golden brown. Pour
spaghetti sauce over eggplant. Sprinkle with cheese. Heat to
boiling. Reduce heat to medium. Cover and cook 3 to 4 minutes
or until eggplant is tender and hot.

~Effie
Karambelas

Serves: 4

Green Peas in Tomato Sauce ☦
Arakas Yiahni

1 cup olive oil
1 medium red onion, chopped
2 cups baby carrots, sliced in 4 long strips
1 cup fresh parsley, chopped
1/2 cup fresh mint, chopped
1 (8-ounce) can tomato sauce
6 cups green peas, frozen
2 cups water
Salt and pepper to taste

In a skillet, sauté onions in olive oil for 1 minute. Add carrots, parsley, mint and tomato sauce. Simmer on medium heat about 10 minutes. Add peas, water and salt and pepper to taste. Bring to a boil. Lower heat to medium and cook for about 30 to 40 minutes.

~Antigone
Koukoumanos

Serves: 6 to 8

Πατάτες στο Φούρνο

Potatoes Roasted in Lamb Juices
Patates sto Fourno

15 potatoes (baking or white), washed, peeled
   and cut lengthwise into fourths
1/4 cup (1/2 stick) margarine or butter
Drippings and liquid from a cooked lamb roast

Prepare and roast the leg of lamb according to any Greek-style recipe. Strain the liquid left in the roasting pan into a jar and refrigerate to separate the fat from the juices. Remove and discard the fat.

Arrange the potatoes in a large baking pan in a single layer. Pour the defatted lamb juices over the potatoes to about half the depth of the pan. Add water if necessary to reach this level. Dot with butter. Bake in a preheated 350 degree oven on a low rack until golden brown, about 25 to 30 minutes.

~ George
Anasis

Serves: 6

Πατάτες Τηγανιτές του Φώτη

Foti's Greek Fries
Patates Tiganites tou Foti

2 pounds (#2 sized) baking potatoes
1/4 cup salt (season to taste)
1/4 cup pepper (season to taste)
1/4 cup ground oregano
1/4 cup garlic powder
1 pound flour

Cavender's (All-Purpose Greek Seasoning)
Shortening (for frying)

Wash the potatoes, but leave the skins on. Cut each potato
in half, lengthwise. With cut side on board, cut each half in
lengthwise strips about 1/2 inch thick. Keep them in water until
ready to flour. Combine the salt, pepper, oregano, garlic powder
and flour. Drain the potatoes in a colander. Heat shortening in
pressure fryer to 350 degrees. Flour the potatoes and arrange
in the basket, making sure not to crowd them. Cook in hot
shortening for 9 minutes. Let them drain and cool slightly.
Season with Cavender's Greek Seasoning. Enjoy with your
favorite dip.

Note: Time and temperature may vary according to your fryer.

Serves: 4

—Fotis and
Jill Kosmas,
Foti's Greek Deli

Roasted Lemon Potatoes
Patates sto Fourno Lemonates

5 yellow Yukon potatoes, peeled and sliced lengthwise
Juice of 3 lemons
2/3 cup olive oil
1 teaspoon oregano, dried
4 large garlic cloves, mashed
Salt and pepper to taste

In a bowl, combine lemon juice, olive oil, oregano, garlic, salt and pepper. Beat this mixture and set aside. Place potatoes in roasting pan and pour marinade over them. Let sit 1 hour. Cover with foil and bake 1 hour in a preheated 375 degree oven. Uncover and cook an additional 30 minutes or until potatoes are browned. Remove pan from the oven and let stand for a few minutes before serving.

~Michael
Antonis

Serves: 4 to 5

I got this recipe from my Yiayia,
Polixeni Antonis. She taught me to
make them because I loved her potatoes
so much she thought I could make them
anytime I felt like having them.
Yasou, Yiayia, these are the best!

Pita,
Pasta &
Pilaf

86

Contents

Spinach Pie
Spanakopita

3 boxes frozen chopped spinach
2 bunches green onions, chopped
1/4 cup olive oil
1/2 cup fresh parsley, minced
2 tablespoons dill, dried
1 pound feta cheese, crumbled
8 eggs, beaten
Salt and pepper to taste

1 box phyllo pastry dough
2 cups (4 sticks) unsalted butter, clarified

Thaw spinach overnight. Squeeze out all excess water. In a skillet, sauté the green onions in olive oil until tender. In a bowl, combine the spinach, parsley, dill, feta cheese and beaten eggs. Add sautéed onions. Season with salt and pepper and mix well.

Butter bottom of a 17 x 12 inch metal baking pan with clarified butter. Line bottom of pan with half of the phyllo dough, buttering between each sheet. Add spinach mixture. Top with remaining phyllo dough, again buttering between each sheet. Make sure you butter top sheet.

Score top layer into diamond shapes with sharp knife. Bake in a preheated 350 degree oven for 45 minutes or until golden brown.

Note: Can be frozen before baking. Remove directly from freezer to hot oven. Do not thaw. Bake on middle rack.

~Pearl Pavlos

Yield: 60 to 70

A family favorite,
for every wedding, baptism
and family gathering.

Σπανακοπιτάκια για Πανηγύρι

Spinach Triangles for a Festival
Spanakopitakia yia Paniyiri

12 (3-pound) boxes frozen chopped spinach
1 bag chopped onion
20 cups green onion, chopped
1/4 cup fresh parsley, chopped
1/4 cup dill, dried or fresh
Fresh mint, as desired
1/2 gallon olive oil
6 cups Parmesan cheese, grated
1/8 cup pepper
1/4 cup salt
1/2 of a 5-gallon tub feta cheese, crumbled
7 dozen eggs
4 (5 pound) containers of cottage cheese

81/2 pounds butter, melted
36 pounds (17 X 25 inch sheets) phyllo dough

Sauté onions and herbs in olive oil until very soft (at least 1/2 hour). Drain excess water from spinach and place in large tubs. Layer ingredients over spinach in tubs. Mix well. Refrigerate overnight, if possible. Mix again.

Cut phyllo sheets into long strips (3-inches wide). Place damp towels over phyllo sheets to protect them from drying. Work with one strip at a time, brushing each with melted butter. Place 2 tablespoons of the spinach mixture near the bottom edge of each strip. fold the corner up and to the left to form a triangle. continue to fold the strip upward at right angles until you reach the end.

Note: These triangles are prepared ahead, sealed and frozen in large plastic containers. At festival time, they are baked to order, in small quantities, and sold in the "Taverna".

Yield: approximately 790 triangles

This is the batch recipe used for the Holy Trinity Greek Orthodox Church Greek Festival, Portland, Oregon. We make 9 batches to yeild 7,100 Spanakopites. Needless to say, they are a major hit!

Σπανακόπιτα

Spinach Pie
Spanakopita

4 packages frozen chopped spinach or
   fresh spinach of equivalent weight
2 tablespoons olive oil
3 eggs, beaten
1 pound feta cheese, chopped
1/2 cup rice, uncooked
1 medium onion, finely chopped
Salt and pepper to taste

Pie crust:
3 cups whole wheat flour
3 cups white flour
1/2 teaspoon salt
1/2 cup oil
2 1/2 cups water

In a saucepan, sauté onion in the oil until soft. Add spinach
and cook until it defrosts completely. Add the rice, cover the
pan and turn the heat off. The rice will absorb the juices from
the spinach.

Meanwhile, prepare the crust. In a bowl combine the flours and
salt. Blend in the oil and water with a fork. Form into a smooth
ball and divide dough in half. With a rolling pin, roll out dough
and place in a 9 x 13 inch pan. Cover the remaining dough and
set aside.

Add beaten eggs and chopped feta to the spinach mixture. Mix
well and pour into pan. Cover with the remaining dough. Pierce
crust with fork in several places. Bake in a preheated 350 degree
oven for 30 to 40 minutes or until golden.

~Diane
Jouganatos Cook

Serves: 8 to 12

*This is a spanakopita with a hearty crust—more a meal than
an appetizer. Many years ago on the island of Cephalonia,
we had a similar pita, but with all variety of greens,
and no cheese or eggs. It was served during Lent.*

Σπανακόπιτα

Spinach Pie
Spanakopita

Filling:
2 bunches fresh spinach, washed and drained
1/2 onion, minced
3/4 cup lowfat cottage cheese
1/2 pound feta cheese, crumbled
2 eggs, beaten slightly
1/4 cup fresh parsley, chopped
1/2 teaspoon dill weed, dried
1/2 cup uncooked rice
1/2 teaspoon pepper

Pie crust:
1 cup whole wheat flour
1 cup unbleached white flour
1/3 cup margarine
1/4 cup water (enough to make a soft ball)

Place flour in a mixing bowl. Blend in margarine with a pastry blender until mixture is crumbly. Sprinkle with cold water. Mix with fork and roll mixture into a ball. Using a little more than 1/2 of the dough, roll it out to cover the bottom of a 12 x 7 1/2-inch baking dish. Bake bottom crust for 10 minutes in a preheated 350 degree oven.

In a bowl tear spinach into small pieces. Add minced onion, cottage cheese, feta cheese, eggs, parsley, dill weed, rice and pepper. Mix well and place mixture onto crust. Cover with the remaining dough. Bake in a preheated 350 degree oven 35 to 45 minutes or until top crust is golden brown in the center.

—Diane
Jonganatos Cook

Serves: 6

Spinach Pie
Spanakopita

3 (10-ounce) packages frozen chopped spinach
1 pound feta cheese
1 pound cottage cheese
1 (8-ounce) package cream cheese
2 eggs
1 teaspoon dill, dried

1 cup (2 sticks) butter, melted
1 pound phyllo dough

Defrost spinach at room temperature and squeeze dry to remove all water. Mix the spinach with the crumbled feta, the cottage cheese and the cream cheese, then add the eggs and dill.

Butter a 9 x 13 inch pan and line it with 9 phyllo sheets. Brush each phyllo sheet with butter as you lay it in the pan. Spread the spinach mixture evenly, then cover with 6 more phyllo sheets, brushing each with butter.

Cut through top layers to mark pieces into square or diamond shapes. Bake 45 minutes in a preheated 350 degree oven.

~Virginia
Rozos

Serves: 15

Σπανακόπιτα

Spinach Pie
Spanakopita

5 bunches fresh spinach or 2¹/2 pounds packaged fresh spinach
¹/4 cup salt
3 bunches green onions, finely chopped
1 teaspoon pepper
¹/2 teaspoon allspice
1 pound feta cheese, grated
4 eggs, lightly beaten
¹/2 cup olive oil
3 tablespoons fresh dill, chopped
1 bunch fresh parsley, chopped

1 cup (2 sticks) butter plus 6 tablespoons (³/4 stick)
1 cup olive oil
1 pound phyllo dough

Wash spinach, and chop. Place in a large bowl and sprinkle with
¹/4 cup salt. Wait 30 minutes to draw moisture out of spinach.
Squeeze spinach well until dry to remove excess moisture. Must
be squeezed at least 3 times or more, as needed. In a bowl,
combine green onions, pepper, allspice, feta cheese, eggs, olive
oil, dill, and parsley and set aside. Add prepared spinach.

In a saucepan over low heat, melt 2 sticks butter, then add
the olive oil. Layer phyllo sheets in a 14 x 7 inch baking pan,
brushing each layer with olive oil and butter. Stop at a half pound
of phyllo. Spread spinach mixture over prepared phyllo. Top with
pats of butter (using the ³/4 stick), then with remaining half pound
of phyllo brushing olive oil/butter mixture between each layer.
Score the top few layers into diamond shape pieces before baking
or freezing. Bake in a preheated 325 degree oven until golden
~Ellen   brown, about 60 minutes. If frozen, take out and bake
Demas Belesin   at 300 degrees about 2 hours until golden brown.

Serves: 6 to 8

*This recipe is in memory of my mother, Anna Stratikos Demas, who
each holiday or special occasion would prepare a spanakopita for our
gatherings. She and her dear friend, Helen Buhler had a tradition
for making a spanakopita together for each of their families for over
20 years. Sharing memories through friendship and food.*

Spinach Pie in a Batter Crust
Messinthra

Batter:
2 1/2 cups flour
1 cup milk
1 cup water
2 eggs, beaten
Pinch of salt

Filling:
2 bunches fresh spinach, washed,
   dried thoroughly and chopped
2 bunches green onions, chopped
1/2 cup fresh dill, chopped
1/2 to 1 cup feta cheese, crumbled
Up to 1/2 cup olive oil

In a bowl, combine flour, milk, water, eggs and salt. Whisk until blended.

In a large bowl, place chopped spinach, green onions, dill and feta cheese. Mix thoroughly.

Coat a 9 x 13 inch casserole with olive oil. Pour half the batter on the bottom of casserole and cover with spinach mixture. Drizzle sparingly with olive oil in a zigzag pattern and top with remaining half of batter. Bake in a preheated 400 degree oven 1 hour and 15 minutes, or until top layer is browned.

Cut in serving size squares for an entrée, or cut into 1 to 1 1/2 inch squares and serve as a delicious hors d'oeuvre, warm or cold.

Hint: To dry spinach, drain very well and pat dry with a kitchen towel.

Serves: 12 as a main course or
        6 dozen (1 1/2-inch) squares as an appetizer

~Sandra
Karafotias

This recipe is from the village of Limnes, near Argos on the Peloponnesus, from Yiayia Eleni.

A CELEBRATION OF FOOD, FAITH & FAMILY

Κολοκυθοτυρόπιτα

Zucchini-Cheese Pie
Kolokithotiropita

3 small zucchini, sliced 1/4 inch thick
1 medium onion, chopped
Butter, oil, and/or margarine as needed
1 teaspoon dill weed, dried
1 teaspoon oregano, dried
1 teaspoon basil, dried
Pepper to taste

1 package refrigerated crescent roll dough
1 1/2 tablespoons Dijon mustard

1/4 cup Parmesan cheese, grated
2 eggs, beaten
1 (8-ounce) package monterey jack cheese, shredded
Chopped fresh parsley
Paprika

In a medium pan, sauté zucchini and onion in as much butter, oil or margarine as needed. Set aside to drain and cool. Add dill, oregano, basil, and pepper to taste and blend well.

Press crescent rolls evenly into an ungreased quiche plate, making sure to press together pieces. Spread mustard over dough. Add zucchini, onion mixture. Sprinkle with Parmesan cheese. Add beaten eggs to shredded cheese and mix well. Spread over zucchini layer, sprinkle with chopped parsley and paprika.

~Demetra
Vlachos

Bake in a preheated 325 degree oven about 30 to 35 minutes. Let stand a few minutes before serving. Bon appetit!

Serves: 4 to 6

Pasta Pie
Makaronopita

1 (12-ounce) package macaroni
3 tablespoons olive oil
2 cups feta cheese, crumbled
5 eggs, well-beaten
Salt and pepper to taste

1/2 cup (1 stick) butter, melted
1/2 cup olive oil
1 pound phyllo dough

In a large pot cook macaroni in salted, boiling water. Rinse
and drain well. Toss with 3 tablespoons olive oil. Add crumbled
feta cheese, eggs and salt and pepper to taste. Mix together
thoroughly.

Combine butter, with 1/2 cup olive oil to use for brushing the
phyllo dough. Use a large baking pan (about the size of the
phyllo dough). Brush the bottom and sides of pan with butter
and oil mixture.

Place 5 sheets of phyllo in bottom of a 9 x 13 inch pan,
brushing each sheet well with butter and oil. Spread some
of the macaroni mixture over phyllo and top with 2 more
sheets, brushing each layer. Repeat process 3 to 4 times until
all the macaroni has been used. Top with 5 more phyllo sheets.
With a sharp knife cut through the top sheets lengthwise in
equal widths. Spray lightly with a little water to prevent curling.

Bake in a preheated 375 degree oven about 1 hour or until
golden brown. Let cool and cut into squares.

~Martha
Polizos

Serves: 6 to 8

Λάχανο με Φιδέ

Cabbage, Celery and Noodles
Lahano me Fithe

1/2 cup olive or vegetable oil
2 large onions, peeled and minced fine
1 small head of cabbage, cut in 1/4 inch slices
8 to 10 ribs celery, cut in 1 inch pieces
1 (8-ounce) can tomato sauce
1 tablespoon tomato paste
Salt and pepper to taste
1/4 pound extra fine noodles or orzo, uncooked
1/2 cup Parmesan cheese, grated (optional)

Heat oil in large heavy casserole and sauté onions, cabbage and celery until lightly browned and limp. Add tomato sauce and paste. Add a little water if mixture is too thick. Simmer over medium heat until vegetables are almost cooked, adding more water if needed. Add salt and pepper and noodles. Simmer only until the noodles are cooked. Sprinkle with grated cheese before serving.

~Georgia
Vareldzis

Serves: 4

One of my favorite vegetarian dinners. It can also be used as a Lenten dish by eliminating the grated cheese.

Μανέστρα

Orzo
Manestra

1 (16-ounce) package orzo
1/4 cup (1/2 stick) butter
1/4 cup olive oil
Mizithra or Parmesan cheese, grated or crumbled feta cheese

~Demetri's
Mediterranean
Restaurant

Boil the orzo for 15 minutes in salted water. Put in strainer and rinse in cold water. In a skillet, heat butter and olive oil. Together add cooked orzo and stir. Add either the mizithra, Parmesan or crumbled feta cheese to your liking.

Serves: 6 to 8

Πιλάφι με Φέτα και Δυόσμο

Feta-Mint Rice
Pilafi me Feta ke Thiosmo

1/2 cup onion, peeled and chopped
2 tablespoons olive oil
2 cups long-grain rice
4 cups chicken broth
5-ounces feta cheese, crumbled
6 tablespoons fresh mint, snipped
1 teaspoon pepper
Fresh whole mint leaves (optional)

In a large saucepan, sauté onion in hot oil until tender. Do not brown. Add uncooked rice and stir for 1 minute. Slowly add the chicken broth and bring to boiling. Reduce heat and cover pan. Simmer 15 to 20 minutes until the broth is absorbed. Gently stir in the cheese, mint and pepper. Serve warm. If desired, garnish with whole mint leaves.

~Paula
Dudunake
Diamond

Serves: 8 (as a side dish)

A 'new' Greek recipe that is easy to prepare and 'fail-proof.'

Popped Rice ✝

1/4 cup olive or vegetable oil
1 cup converted long grain rice
2 1/2 cups warm water
Salt and pepper to taste
1 small tomato, diced

In a Dutch oven, heat oil until hot, but not smoking. Add rice and wait until most of the rice has popped (turned white). Add water, salt and pepper. Cook until water comes to a boil. Place in a preheated 400 degree oven and cook covered for 15 to 18 minutes. If not completely cooked, add a small amount of water and cook another 3 to 5 minutes. Add tomatoes.

In addition, pine nuts, walnuts or raisins can be added before rice is completely cooked.

~Helen M.
Lampus

Serves: 6

My mother's recipe. This rice can be made ahead of time and doesn't get mushy.

Rice with Vermicelli ☦
Pilafi me Fithe

1 cup vermicelli (break into 1/2-inch pieces)
1/2 cup (1 stick) margarine or butter
1 cup uncooked long grain rice
2 cups water
1 tablespoon salt
1/4 teaspoon pepper
1/4 teaspoon cinnamon

In a saucepan, brown vermicelli in margarine or butter until golden brown. Add rice, water and spices. Cover and bring to a boil. Reduce heat and cook 20 minutes until all the water is absorbed.

~Catherine
Diamond Owen

Note: After you bring rice to a boil, taste water to see if there is enough salt.

Serves: 4

My children Lori and Heather love this dish when served with plain yogurt. Excellent as a side dish with lamb or chicken or as a Lenten dish.

Rice and Vermicelli
Pilafi me Fithe

1/2 cup (1 stick) butter
2 green onions, chopped
1 cup sliced mushrooms
1 1/2 cups rice
2 vermicelli swirls, broken into pieces
3 1/4 cups chicken broth

Melt butter in skillet. Add onions and mushrooms and brown lightly. Add rice and vermicelli. Sauté until golden brown. Add chicken broth and bring to boil. Remove from heat and transfer into a covered baking dish. Bake in a preheated 300 degree oven for 30 minutes.

Serves: 8 to 10

~Lisa
Buhler
Psihogios

This is a wonderful side dish to your favorite lamb or chicken recipe. My family loves this rice.

Πιλάφι

Rice Pilaf
Pilafi

1 small onion, chopped
1/4 cup (1/2 stick) butter
2 cups rice
4 cups chicken broth

~Georgia Belesin

Melt butter in saucepan. Add chopped onion and sauté for one minute. Add rice and sauté for one more minute. Add broth and bring to a boil. Cover and reduce heat to low; simmer for 20 minutes or until rice is done.

Serves: 6 to 8

Serve with a dollop of plain yogurt on top of rice.

Spinach Rice ✟
Spanakorizo

10 cups (3 bunches) fresh, cleaned packed spinach
1/2 cup olive oil
6 to 8 green onions, chopped
1/2 cup fresh dill, chopped
1/2 cup fresh parsley, chopped
1 (14-ounce) can diced tomatoes
Salt and pepper to taste
1/4 cup rice plus 1 tablespoon

Thoroughly wash spinach, drain and set aside. In a large pot heat oil and sauté onions. Add spinach and simmer for 5 minutes, stirring with a wooden spoon until the spinach is wilted. Add dill, parsley, tomatoes, salt and pepper and bring to a boil. Add rice; cover and reduce heat. Cook for 20 minutes or until rice is done.

~Georgia
Belesin

Serves: 4

Σπανακόρυζο

Spinach Rice ☦
Spanakorizo

2 pounds fresh spinach, washed and drained
3/4 cup olive or vegetable oil
1 bunch leeks, cleaned and washed
1 teaspoon fresh dill or 1/2 teaspoon, dried
2 tablespoons tomato paste
2 1/2 cups water
1 cup rice
Salt and pepper to taste
Lemon wedges

Heat oil in a heavy saucepan and sauté leeks until translucent, about 5 minutes. Add spinach and sauté until spinach has wilted. Add dill and tomato paste diluted in the 2 1/2 cups water. Bring to a boil and add the rice. Stir, cover and simmer for 20 minutes until the rice is done and liquid is absorbed. Add salt and pepper to taste. Garnish with lemon wedges before serving.

~Georgia
Vareldzis

Serves: 4 to 6

A Lenten dish that also serves as a delicious side dish with chicken or meat; especially lamb. Sliced tomatoes make a colorful and complete accompaniment.

Stuffed Tomatoes ☦
Domates Yemistes

8 medium-sized tomatoes
1 cup olive oil
2 cups chopped onions
Reserved tomato pulp
1 (8-ounce) can tomato sauce
1¼ cup rice
½ cup fresh parsley, chopped
¼ cup fresh mint, chopped
4 to 5 garlic cloves, chopped
Salt and pepper to taste

Wash tomatoes and cut a thin slice off the bottom ends; reserve
to use as lids. Scoop pulp and seeds from tomatoes and reserve.
Turn tomatoes upside down to drain. In a saucepan sauté onion
in half the oil. Add chopped tomato pulp and tomato sauce.
Cook over medium heat for a few minutes, then add rice and
remaining ingredients. Mix well. Fill tomatoes almost full with
the rice mixture and cover with tomato lids. Arrange them in
a baking dish and pour over the remaining oil. Bake in a
preheated 375 degree oven for 1 hour.

~Georgia
Belesiu

Serves: 4 (as a main course)

Τζούντρα

Lentils with Rice ☦
Juddra

1 cup uncooked lentils
4 cups water
1 large onion, chopped
1/2 cup olive oil
1/2 cup uncooked rice
1 tablespoon salt
1/8 teaspoon pepper
2 tablespoons fresh lemon juice (optional)

Rinse lentils and put into a heavy saucepan with the water. Bring to a boil and cook over medium heat 15 minutes. Add the chopped onion, oil and rice. Cover and cook 20 to 25 minutes, until rice and lentils are cooked, stirring occasionally. Add salt and pepper. Serve on a platter.

~Lori (Owen) Thompson and Heather Owen

This may be served hot or cold. The juice of 1/2 lemon may be added if desired.

Serves: 4

Our grandmother, Violet Diamond, fixed rice with lentils. She served it with plain yogurt and Greek salad. We always had our grandmother make this dish when we went to visit her.

Beef,
Pork &
Lamb

Contents

All-Purpose Greek Marinade
Marinata

Equal amounts of:
Lemon juice (fresh or bottled)
Olive Oil
1/2 cup garlic cloves (before chopped)
Salt and pepper to taste
Oregano to taste

Blend all the ingredients together in a food processor until the consistency of a thick paste.

Note: Use on chicken, lamb or beef.

~Mike
Diamond and
George Lampus

Greek Meatballs
Keftethes

5 pounds ground beef
2 cups bread crumbs
Dash of thyme
1/2 teaspoon black pepper
1/2 teaspoon red pepper
Dash of allspice
1/4 teaspoon coriander
1/4 teaspoon oregano
1/4 teaspoon basil
1/2 teaspoon garlic, crushed
4 teaspoons salt
2 eggs
1/4 cup olive oil
1/4 cup lemon juice
2 cups finely chopped onion
1/2 cup Romano or Parmesan cheese, grated

Tomato juice (8 ounces for every 6 meatballs)

Combine all ingredients except tomato juice and mix well. Form into small balls and flatten slightly. Heat oil in a large skillet and fry the meatballs, turning to brown on all sides. Remove with slotted spoon and drain on paper towels.

~Saki and John Tzantarmas, New Copper Penny Restaurant

After meatballs are cooked, heat tomato juice in a saucepan. Bring to boiling and reduce juice until thickened (about 3 minutes) Combine meatballs with tomato juice and keep warm in a chafing dish.

This recipe is delicious as an appetizer or served as a main course. Don't be surprised to see the adults as well as the children start fighting over that last meatball!

Greek Spaghetti
Makaronatha

1/2 cup (1 stick) butter or olive oil
3 onions, finely chopped
5 pounds ground beef or turkey
1 (16-ounce) can diced tomatoes
3 tablespoons fresh or dried parsley
6 tablespoons tomato paste
2 sticks cinnamon
5 bay leaves
2 tablespoons salt
1 tablespoon pepper

2 3-pound packages spaghetti plus 1/2 teaspoon salt
1 cup (2 sticks) butter
Garlic to taste
Grated Parmesan or mizithra cheese

In a sauté pan over medium-high heat sauté the onions in olive oil or butter until translucent. Add the meat and cook until well browned. Add the remaining ingredients and simmer for 1 hour.

In a large pot cook the spaghetti, according to directions in boiling, salted water.

Brown garlic cloves in 2 sticks of butter and mix thoroughly with cooked spaghetti. Serve with sauce and top with grated cheese.

Serves: 25

*Saki and
John Tzantarmas,
New Copper
Penny
Restaurant*

Meatballs
Keftethes

1 pound lean ground beef
1 medium onion, finely grated
1 teaspoon oregano, dried
1/2 cup bread crumbs
1 egg, slightly beaten
1 teaspoon tomato paste
1 teaspoon salt
1/2 teaspoon pepper
3 tablespoons oil

Tomato Sauce:
2 tablespoons tomato paste
2 tablespoons vinegar
1/2 teaspoon allspice
Salt and pepper to taste

In a bowl, combine beef, onion, oregano, bread crumbs, egg, tomato paste, salt and pepper. Knead lightly. Form into small balls. Heat the oil in a shallow pan and fry for 10 to 15 minutes, turning until brown. Remove from pan and place in a serving dish.

Combine tomato paste, vinegar, allspice, salt and pepper in the same pan used to prepare meatballs. Bring to a quick boil. Strain and pour over the meatballs. Serve hot.

~Georgia
Maletis Miller

Yield: Approximately 30 meatballs.

This is my mother-in-law's recipe and is excellent.

Violet Lampros' Spaghetti Sauce
Saltsa yia Makaronia

2 tablespoons olive oil
2 1/2 pounds lean ground round
1/2 pound pork sausage
1 green pepper, chopped
1 large onion, chopped
5 garlic cloves, chopped
1 large (14 1/2-ounce) can stewed tomatoes flavored
    with green pepper or herbs
2 (8-ounce) cans tomato sauce
Dash of catsup
Dash of Worcestershire sauce
3/4 pound mushrooms, sliced
1 cup fresh parsley, chopped
2 tablespoons oregano, dried
2 teaspoons cinnamon
1 teaspoon spaghetti sauce seasoning
Salt and pepper

In a skillet over medium-high heat, sauté ground beef in
2 tablespoons olive oil. Add sausage, green pepper, onion
and garlic. Mash the stewed tomatoes and add to meat mixture.
Then add the tomato sauce, catsup and Worcestershire sauce.
Simmer 30 minutes.

In a separate pan, sauté sliced mushrooms and set aside.
Add mushrooms, parsley, oregano, cinnamon and spaghetti
seasoning to the sauce and simmer another 30 to 45 minutes.
Add salt and pepper to taste.

~Elaine
Lampros

Serves: 10

*It was tradition for the Lampros family to
have this dish on Christmas Eve.
It is very easy to prepare and a
wonderful recipe for a large group.*

Κεφτέδες με Σάλτσα Ντομάτας

Meatballs in Tomato Sauce
Keftethes me Saltsa Domatas

2 to 2 1/2 pounds lean ground beef
1 large onion, finely chopped
3 garlic cloves, finely chopped
4 to 5 slices bread, toasted and made into crumbs
1/2 bunch fresh parsley, chopped
2 eggs, beaten
1/2 cup broth or water
1 3/4 teaspoon salt
1/2 teaspoon oregano
1/2 teaspoon ground pepper
3 tablespoons corn or olive oil for frying

Tomato Sauce:
3 (8-ounce) cans tomato sauce
2 tablespoons catsup
1 cup broth or water
1 carrot, approximately 4 inches long, finely chopped
A few inner leaves of celery, finely chopped or
    1 celery stalk, finely chopped
1 tablespoon onion, finely chopped
1 or 2 sprigs parsley, finely chopped
1/4 teaspoon salt
1/8 teaspoon ground pepper
1 garlic clove, finely ground
1/2 teaspoon oregano, dried

In a large bowl mix all ingredients for meatballs. Form into balls
(approximately 45 to 50 medium sized meatballs) and roll in flour.
In a skillet over medium-high heat, brown meatballs in the oil. Set
aside while making sauce.

Tomato sauce: combine ingredients in a saucepan. Bring to a boil,
lower heat and simmer for approximately 5 minutes. (Sauce and
meatballs will be thoroughly cooked later in the roasting pan.)
Place a layer of meatballs in roasting pan and pour just enough
sauce to cover. Shake pan to allow sauce to go to bottom of the
pan. Add rest of the meatballs and cover with remainder of sauce.

Bake in a preheated 350 degree oven, uncovered, for 10 minutes.
Cover and cook for another 35 to 45 minutes. Baste meatballs
with sauce once or twice while cooking. It is important that all
meatballs are covered with sauce while cooking to avoid drying

out. Add more water, if necessary. Serve hot. Meatballs are especially delicious when served with cooked noodles, baked with browned butter and Parmesan cheese.

Helpful hints: meatballs may be prepared the day prior to serving. Brown meatballs, place in roasting pan, cover and refrigerate. Bake with tomato sauce immediately prior to serving.

~Nicolas G.
Hanches

Serves: 10

Of all the delicious meals my mother has prepared over the years, her meatballs in tomato sauce are by far my favorite. My mother, Mrs. Gus Hanches, now lives in Seattle. Our friends and relatives in Spokane, Washington, where I grew up, have raved about her meatballs for years.

Σάλτσα με Κιμά για Μακαρόνια

Meat Sauce for Spaghetti
Saltsa me Kima yia Makaronia

¹/4 cup olive oil
1 small onion, chopped
1 pound ground beef or chicken
10 bay leaves
1 (8-ounce) can tomato sauce
Salt and pepper to taste
1 cup kefalotiri cheese, grated

In a saucepan sauté onions in olive oil until translucent. Add ground beef or chicken and brown. Add bay leaves, tomato sauce, salt and pepper. Cover and simmer for 20 minutes. Remove bay leaves. Drain any excess fat and stir in cheese. Serve over your favorite pasta.

~Christine
Rulli

This recipe is from my cousin who came from Mytilene.

Κεφτέδες της Μαμάς

Mama's Meatballs
Keftethes tis Mamas

2 medium potatoes, peeled and quartered
3 large onions, quartered
2 pounds lean ground beef
1 egg, beaten
3 teaspoons Parmesan cheese, grated
1 tablespoon oregano, dried
Salt and pepper to taste

Flour, for dusting
Vegetable oil, for frying

In a large pot, boil peeled potatoes until soft. Boil onions until soft. Drain water from potatoes and onions and mash them together. Add the ground beef to the potatoes and onions. Add beaten egg to meat mixture and mix well. Add the grated cheese, oregano, salt and pepper and mix well.

~Fifi
Thomas
Prihogios

Form into balls the size of golf balls and flatten slightly. Dust each meatball with flour and fry in hot vegetable oil. Fry until meat is cooked all the way through. (Cooking time will vary according to size.) These are excellent served either hot or cold.

This is my mother's recipe for keftethes from Samos. Whenever we vacationed in Iowa visiting my parents, Mama always made lots of keftethes for us to eat as we drove back to Oregon. They became a family favorite and eating them always brings back many happy memories.

"Vineyard" Meatballs
Keftethes Ambelion

1 egg
1 1/4 cups fine soft bread crumbs
2 tablespoons instant minced onion
1/4 cup fresh parsley, chopped
1/4 teaspoon basil
1/2 teaspoon salt
1 teaspoon garlic salt
1/4 teaspoon pepper
3/4 cup Burgundy
1/4 cup water
1 1/2 pounds lean ground beef
1 tablespoon oil for frying

Spaghetti sauce:
1 1/2 ounce envelope spaghetti sauce mix
1 (16-ounce) can tomatoes

1 (16-ounce) package spaghetti
Butter
Parmesan cheese, grated

In a bowl beat egg lightly. Combine with bread crumbs, onion,
parsley, basil, salt, garlic salt, pepper, 1/4 cup wine and water.
Let stand until crumbs are soft. Add beef and mix well. Using
a rounded tablespoonful for each, shape into balls.

In a saucepan, combine spaghetti sauce mix with remaining
1/2 cup wine; add tomatoes, breaking them up. In a separate pan,
simmer the sauce while browning meatballs in oil. Drain off fat
from meatballs. Add sauce, cover and simmer 15 to 20 minutes.

Serve with spaghetti that has been boiled, drained and drizzled
lightly with melted butter and mixed with a little Parmesan
cheese. It's the Burgundy that makes the difference! Men love it.

~Katherine
Vlahos Lockie

Serves: 8

*Another yellowed newsprint recipe from
Yiayia Marina Vlahos' little green
plastic cooking box!*

Meatballs in Egg-Lemon Sauce
Youvarlakia Avgolemono

1 pound lean ground beef
1/4 cup rice
1 egg
1 medium onion, finely chopped
1/2 cup fresh parsley, chopped
1 teaspoon salt
1/4 teaspoon pepper
Water for boiling
2 tablespoons oil

Egg-Lemon Sauce (Avgolemono):
2 eggs
Juice of 1/2 lemon, freshly squeezed
  (may desire more to taste)

In a large bowl combine the ground beef, rice, egg, onion, parsley, salt and pepper; mix well. Take enough of the meat mixture to create meatballs (approximately 30) the size of large walnuts. Set aside.

Fill a medium size pot with enough water to cover the meatballs. Add oil to the water and bring to a boil. As the water is boiling, gradually add the meatballs one at a time to keep them from sticking together. Continue boiling until meatballs are cooked thoroughly and the rice is done (approximately 30 minutes). Remove from heat.

Egg-Lemon Sauce (Avgolemono): Using a small ladle, remove 1 cup broth from the pot and set aside to cool. Beat eggs and slowly add lemon juice. Gradually add broth to egg mixture; slowly add lemon sauce to the pot with the meatballs to keep eggs from curdling.

Serves: 6 (30 meatballs)

~ Angeliki
Anasis

Meatballs
Youvarlakia

2 pounds ground beef
1 onion, grated
4 to 5 large garlic cloves, minced
3 tablespoons fresh mint
1/8 teaspoon allspice
1/2 teaspoon oregano, dried
1/2 cup plus 2 tablespoons rice
1/2 cup white wine
Salt and pepper to taste
1 (10 1/2-ounce) can tomato soup, undiluted

Mix all of the above ingredients together except tomato soup.
Add some water into mixture and form into balls. Place
meatballs in baking pan and pour tomato soup over the top.
Dot meatballs with butter. Put pan into the oven and bake in
a preheated 375 degree oven for about 40 minutes.

~Elena
Phoutrides

Note: The garlic cloves should be very large.

Serves: 4 to 6

*This recipe is from my Yiayia Betty.
I copied it down from her recipe
when I was about 5 years old.*

Meatballs in Egg-Lemon Sauce
Youvarlakia Avgolemono

2 pounds ground beef
1/2 cup short grain rice
1/2 cup fresh parsley, finely chopped
3 tablespoons fresh mint, finely chopped
1 egg
2 teaspoons salt
1 teaspoon pepper
1 medium onion, finely chopped
2 tablespoons olive oil
5 cups water
1 (8-ounce) can tomato sauce

Egg-Lemon Sauce (Avgolemono):
3 egg yolks
1/4 cup freshly squeezed lemon juice

In a large bowl combine the ground meat, rice, parsley, mint,
one egg, salt, pepper and 3/4 of the chopped onion. Knead until
thoroughly mixed, then shape into medium-size (30 to 35) balls.
Set aside. In a large pot sauté 1/4 cup chopped onion in olive oil.
Add 5 cups water and tomato sauce and bring to a boil. Add
meatballs slowly to avoid interrupting the boil. Reduce heat
and simmer covered for 1 hour.

Egg-Lemon Sauce (Avgolemono): Lightly beat the egg yolks
together with the lemon juice. Very slowly add 2 to 4 ladlefuls of
broth at a time to egg mixture, beating vigorously to keep eggs
from curdling. Remove meatballs from heat. Add egg-lemon
mixture to pot. Return to heat and bring to a boil. Turn heat off
and let sit for awhile before serving. Makes 30 to 35 meatballs.

*~Antoinette
Belesin
Papailiou*

Serves: 6

A family favorite.

Kamari Stew
Stifatho Kamariotiko

1/3 cup olive oil
2 pounds lean beef, cut into small cubes
2 pounds sweet white or new yellow onions, chopped
2 garlic cloves, minced
2 bay leaves
1/4 cup red vinegar
2 cups tomato purée
Salt to taste

Heat oil in Dutch oven. Add meat (do not brown) and all other ingredients and mix together. Simmer for 2 hours or until meat is tender. I prefer to serve this dish on a plate over boiled noodles along with a cucumber, radish and lettuce salad with olive oil and vinegar dressing. French bread and dry red wine are also a good accompaniment. Traditionally Greeks do not eat desserts except for fruit, but I prefer to serve apple pie to make the dinner complete.

~Jeanette
Michas

Serves: 4

Kamari is a village in Tripoli. My mother, Bessie Kosebas, is one of the "to be envied cooks" who knows exactly how much of what to put into the preparation of any dish without employing any measuring devices. "One or two handfuls, a fistful, a pinch, a little of this, more of that, a little more of whatever, a squirt of, a dash." Her dishes proved beyond any doubt that this method of cooking is ideal for her. Trying to follow one of her recipes is strictly another matter. Here is a word for word translation of a recipe she gave me almost 50 years ago when I was a new bride.

Athenian Moussaka
Athinaiko Moussaka

2 large eggplants, trimmed and cut lengthwise
   into 1/4 inch thick slices
Salt
1/2 cup olive oil, divided

Meat Sauce:
2 tablespoons olive oil
2 medium onions, chopped
2 1/2 pounds ground beef or ground lamb
2 teaspoons salt
2 (6-ounce) cans tomato paste
1 1/4 cups red wine
1/4 cup fresh parsley, chopped
1 stick cinnamon
2 garlic cloves, minced
3 tablespoons fine bread crumbs
1 cup Parmesan cheese, grated

Béchamel Sauce:
1/3 cup butter
1/2 cup flour
1 quart milk
1 teaspoon salt
1/4 teaspoon nutmeg
6 eggs, lightly beaten
1/2 cup Parmesan cheese, grated

Sprinkle eggplant slices with salt and let sit for 30 minutes.
Rinse and drain. Pour olive oil into two large baking pans;
turn over eggplant to coat both sides. Bake in single layer in
a preheated 425 degree oven for 30 minutes.

In a heavy skillet sauté onions in 2 tablespoon olive oil. Add
ground meat and cook, stirring until crumbly. Add salt, tomato
paste, red wine, parsley, cinnamon and garlic. Cover and simmer

30 minutes. Remove cover and cinnamon stick. Continue cooking until liquid has evaporated. Stir in bread crumbs and Parmesan cheese.

Béchamel Sauce: Melt $1/3$ cup butter and blend in $1/2$ cup flour. Cook, stirring constantly for 2 minutes. Gradually stir in milk. Continue until mixture boils and thickens. Add salt, nutmeg and Parmesan. Stir hot sauce slowly into 6 slightly beaten eggs.

Lay half the eggplant slices in a 9 x 13 inch pan. Spoon meat sauce evenly and top with remaining eggplant. Pour on the Béchamel sauce and sprinkle with grated cheese. Bake uncovered in a preheated 350 degree oven for 1 hour. Let stand a few minutes before cutting.

~Kathy
Phoutrides

Serves: 10 to 12

A family favorite.

Baked Eggplant and Beef
Moussaka Romano

1 medium eggplant, peeled and sliced 3/8 inches thick
Oil
1 pound lasagna noodle
1 pound ground beef
1/2 cup onion, chopped
2 (6-ounce) cans tomato paste
2 teaspoons salt
1/2 teaspoon pepper
1 teaspoon garlic powder
1 teaspoon oregano, crushed
1 teaspoon sweet basil, crushed
4 cups water

Béchamel Sauce:
1/4 cup (1/2 stick) butter
1/4 cup flour
1/2 teaspoon salt
2 cups milk
1 (15-ounce) carton ricotta cheese
1/4 teaspoon cinnamon
3 eggs

1/2 cup grated Parmesan cheese

In a heavy skillet, fry eggplant lightly in oil. Set aside. Cook lasagna noodles in boiling salted water (1 gallon water plus 2 tablespoons salt) until slightly undercooked, about 12 minutes. Rinse with cold water and drain. Pat off all excess moisture. Set aside. Brown ground beef. Add onion and cook 5 minutes. Add tomato paste, salt, pepper, garlic powder, oregano and basil. Stir in 4 cups of water. Simmer uncovered for 1 hour.

Béchamel Sauce: In a medium saucepan, melt butter. Add flour and 1/2 teaspoon salt to make a paste. Stir in milk slowly and cook, until sauce is thick and smooth. In a small bowl, combine white sauce with ricotta cheese, cinnamon and eggs.

Cover bottom of 15 x 10 x 2 inch baking pan with 1/3 of the ricotta cheese mixture and 1/2 of the lasagna noodles. Layer the eggplant slices over noodles adding the meat sauce, reserving 1 cup. Repeat layers. Dot top with remaining ricotta cheese mixture. Ladle 1 cup meat mixture around dots of ricotta mixture; swirl together with a spoon. Sprinkle Parmesan cheese over top.

Bake in a preheated 350 degree oven for 45 minutes. Allow to set 10 minutes. Cut in squares and serve with sauce.

~Katherine
Vlahos Lockie

Serves: 8 to 10

Found in Yiayia Marina Vlahos' little green plastic recipe box printed on very yellowed newsprint.

Light and Easy Moussaka

1 medium eggplant, sliced 1/2 inch thick
1 tablespoon olive oil
12 ounces extra lean ground beef
1 onion, chopped
1/2 cup fresh parsley
1 large fresh tomato, chopped
2 tablespoons green pepper, chopped
2 tablespoons celery, chopped
1 garlic clove, minced
1/4 cup red wine
Scant 1/8 teaspoon cinnamon
4 ounces shredded mozzarella cheese

Brush eggplant slices with olive oil. Broil eggplant slices on baking sheet about 5 minutes until tender, but still firm. Set aside.

Sauté ground beef with the onion until red from meat disappears. Add parsley, tomato, green pepper, celery and garlic. Simmer for 25 minutes. Add wine and cinnamon.

Arrange half the eggplant slices in a casserole dish to make the bottom layer. Spread meat sauce over eggplant. Add remaining eggplant layer. Sprinkle with mozzarella cheese.

Bake in a preheated 350 degree oven 25 to 30 minutes. May brown under broiler for last few minutes if desired.

~Diane
Jouganatos Cook

Serves: 4

Μουσακάς

Baked Eggplant and Beef
Moussaka

4 medium eggplants
Salt
1/4 cup (1/2 stick) butter
2 pounds ground beef
2 onions, chopped
2 tablespoons tomato paste
1/4 cup parsley, chopped
1/2 cup red wine
Salt and pepper to taste
1/2 cup water
1/8 teaspoon cinnamon
3 eggs, beaten
1/2 cup Parmesan cheese, grated
1/2 cup bread crumbs

Béchamel Sauce:
6 tablespoons butter
6 tablespoons four
3 cups hot milk
Salt and pepper to taste
1/2 teaspoon nutmeg
4 egg yolks, lightly beaten

Oil, for frying
Cheese, grated

Peel eggplants and cut into slices. Sprinkle with salt and let stand between 2 heavy plates while browning meat and preparing sauce. In frying pan, melt butter; sauté meat and onions until brown. Add tomato paste, parsley, wine, salt and pepper and water. Simmer until liquid is absorbed. Cool. Stir in cinnamon, eggs, cheese and half the bread crumbs.

In a heavy skillet, brown eggplant slices on both sides in hot oil. (Add oil as needed). Grease an oven-proof casserole and sprinkle bottom with remaining bread crumbs. Cover with layer of eggplant slices, then a layer of meat. Continue layering until all eggplant and meat is used, finishing with one layer of eggplant. Set aside while making béchamel sauce.

Béchamel Sauce: In a saucepan melt 6 tablespoons butter over low heat. Add flour and stir until well blended. Remove from heat. Gradually stir in milk and return to heat. Cook, stirring until sauce is thick and smooth. Add salt and pepper to taste. Add nutmeg. Combine egg yolks with a little of the hot sauce. Stir egg mixture into the sauce and cook over very low heat for 2 minutes, stirring constantly. Cover the eggplant with sauce and sprinkle with additional grated cheese.

Bake in a preheated 350 degree oven for one hour. Serve hot.

Serves: 10 to 12

~Nick
Vanikiotis

Baked Eggplant and Beef
Moussaka

1 medium eggplant, cut into 1/3 inch slices
6 medium potatoes, peeled and thinly sliced
Olive oil
1 medium onion, chopped
1 garlic clove, minced
1 1/2 pounds lean ground beef
1 (8-ounce) can tomato sauce
2 teaspoons cinnamon
Salt and pepper to taste
1 egg
1/4 cup Parmesan cheese, grated

Béchamel Sauce:
1/4 cup (1/2 stick) butter
4 tablespoons flour
2 cups milk
1 egg yolk, lightly beaten
1/4 cup Parmesan cheese, grated

In a large skillet fry the sliced eggplant and potatoes separately in olive oil and set aside.

Sauté the chopped onion and minced garlic in olive oil until golden brown. Add the ground beef and cook until brown; pour off excess fat. Add the tomato sauce, cinnamon, salt and pepper and simmer for 20 minutes. Allow to cool slightly, then add one egg to the meat mixture. Stir well. Add the Parmesan, stir and set aside.

Béchamel Sauce: In a saucepan, melt butter and stir in flour. Slowly add 2 cups of milk, stirring constantly over medium heat until it thickens. Remove from heat. Stir in egg yolk then the Parmesan cheese.

In a 5 quart casserole dish layer ¹/₂ the potatoes, ¹/₂ the eggplant, all the meat mixture, remaining eggplant, and remaining potatoes. Top with sauce.

Bake in a preheated 350 degree oven about 45 minutes until it bubbles. Check the interior temperature with a knife. Allow to cool 20 minutes before cutting and serving.

Note: Moussaka can be made ahead and kept in the refrigerator until ready to bake. It can also be frozen. Do not thaw prior to baking.

~Catherine J. Lingas

Serves: 6

When I was first married, a school friend of my husband, then a first officer on a Greek ship, came to Vancouver, BC. He said "since I was now married to a Greek I needed to learn how to cook like a Greek." He told me what to buy and came over one afternoon to show me step by step how to make Moussaka.

Beef Stew with Onions
Stifatho

2 pounds boneless beef, cut into small cubes
1/2 cup olive oil
4 pounds boiling onions, peeled and left whole
1/2 cup red wine vinegar
1 (6-ounce) can tomato sauce
5 garlic cloves
4 bay leaves
1 cinnamon stick
5 to 6 whole cloves
1 large "Golden Delicious" apple, sliced unpeeled
Salt and pepper to taste

In a heavy bottom pan with a lid, over medium-high heat, brown meat in olive oil. Add onions. Add the remaining ingredients, salt and pepper to taste. Add enough water to pot so that all ingredients are covered. Cover pot and bake in a preheated 375 degree oven for 2 hours.

~Anastasia
Couris

Beef Stew with Onions
Stifatho

2 1/2 pounds top sirloin, cut in 1 1/2-inch pieces
3 tablespoons butter
2 tablespoons olive oil
1 medium onion, finely chopped
4 garlic cloves, minced
1 cup dry red wine
3 tablespoons red wine vinegar
4 teaspoons tomato paste
1 tablespoon brown sugar
1 tablespoon mixed pickling spices (in a cheesecloth bag)
1 stick cinnamon
Salt and pepper to taste
2 pounds small onions

In a skillet brown meat on all sides in butter and oil. Remove meat and place in a Dutch oven. Using the same skillet, sauté onions and garlic. Add red wine, red wine vinegar, tomato paste and brown sugar. Stir and cook for 5 minutes. Pour sauce over the beef. Add the spice bag, cinnamon stick and salt and pepper to taste. Cover and cook over low heat for 1 hour.

Peel onions. Make a small cut in the root end of each to prevent bursting. Add onions to the meat mixture and simmer 1 hour longer until meat and onions are tender and sauce has thickened. Serve with noodles, macaroni or rice.

~Sophia
Kriara

Serves: 8

Στιφάδο

Beef Stew with Onions
Stifatho

1 pound lean sirloin, flank or round steak,
   cut into serving-size portions
2 cups tomatoes, peeled and chopped
1 pound small boiling onions
1 garlic clove
Bay leaf
1 teaspoon whole pickling spice
1/2 cup red wine
1 teaspoon pepper

1/4 pound feta cheese, cubed
1/4 cup walnuts, coarsely chopped

In a saucepan brown the meat in its own juices. Add tomatoes
and simmer for 20 minutes. Peel onions and leave whole,
and add to stew. Place garlic, bay leaf, and spices in a clean
cheesecloth. Add this plus wine to mixture. Add a small amount
of water as liquid becomes reduced. Cook tightly covered until
onions are tender, about 30 minutes. Before serving toss feta
cheese cubes and walnuts into the stew.

~Diane
Jonganatos
Cook

Serves: 4

Στιφάδο

Beef Stew with Onions
Stifatho

1/2 cup olive oil
2 pounds lean beef cut in 2-inch cubes
2 teaspoons salt
1/4 teaspoon pepper
4 garlic cloves, crushed
1 stick cinnamon
3 bay leaves
8 to 10 whole black peppercorns
1 cup dry red wine
1 cup tomato sauce
3 tablespoons wine vinegar
1 tablespoon brown sugar
3 pounds small whole boiling onions

Heat oil in a heavy saucepan. Add meat and brown on all sides; season with salt, pepper and garlic. Add cinnamon stick, bay leaves and peppercorns. Pour in the red wine, tomato sauce, vinegar and brown sugar. Cover and simmer for 1 hour.

Peel the onions and make a small cut in the root end of each to prevent bursting. Add the onions and simmer an additional 30 minutes or until the onions and meat are tender and the sauce is thick.

Serves: 4 to 6

~Angeliki
Anasis

Beef Stew with Onions
Stifatho

2 tablespoons olive oil
3 pounds lean stew meat (beef or lamb)
   cut into 1 1/2-inch cubes
2 cups yellow onions, chopped
2 (16-ounce) cans pear tomatoes in juice
1/2 cup tomato paste
2 teaspoons salt
1 cup water
1/2 cup whole peeled garlic
15 whole peeled shallots or small onions
1/4 cup red wine vinegar
1/4 cup honey
2 cinnamon sticks
1 teaspoon whole black peppercorns
1/2 teaspoon whole cloves
1/2 teaspoon ground allspice

On stovetop in a heavy large pot with a tight-fitting lid, heat olive oil. Brown meat and chopped onions. Add tomatoes, tomato paste, salt and water. Cover and bake in a preheated 400 degree oven for 1 hour and 15 minutes. Add garlic, shallots, vinegar, honey, cinnamon, peppercorns, cloves and allspice. Bake covered an additional 1 1/2 hours. Serve with your favorite potato, rice or pasta.

~Berbati
Restaurant

Serves: 6

Stuffed Grapevine Leaves
Dolmathes

1 1/2 pounds ground beef
1/2 cup long grain rice
1 onion, chopped
1/4 cup fresh parsley, chopped
1 teaspoon fresh mint, chopped
1 egg, slightly beaten
3 tablespoons tomato sauce, optional
1 teaspoon fennel, optional
1 cup beef broth or water
2 tablespoons butter, melted
Salt and pepper to taste
50 to 60 grape leaves, fresh or canned

Blend beef, rice, onion, parsley, mint, egg, tomato sauce,
fennel, beef broth, butter, salt and pepper and mix well. Place
1 teaspoon filling in center of grape leaf, making sure that shiny
side of leaf is on the outside when rolling and tucking in the
ends of the leaf. Continue in this manner until all meat is used.

Line the bottom of a stockpot with coarser leaves. Arrange
dolmathes side by side in layers. Invert a heavy plate on top
to hold dolmathes in place. Add enough water to cover
dolmathes. Cover with lid, bring to a boil and then lower
heat to simmer for 1 1/2 hours. Can be served as a main course
or appetizer. Delicious served with plain yogurt, if desired.

Note: Fresh grape leaves should be put in hot water for about
5 minutes to make them pliable. Canned leaves should be
rinsed in water.

~Pearl Pavlos

Yield: 50 to 70

*This is our family must for birthdays, dinners,
baptisms, weddings and just because. We try to make up
the mixture the night before and let set in the refrigerator
overnight. This blends all the flavors together nicely. Also, they
seem to roll easier and faster. Have rolled and fast frozen to be
cooked later. Have rolled, cooked and then frozen.
Have rolled, cooked and eaten same day!*

Ντολμάδες

Stuffed Grapevine Leaves
Dolmathes

1 jar (1 pint) grape leaves
2 tablespoons vegetable oil
1 garlic clove, chopped
2 onions, grated
1 1/2 pounds ground beef or
   1 pound ground beef and 1/2 pound ground pork
1 cup long grain rice
2 1/2 teaspoons salt
Pepper to taste
1/2 cup fresh parsley, chopped
1/4 cup fresh dill, chopped
1/4 cup fresh mint, chopped
1/4 cup (1/2 stick) butter
2 cups beef or chicken broth
Juice of 1 1/2 lemons

Egg-Lemon Sauce (Avgolemono):
3 eggs, well-beaten
1/4 cup water
1 heaping teaspoon cornstarch
Juice of 2 lemons

Rinse leaves in cold water. Let stand in warm water as
dolmathes are being prepared. (If necessary, simmer leaves
in water for 10 minutes to soften.)

Sauté garlic and onions in the oil and add to the meat mixture.
Add the next six ingredients plus 3/4 cup water to make a softer
mixture. Place 1 teaspoon filling in center of grapevine leaf
(ribbed side) and shape in a narrow roll. (May be frozen at
this point.)

Line deep saucepan with grapevine leaves and arrange
dolmathes in layers. Add butter, broth, lemon juice and cover
with inverted plate.

Egg-Lemon Sauce (Avgolemono): In a mixing bowl, beat eggs until light and fluffy. Add cornstarch and water, blending until stiff. Add lemon juice and gradually add hot liquid from the dolmathes, a little at a time, until eggs are lukewarm. Beat constantly. Remove saucepan from heat. Pour egg-lemon sauce slowly over dolmathes. Shake saucepan gently to spread sauce evenly. Serve at once.

Hint: Tender leaves picked from the vines are the best. After they are picked they should be rinsed, then blanched. They can also be frozen. Lay them flat before putting them into the freezer.

Yield: 65 rolls

~Anthony Gianopolous and Helen Gianopolous Tzakis

Every time we have a gathering my father is asked to bring his famous dolmathes. Everyone goes wild for them. I finally got him to tell me his recipe. Hope you enjoy eating them as much as we do.

Baked Pasta with Beef
Youvetsi

2 tablespoons olive oil
3 pounds lean chuck roast
3 garlic cloves, halved
Salt and pepper to taste
2 (8-ounce) cans tomato sauce
1 cup water
1 cup white wine
1 teaspoon sugar
1 1/2 cups orzo pasta (manestra)
Mizithra cheese, grated to sprinkle over pasta

Coat the bottom of a roasting pan with olive oil. Make equally spaced cross cuts in the meat and insert garlic pieces, then salt and pepper both sides. Place roast in the pan and brown in the oven (bottom rack) uncovered 20 to 30 minutes on each side. Pour in the tomato sauce. Add water and white wine. Cover and bake in a preheated 375 degree oven for 35 minutes. Sprinkle sugar into sauce. Turn roast over, cover and cook another 35 minutes. Roast should be "pull apart" done (longer cooking time may be needed depending on size and cut of roast). Remove roast from pan with some of the pan juices, cover and set aside.

Par boil pasta. Rinse, then add it to the sauce in the pan. An adequate amount of hot water may be added to the sauce to boil the pasta. Increase oven temperature to 425 degrees. Boil the pasta uncovered until done stirring every 10 minutes. Consistency should be thick (not soupy, but not totally dry). Arrange on serving platter with roast and sprinkle manestra with Mizithra cheese.

Substituting any roast is okay although cooking time will vary considerably. As long as there is adequate liquid and the roasting pan is covered, cooking time can be extended as required to achieve the "pull apart" quality.

~Eleni
Vokos
Marschman

This was always one of my favorite dinners growing up!
It is dedicated to my father and mother Christ and Katy
Vokos who taught me how to prepare this and many other
wonderful dishes and encouraged me to bake and cook since
I was tall enough to see over the counter!

Baked Macaroni with Beef
Pastitsio

1 large onion, chopped
1/2 cup (1 stick) butter
3 pounds ground beef
1 tablespoon salt
1/2 teaspoon pepper
Sprig of mint
1 (6-ounce) can tomato paste
1/2 cup water
Cinnamon and Nutmeg to taste
2 teaspoons fresh parsley, chopped

Béchamel Sauce:
2 quarts milk
1/2 cup flour
3 tablespoons butter
1 cup of milk
2 eggs
1 cup Parmesan cheese, grated

1 (32-ounce) package macaroni
10 eggs, beaten
1 cup (2 sticks) butter
1 1/2 cups Parmesan cheese, grated

In a large pot, combine the first set of ingredients and bring to a boil. Simmer for 2 hours over low heat.

Béchamel Sauce: In a saucepan heat the milk. In a separate saucepan make paste with flour and butter then add hot milk. Cook until thick and creamy, beating constantly. Add eggs and grated cheese and cook a little longer, just until well blended.

In 2 quarts of salted boiling water add 2 pounds macaroni. Boil until macaroni is tender. Strain and put in a large bowl. Add the beaten eggs, butter and grated cheese. Mix together and pour half of the macaroni mixture into a buttered baking pan. Add the meat sauce and spread evenly. Cover with remaining macaroni mixture. Spread cream sauce over macaroni. Beat 1 egg and spread over the cream sauce. Sprinkle top with grated cheese. Bake in a preheated 350 degree oven for 30 to 35 minutes.

~Rene
Contakos

Serves: 10

This has been passed down through three generations. It is Yiayia's version and Mother's version.

Παστίτσιο αλά Αναστασία

Baked Macaroni with Beef
Pastitsio ala Anastasia

2 pounds macaroni (Italians sell it as "Mezzani")
2 tablespoons oil
3 pounds ground beef
1 medium onion, diced
1 (15-ounce) can tomato sauce
1 (10½-ounce) can tomato soup
1 teaspoon salt
½ teaspoon black pepper
1 tablespoon oregano
1 tablespoon Worcestershire sauce
1 teaspoon allspice
1 teaspoon cinnamon
8 ounces red wine

Sauce:
½ cup (1 stick) butter
½ cup flour
2 (10½-ounce) cans cream of chicken soup
4 cups milk
12 eggs
8 ounces mizithra cheese, grated

Boil the macaroni in lightly salted water for approximately
9 minutes. Drain and cool pasta; set aside. In a large sauté
pan over medium-high heat, brown ground beef and onion in
oil. Drain the fat. Add the tomato sauce, tomato soup, salt,
pepper, oregano, Worcestershire, allspice, cinnamon and wine.
Return to heat and simmer until liquid is reduced (about 10 to
15 minutes). Remove from heat and let cool.

In a saucepan, melt the butter over medium heat. Add the
flour and cook for 2 minutes, stirring continuously. Add the
milk and continue to cook. As the sauce thickens, add the
cream of chicken soup and continue to cook (approximately
15 to 20 minutes total cooking time). Set the sauce aside to cool;
refrigerate if necessary. Beat the eggs with a wire whip until
they double in volume. Fold the beaten eggs into the cooled

chicken soup and milk sauce. To assemble the dish, mix the
macaroni and meat mixture together with 6 ounces mizithra
cheese. Adjust salt and pepper to taste. Spread evenly in a lightly
buttered baking dish of sufficient size to accommodate the
mixture (with an inch to spare to allow for the cream sauce).
Sprinkle the remaining 2 ounces of mizithra cheese over the
top of the macaroni and meat mixture. Pour the cream sauce
over the top. Bake in preheated 350 degree oven for 1 hour.

This dish is best when made a day ahead and allowed to cool
and setup completely. Servings can then be cut that will hold
their shape for reheating. Any extra servings can be wrapped
individually in plastic wrap and then aluminum foil and frozen
for future reheating (works great in the microwave!).

*~Georgia
Dariotis,
Guss Dussin
and Alice Pulos*

Serves: 20 to 24 generous portions

*Among her contemporaries,
Anastasia Dussin was considered one of
the finest and most innovative cooks
in Portland. We know she took great
pride in her culinary accomplishments and
her Baklava, in particular, was highly
regarded by the cognoscenti of Portland.*

Baked Macaroni with Beef
Pastitsio

Meat Sauce:
3 1/2 pounds ground beef
1/2 cup (1 stick) butter
2 large onions, grated
1 teaspoon salt
1 teaspoon pepper
1 teaspoon cinnamon
1/4 teaspoon nutmeg
1/3 cup dry white wine
2 1/2 (8-ounce) cans tomato sauce
2 1/2 cups water
1/2 teaspoon sugar
2 tablespoons Romano cheese, grated

Macaroni:
3 quarts boiling water
1 1/4 pounds long macaroni, broken in half
2 tablespoons salt
5 large eggs, well beaten
1 cup Romano cheese, grated

Béchamel Sauce:
5 cups whole milk
1 teaspoon salt
4 heaping tablespoons cornstarch
1/2 cup (1 stick) plus 2 tablespoons butter

Melt the butter in a heavy skillet. Add the grated onions and
salt to the melted butter. Sauté onions over high heat and stir
occasionally until translucent. Add the ground beef to the skillet.
Break up the meat with a wooden spoon until the texture is
even. Cook until browned. Add pepper, cinnamon, and nutmeg.
Stir in wine, tomato sauce, water, and sugar. Bring the meat
sauce to a boil. Lower heat to simmer and cook for 1 1/2 hours.
Remove from heat. Stir in grated Romano cheese. Mix well.

Pour 3 quarts of water into a deep pot with lid. Bring the water
to a rapid boil. Add the salt and the macaroni. Boil the macaroni

for 15 to 18 minutes until nearly done. It should be a little undercooked. Remove the macaroni from the heat and drain in a colander. Return the macaroni to the pot. Add the beaten eggs and the grated cheese to the macaroni and mix thoroughly.

Pour 4 cups of the milk into a saucepan. Mix cornstarch with the remaining cup of milk. Mix well until the cornstarch dissolves. Add the cup of milk with dissolved cornstarch to the 4 cups of milk in the saucepan. Add salt. Cook over high temperature, stirring constantly with a wooden spoon until milk comes to a boil and has thickened (be careful not to scorch milk). Remove from heat. Add butter. Gently stir in butter until it melts completely.

Grease a 17 x 11 x 2 inch pan with butter. Layer half of the macaroni into the bottom of the pan. Spoon the meat sauce evenly on top of the layer of macaroni. Layer remaining macaroni on top of the meat sauce. Spoon cream sauce evenly on top the second layer of macaroni. Bake in a preheated 375 degree oven for approximately 30 minutes until golden brown. Let sit about 20 minutes before cutting and serving.

—Maria Karis Iwasyk, George Karis and Chrisanthy Karis

Serves: 10 to 12

Pastitsio is a delicious Greek dish. It consists of two layers of macaroni and a layer of spicy meat sauce covered by a layer of luscious béchamel cream sauce. Although it takes time to prepare (approximately three hours), it is well worth the effort. Because the flavors improve on the second and even the third day, you can look forward to tasty leftovers! Pastitsio can also be prepared weeks in advance as it freezes very well.

Παστίτσιο

Baked Macaroni with Beef
Pastitsio

2 tablespoons oil
2 onions, finely chopped
2 garlic cloves, finely chopped
2 pounds lean ground beef
1 1/2 teaspoon salt
Pepper to taste
1/2 teaspoon allspice
1/2 teaspoon cinnamon
1 (8-ounce) can tomato sauce
1 cup water
1 (16-ounce) package elbow macaroni
1/4 cup (1/2 stick) butter
1 cup Romano cheese, grated

Béchamel Sauce:
15 eggs
1 tablespoon flour
1 quart milk

In a sauté pan over medium high heat, sauté onions and garlic in the oil. Reduce heat and simmer until lightly browned, then add the meat, salt and pepper, allspice and cinnamon. Brown the meat well, breaking it up into small particles. Cook until all juices are absorbed. Add the tomato sauce and water. Simmer meat while preparing the rest of the ingredients.

Cook the macaroni according to package directions (20 to 25 minutes). Drain well and put into a large bowl.

Melt butter in a small pan. Use a little to grease the baking pan and pour the rest over the cooked macaroni. Add the grated cheese to the macaroni while it is hot, so it will melt. Stir carefully, but well. Add meat sauce to the macaroni mixture. In a separate bowl, beat eggs and flour, then add milk. Strain 1 cup of the mixture over the macaroni. Place macaroni in a 12 x 18 inch baking pan. Strain the rest of the egg-milk mixture over the top of the pan.

~Nick
Vanikiotis

Bake in a preheated 375 degree oven for 10 minutes, then lower to 325 degrees for 35 minutes. Test with a knife. Cool 15 minutes. Cut into squares and serve.

Baked Macaroni with Beef
Pastitsio

1 pound ground beef
Oil or butter
Garlic to taste
1 medium onion or 1 envelope onion soup mix
   (omit salt if using mix)
Salt and pepper to taste

3 cups elbow macaroni
1/2 cup Parmesan cheese, grated

Béchamel Sauce:
3 cups milk
4 eggs, lightly beaten
1/2 cup Parmesan cheese, grated
Salt and pepper, to taste
1/2 cup (1 stick) butter
1/2 cup flour

Cinnamon

In skillet cook ground beef with oil or butter until brown. Add
garlic and onion (or soup mix). Set aside.

Cook macaroni according to package directions. Drain well and
set aside.

Béchamel Sauce: Mix all of the ingredients in a saucepan. Place
on burner; increase heat and stir sauce until slightly thickened.

Place half of the macaroni in a 9 x 13 inch pan. Top with half
the ground beef. Sprinkle with Parmesan cheese. Repeat for
second layer. Pour sauce over macaroni. Mix thoroughly with a
fork (it is best to add sauce half at a time while adding macaroni
for good distribution). Sprinkle with cinnamon. Bake in a 350
degree preheated oven for about 30 minutes. Pastitsio is done
when inserted knife comes out clean.

~ Evangeline
Dumas

Serves: 4 to 6

*This dish has been simplified for
a quick and easy dinner.*

Baked Macaroni with Beef
Pastitsio

1 pound ground lamb, beef, or a combination of both
1/4 cup (1/2 stick) butter
1 small onion, finely chopped
1 garlic clove, crushed
Salt and pepper to taste
1 (8-ounce) can tomato sauce
1/2 cup red wine
1/2 cup water
1/2 cup fresh parsley, chopped
1 (1-inch) piece cinnamon stick
1 pound long macaroni or thick spaghetti, i.e. bucatelli

1/2 cup (1 stick) butter
1 cup Parmesan or mizithra cheese, grated

4 eggs
2 cups milk

Béchamel sauce:
6 tablespoons (3/4 stick) butter
6 tablespoons flour
3 cups milk
3 egg yolks
Salt and pepper to taste
1/2 teaspoon nutmeg (optional)

Parmesan or mizithra cheese, grated, for topping

Sauté ground meat, onion and garlic in butter. Season with salt and pepper. Add tomato sauce, wine, water and seasonings. Simmer until moisture is absorbed, about 30 minutes. Remove from heat and discard cinnamon stick. Set aside.

While meat sauce is simmering, cook macaroni in salted water until almost tender. Drain and mix with melted butter and grated cheese. Mix meat and macaroni together in a 9 x 13 inch pan. Beat eggs until light and fluffy and blend in the milk. Carefully pour over the meat-macaroni mixture. Set aside.

Béchamel Sauce: In a saucepan melt butter over medium heat. Add flour slowly and cook until mixture is golden (about 10 minutes or less). Gradually stir in 3 cups milk and cook until slightly thickened, stirring constantly (it will come to a slow boil). Carefully combine with egg yolks and cook over low heat until thickened, stirring constantly. Season with salt and pepper. Add ½ teaspoon nutmeg if desired. Pour over mixture into pan.

Bake in a preheated 350 degree oven 45 minutes. Cut into squares of desired size when cooled to room temperature. Reheat, if needed, at 300 degrees for 20 to 30 minutes or until hot through the center. If you are serving this dish immediately, allow 20 minutes to set before cutting.

~Georgia
Vareldzis

My father was a great chef, and he taught me all about making Pastitsio, and I have continued to develop the recipe until it was the way my family liked it. It is one of my favorite dishes.

Σουτζουκάκια

Spicy Sausage-Shaped Meatballs
Soutzoukakia

1 (16-ounce) can tomatoes
1 tablespoon tomato paste
1 teaspoon sugar
Salt and pepper
3 large garlic cloves, minced
1 1/2 teaspoon cumin seed
1 1/2 pounds ground sirloin or lean ground beef
2 slices bread (soaked in red wine)
Oil for frying

Combine tomatoes, tomato paste, sugar, salt and pepper,
1 minced garlic clove and 1/2 teaspoon cumin seed in saucepan.
Heat and simmer for 30 minutes. Combine ground beef, 2 cloves
of the minced garlic, bread and remaining 1 teaspoon cumin,
salt and pepper. Mix well. Form into sausage shapes (about

~Theodora   3 inches long). Drop Soutzoukakia into tomato sauce, cover and
Vlachos   simmer on low flame for 20 minutes. Serve hot over rice pilaf.

Σουτζουκάκια

Spicy Sausage-Shaped Meatballs
Soutzoukakia

1 pound ground beef
2 slices bread
1/2 cup red wine
1 egg
Salt and pepper to taste
Garlic powder to taste
Butter for frying

Tomato Sauce:
1 (15-ounce) can tomatoes
1 cinnamon stick
1 garlic clove, crushed or 1/2 teaspoon garlic powder
2 whole cloves

Place ground beef in a mixing bowl. Add 2 slices of bread that
have been soaked in 1/2 cup wine. Mix in whole egg. Sprinkle
salt, pepper and garlic over meat mixture and mix together well.
Form into meatballs shaped like a football (not round). Brown in
butter in frying pan.

Tomato sauce can be cooking while you are frying the
soutzoukakia. Using a large saucepan, cook together the
tomatoes, cinnamon, garlic and cloves. Place the browned
soutzoukakia in hot tomato sauce and cook until done.

These are great with French bread for dipping in the sauce.
This recipe doubles easily for more servings.

~George
Peter Psihogios

Serves: 4

*These "Souzous" have been a favorite of
mine since childhood. Our house smelled so
good when I came home from school and
Mom was fixing soutzoukakia for dinner.*

Cephalonian Meat Pie
Kreatopita Kefalonias

Phyllo Dough:
4 cups flour
1 egg
1 cup white wine
1/2 cup cold water

Meat Filling:
1/2 cup oil
2 to 2 1/2 pounds beef (leg of lamb or goat kid if preferred),
    cut into small cubes
3 onions, finely chopped (optional)
4 garlic cloves, finely chopped (optional)
1 (14-ounce) can chopped tomatoes or
    14 ounces fresh tomatoes, chopped
1 tablespoon tomato paste dissolved in just enough water
    to produce a rich color when added to the filling
1/2 cup red or white wine
2 potatoes, cut into small cubes
1 tablespoon marjoram or bouquet garni
Salt and pepper to taste
1 cup Parmesan, grated

1/2 cup long grain rice
1 egg white for top (optional)

Sift 3 cups flour into a large bowl. In another bowl beat the
egg, add wine and water and beat until well mixed. Make a
well in the flour and add the egg wine mixture. Stir with a fork
until all ingredients are combined. Knead dough until smooth
and elastic, 5 to 7 minutes, adding remaining 1 cup flour, if
necessary. Form dough into a large ball and cover with plastic
wrap. Refrigerate for 1 hour.

In a large heavy pot heat some of the oil and brown the meat
in 3 separate batches. Add the rest of the ingredients except
the rice and cook over low heat until meat is cooked.

Butter a 9 or 10-inch pie dish (3 inches deep). Prepare an area to roll out the pastry dough, and dust it with flour.

Remove 2/3 of the chilled dough from the refrigerator. Roll out slightly larger than the pie dish. Place the rolled out dough in the pie dish so that it sits in the base and falls over the sides of the dish. Spoon the meat mixture into pie and spread evenly. Sprinkle the rice over the meat evenly. Roll out the remaining dough to fit over the pie and to overlap over the rim of the dish. Place this over the pie, and press the overlapping pastry at the rim with your fingers. The excess pastry will fall away on its own with the weight. Do this for the whole perimeter of the dish. With a fork pierce holes in the top pastry.

Brush top with water (or if you prefer with egg white and water beaten together). Bake in a preheated 350 degree oven approximately 1 hour.

*Adamandia
Niki Swanepoel*

Pork in Egg-Lemon Sauce
Hirino Avgolemono

2 tablespoons olive oil
1 1/2 pounds pork, cut into 1 inch cubes
2 onions, sliced into rings
12 large celery ribs, cut into 2 inch pieces

Egg-Lemon Sauce (Avgolemono):
3 egg whites (room temperature)
1 egg yolk
Juice of 1 fresh lemon

In a large skillet, brown pork on all sides in olive oil; remove meat and add onion to same pot. Sauté until golden. Return pork to pot and add just enough water to cover; salt to taste. Cover and bring to a boil. Reduce heat and simmer for 30 minutes; then add celery. Continue simmering for another 40 minutes, or until meat is tender. Remove from heat and pour off the broth to cool. Put pork in a large serving dish that will also accommodate the broth; keep dish warm.

Egg-Lemon Sauce (Avgolemono): In a medium bowl, beat egg whites until light and fluffy. Slowly beat in one egg yolk, then lemon juice. Ensure broth is cool (to keep from cooking the eggs) then gradually whisk the broth into the egg mixture, one tablespoon at a time. Pour sauce over pork. Serve immediately.

~ Katina
Joannides

Serves: 4 to 6

This recipe is from my great aunt, Demetra Tripilas. You can't believe how good it is! I think it is unique. She was from the Peloponnesus (Methoni).

Seasoned Skewered Meat
Souvlakia

3 pounds lean lamb or pork cut from the leg or shoulder
2 garlic cloves, crushed
1 teaspoon Greek oregano, dried
Salt and pepper to taste
Freshly squeezed juice of 2 lemons
1/2 cup olive oil

Cut meat into pieces the size of a walnut. In a bowl combine
all ingredients. Marinate in the refrigerator for 30 minutes or
longer. Put meat on small skewers and cook over charcoal
broiler to desired doneness. Serve immediately with Greek salad.

~Voula
Bakouros

Σουβλάκια

Seasoned Skewered Meat
Souvlakia

2 pounds pork or lamb, cut into bite size pieces
Salt and pepper to taste
Greek oregano, dried, to taste
Olive oil
Dash of Retsina wine

Bamboo skewers for grilling

Combine all ingredients for the marinade and mix well with the
meat. Skewer and cook on a grill over coals. Do not overcook.
Serve immediately with fried potatoes and a salad.

~Isidoros
Garifalakis

Pan-fried Pork Chops
Hirines Brizoles sto Tigani

4 pork loin, rib, or shoulder chops, cut 1 inch thick
Salt and pepper to taste
1/4 cup extra virgin olive oil or butter
1/4 cup dry white wine

Season the chops with salt and pepper and set aside. Heat a large
heavy duty sauté pan over medium heat. Add the oil or butter and
place chops one at a time in the pan. Fry one side until golden
brown, for approximately 5 minutes. Turn them over and fry the
other side until golden brown. Make a cut next to the bone and if the
juices run clear the chops are done. Season with salt and pepper and
transfer them to a hot platter. Add the wine to the pan and de-glaze
it. Cook over high heat for 2 minutes to reduce the sauce and pour
over the chops. Serve with boiled greens or manestra with mizithra
cheese. Red Naousa wine is recommended.

~George
Papas

Serves: 4

Pork with Celery
Hirino me Selino

1 1/2 pound pork, cut into cubes
2 celery roots, peeled and cut into cubes
8 celery stalks, strings removed and cut into 1 inch sections
1 onion, chopped
1/4 cup (1/2 stick) butter
4 tablespoons flour
2 eggs
Freshly squeezed juice of 1 lemon

In heavy pot sauté pork cubes and onion in butter, until browned.
Add flour and brown 2 to 3 minutes. Cover with water and season
with salt and pepper. Simmer until tender. Blanch celery root cubes
and stalks. Add to pork and cook until tender. Beat eggs until light;
blend in lemon juice. Using a wire whisk, gradually blend in broth
from pork, beating constantly. Slowly pour back into the pot with
pork and celery, stirring constantly.

~Vassie
Stoumbos

Serves: 4 to 6

Spiced Stewed Meat with Pasta
Καραma

1/4 cup oil
5 to 6 pounds beef stew meat
   (can use 1/2 lamb or all lamb)*
3 (8-ounce) cans tomato sauce
2 (16-ounce) cans whole tomatoes, crushed
1 medium onion, peeled
12 whole cloves
1/2 to 1 whole orange
2 to 3 sticks cinnamon
Salt and pepper to taste
4 pounds macaroni
1/2 cup (1 stick) butter
1 cup mizithra cheese, grated (or to taste)

In a large stockpot, over medium-high heat brown meat in oil.
Add tomato sauce and tomatoes to stock. Stick cloves in onion.
Add to stock. Cut top and bottom off orange (so that the juice
can escape). Add to stock along with cinnamon sticks and salt
and pepper. Add water to a level that covers the meat. (Add
water to stock.) Cook for 50 to 60 minutes or until meat is
tender. While the meat cooks, fill a pot with water. Boil
macaroni according to package directions. Drain and place
on a serving platter. In a saucepan, melt butter just until
browned. Pour over macaroni. Add mizithra cheese. Serve
along with kapama.

~Anastasia
Gianopoulos

*Ask your butcher to cut lamb chunks with bones if so desired
(adds to flavor).

Serves: 12 to 18

*This recipe has been in our family for three
generations. My Aunt Angie made
this for our Sunday dinners.*

Moroccan Lamb
Arni ala Maroko

1/4 cup olive oil
1/4 cup (1/2 stick) butter
1 large onion, very thinly sliced
1 teaspoon salt
1/2 teaspoon ground ginger
1/4 teaspoon coarsely ground black pepper
1/8 teaspoon saffron
1 stick cinnamon, 2 inches long
2 pounds boneless leg of lamb, cut in 2-inch cubes
3/4 cup ready-to-eat prunes, pitted
1 tablespoon honey
1 tablespoon orange flower water or lemon juice
1 tablespoon toasted sesame seeds

Heat oil and butter together in a heavy Dutch oven. Stir in onion, salt, ground ginger, ground black pepper, saffron and cinnamon. Add lamb and turn to coat with onion mixture. Cover and simmer, stirring occasionally, 1 1/2 hours or until meat is very tender. Add prunes and cook 15 minutes. Add honey and cook 5 minutes longer. Remove meat to warm serving platter. Arrange prunes on top and keep warm. Continue cooking liquid, stirring over high heat until reduced to a sauce. Stir in orange flower water or lemon juice. Pour over lamb and prunes and sprinkle with sesame seeds. Serve with crusty bread and a salad.

~Carolyn Damis

Serves: 6 to 8

In memory of Virginia J. Damis. My mother-in-law, Virginia, was a wonderful cook. While this is not "Greek," it was a recipe she often served at special family gatherings.

Braised Lamb Shanks
Arni Kokinisto

4 lamb shanks
1 large onion, finely chopped
1/2 cup olive oil
1 (12-ounce) can tomato paste
1 (12-ounce) can tomato sauce
2 cups water
3 teaspoons sugar
1 teaspoon cinnamon or 1 (2-inch) cinnamon stick
Salt and pepper to taste
Red wine

Rinse lamb shanks. Put into a saucepan with enough water
to cover. Bring to a boil, reduce heat and simmer for
30 minutes. Drain well.

In a stockpot over medium-high heat, sauté onion in hot olive
oil, until translucent. Add tomato paste and tomato sauce. Add
16 ounces of water. Cook over medium heat for 30 minutes.

In another pan, brown boiled lamb shanks in remaining 1/4 cup
oil on all sides. Remove shanks and add to tomato sauce. Add
sugar, cinnamon, salt and pepper to taste, and red wine. Cover
shanks with water. Cover with lid and simmer on low heat for
2 hours. Check periodically adding water as needed. Do not
reduce sauce completely. Serve shanks smothered in sauce.
Enjoy!

~Demetri's
Mediterranean
Restaurant

Serves: 2 to 4

Lamb Fricassée
Arni Frikasse me Aginares

3 pounds stewing lamb, washed and cut
    into serving size portions
1/2 cup water
1 small onion, chopped
1/4 cup (1/2 stick) butter
1 (8-ounce) can tomato sauce
1 tablespoon tomato paste
1/4 cup fresh dill, chopped
Salt and pepper to taste
12 to 15 frozen artichokes
3 egg yolks
1/2 cup freshly squeezed lemon juice

In a large saucepan cook onion in 1/2 cup water until onion
is soft and water is absorbed. Add butter and lamb and sauté
for 3 minutes. Add tomato sauce, tomato paste, dill, salt and
pepper. Cover with water and bring to a boil. Reduce heat and
simmer until lamb is tender, about 1 1/2 hours. Add artichokes
and cook until artichokes are fork tender. Beat egg yolks with
1 tablespoon water. Add lemon juice. Remove lamb from heat.
With a wire whisk slowly add broth from lamb to egg mixture,
then gradually add egg mixture to lamb in saucepan. Return to
heat and bring to a boil, slowly, then turn off heat.

~ Georgia
Belesin

Serves: 4 to 5

Κεφτέδες από Αρνί

Lamb Keftethes
Keftethes apo Arni

1 pound lean ground lamb
1 small red onion, finely chopped
2 slices whole wheat bread, soaked in water and squeezed
1 egg
2 cloves garlic, chopped
1/4 teaspoon salt
1/3 teaspoon ground cumin
1/2 teaspoon ground black pepper
1/2 teaspoon mint, dried
1/3 of one bunch fresh parsley leaves, finely chopped
1/4 cup water

Combine all ingredients in a bowl. Mix by hand and let mixture stand for 5 minutes. Using a soup spoon scoop large golf ball size rounds from mixture. Wet your hands with cold water and roll mixture in the palms of your hands until a round, slightly flat, shape is formed. Pour 1/4 cup water into a baking pan. Carefully arrange keftethes in the baking pan in a single layer. Bake in a preheated 350 degree oven 30 to 40 minutes. Halfway through baking time turn over all keftethes in order to cook evenly on both sides.

~Vevee B.
Aspros

Serves: 4

In memory of my mother-in-law
Chrisula Aspros.

Αρνί με Αγκινάρες

Lamb with Artichokes
Arni me Aginares

1 tablespoon olive oil
1 cup onion, chopped
1 garlic clove, minced
2 cups frozen artichoke hearts
2 cups mushrooms, sliced
1 1/2 cups water
1 tablespoon tomato paste
2 tablespoons dry red wine
1 tablespoon lemon juice
4 lamb chops, (5 to 6 ounces each) with bone

In a skillet sauté onion and garlic in oil until onion is translucent. Add artichoke hearts, mushrooms, water, tomato paste, wine and lemon juice; set aside. Broil chops on rack for about 2 minutes on each side. Transfer chops to a baking dish. Top with artichoke mixture. Bake in a preheated 350 degree oven for 20 minutes.

~Diane
Jouganatos Cook

Serves: 4

Roast Leg of Lamb
Bouti Arnissio sto Fourno

1 (4 pound) leg of lamb
Salt and freshly ground pepper
1 tablespoon Greek oregano, crushed, divided
1 cup olive oil, divided
2 to 4 garlic cloves, peeled and cut in half
2 pounds small red potatoes
Salt and freshly ground pepper
2 garlic cloves, peeled and crushed
Juice of 1 or 2 lemons, freshly squeezed

Wash the lamb and let it drain. Season lamb with salt, pepper
and 1/2 tablespoon Greek oregano. Sprinkle lamb with 3/4 cup
olive oil. Make deep slits in the meat with a sharp knife and
insert cut garlic cloves. Place the lamb in a greased baking pan.
Peel, wash and dry the potatoes. Put the potatoes in a large
bowl and season with salt, pepper, remaining oregano, crushed
garlic, lemon juice and remaining 1/4 cup olive oil. Mix well.
Place the potatoes around the lamb. Bake uncovered in a
preheated 350 degree oven for 2 hours or to desired doneness.

~Voula
Bakouros

Roast Leg of Lamb
Bouti Arnissio sto Fourno

1 leg of lamb, about 8 to 10 pounds
2 lemons
8 to 10 garlic cloves
Salt and pepper to taste
Oregano to taste

Trim fat from lamb. Wash and place in a roasting pan. Make
incisions in the meat and insert garlic cloves. Pour lemon juice
over meat and season with salt, pepper and oregano. Add 1 to
2 cups of water into the pan and bake uncovered, in a preheated
375 degree oven for approximately 2 to 2 1/2 hours or until meat
is cooked. Baste the meat often, adding water to keep the pan
from getting dry.

Note: Reserve the pan juices for baking potatoes (see page 82).

~George
Anasis

Serves: 8 to 10

Marinated Stuffed Lamb with Zinfandel Sauce
Arni Yemisto Krassato

Marinade:
1/4 cup light soy sauce
1/2 cup olive oil
1/4 cup sesame oil
1/4 cup fresh parsley leaves, chopped
2 garlic cloves, mashed
1 1/2 teaspoons thyme
1 teaspoon rosemary
1 teaspoon dry mustard
1/2 teaspoon mace
1/2 teaspoon oregano

1 (5 to 6 pounds) boned leg of lamb
  (can be butterflied by your butcher)
3 tablespoons olive oil
8 garlic cloves, chopped
1 pound cooked spinach, well drained and squeezed dry
1 cup fresh mint leaves, chopped
1/2 pound feta cheese, crumbled
1 teaspoon dried thyme
1 tablespoon crushed dried rosemary
1/4 teaspoon salt
1 teaspoon pepper, coarsely ground
1 egg, well beaten
Parsley sprigs for garnish
1 cup Zinfandel wine, to be reserved

Combine marinade ingredients in food processor or blender and mix. Transfer 1/2 cup to small saucepan.

Lay lamb on a flat surface. Trim excess fat. Heat olive oil in a skillet over low heat. Add chopped garlic, cooked spinach and mint. Sauté for 2 to 3 minutes. In a medium bowl, stir together spinach mixture, feta, thyme, rosemary, salt and pepper. Pour

in egg and stir well. With a thin spatula or knife, spread entire
mixture completely over one side of the lamb. Carefully roll the
lamb lengthwise to form a thin, long roast. Tie at intervals with
butcher's string. Lay lamb, seam side down in a shallow roasting
pan. Pour marinade evenly over meat. Roast in a preheated 400
degree oven for 20 minutes, then reduce heat to 350 degrees.
Baste with juices and roast another 50 minutes.

About 10 minutes before serving, combine wine with reserved
$1/2$ cup marinade and simmer, stirring occasionally. Remove
lamb from oven and let sit for 15 minutes. Serve sliced lamb
on heated platter and garnish with parsley. Pour sauce into
sauceboat and pass separately. This dish is well worth the effort!

*~Christine
Rulli*

Serves: 8 to 10

Cabbage Dolmathes
Lahanodolmathes

1 large cabbage, tough core removed
1/2 teaspoon salt
Water

2 pounds ground beef
1 onion, finely chopped
2 tablespoons fresh parsley, chopped
1 cup rice
2 eggs, lightly beaten
Pepper and salt to taste (up to 1 tablespoon salt)
Juice of 1/2 lemon

2 tablespoons tomato paste
1 cup water

Place the cabbage in a large pot, add salt and enough water to almost cover. Bring to a boil and simmer until the outer leaves start to open up. Remove each leaf as it loosens and set aside to drain. Cut out the thickest tough part from the center of each leaf and line the bottom of a large pot with them. Place over it a flattened large cabbage leaf.

In a large bowl, mix together the meat, onion, parsley, rice, eggs, salt and pepper and lemon juice. Taste for adequate salt and add more if necessary.

Take a heaping spoonful of the mixture and fill the center of one end of a cabbage leaf. Enclose the meat, folding over both sides and the end. Wrap up the meat by rolling it into a tidy "dolma." Place seam-side down in the bottom of the cabbage-lined pot. Wrap up all the meat and leaves, packing them snugly in layers in the pot.

In a saucepan, bring the tomato paste and 1 cup of water to a boil and pour over the dolmathes. To prevent them from moving and breaking apart, weigh them down with a plate that fits into the pot. Bring to a boil and lower heat to a simmer. Cover and cook about about 1 hour or until the rice is tender. Check the pot and add a little water if the liquid seems to be cooking away rapidly. Some extra liquid in the pot at the end of cooking is not a worry.

~ Bessie Carles

Poultry
&
Game

Contents

ΚΟΤόΠιΤΕΣ

Chicken Breasts in Phyllo
Kotopites

1 cup (2 sticks) butter
1 onion, finely minced
1/2 pound mushrooms, sliced
2 tablespoons fresh parsley, minced
2 to 3 garlic cloves, chopped
Salt to taste
1 tablespoon flour
1/4 cup dry white wine
2 whole chicken breasts (skinless, boneless, halved)
2 tablespoons olive oil
1/2 pound feta cheese

8 sheets phyllo dough
2 cups bread crumbs
1 1/2 cups (3 sticks) butter, melted

In a skillet, sauté onion until golden in 2 to 3 tablespoons of the butter. Remove onion and set aside. Add 3 more tablespoons of the butter and sauté the mushrooms until all juices are absorbed. Return onions to the pan and add parsley and garlic. Sauté 1 minute. Salt to taste. Stir in the flour and blend well. Add the wine and stir over moderate heat until thick. Remove onion mixture from the pan and set aside. Add 4 more tablespoons of the butter plus the olive oil and sauté chicken breasts until golden brown (approximately 2 minutes on each side). Salt lightly.

Lay out 1 sheet of phyllo. Brush with butter and sprinkle with bread crumbs. Place a second sheet of phyllo on top and brush with butter. Place 1 halved chicken breast on the lower part of the phyllo. In the center, add 1/4 of the onion, mushroom mixture and 1/4 of the feta. Roll phyllo over chicken at bottom, then fold over each side of phyllo envelope style and finish by rolling from the bottom up. Brush the packet with butter. Repeat the same with the rest of the ingredients. (At this point, the chicken can be frozen and baked at a later date. Bake without thawing for about 50 minutes.)

Place chicken packets seam side down on a baking sheet. Bake in a preheated 350 degree oven 35 minutes until golden brown.

~ Nancy
Fasilis

Serves: 4

Chicken Pilaf
Kotopoulo me Rizi

1 whole chicken, cut into pieces
1/4 cup (1/2 stick) butter
1 cup onion, chopped
1/4 cup wine
1 can chopped tomatoes or 3 tablespoons tomato paste
Salt and pepper to taste
2 cups rice or orzo

In a large saucepan over medium heat, sauté chicken, butter and onions, stirring occasionally until golden brown. Add wine, tomatoes, salt and pepper. Cook until chicken is tender. Prepare rice as directed on package. Remove chicken to a platter. Serve over rice with the sauce.

~ Georgia Belesin

Serves: 8

Oregano Roast Chicken
Kota Riganati

1/4 cup olive oil
Juice of 1 large lemon
1 1/2 teaspoons salt
1/4 teaspoon pepper
2 garlic cloves, crushed
3 teaspoons Greek oregano
1 whole chicken, cut into pieces
3 tablespoons butter

Combine first six ingredients in a bowl. Beat with a fork until blended. Dip chicken pieces in marinade and arrange in a baking dish. Pour remaining marinade over chicken. Dot with butter. Bake uncovered in a preheated 375 degree oven for approximately 1 hour until chicken is tender and slightly brown on top.

~Nikki
Diamond

Serves: 4

This is the first main dish I learned how to make, because it's fast, simple and so tasty!

Κότα Γιουβέτσι

Baked Chicken with Pasta
Kota Youvetsi

1 chicken, cut in half
Salt and pepper to taste
1 1/2 (14 1/2-ounce) cans diced tomatoes
4 to 5 garlic cloves, chopped
1/4 cup olive oil
1 cinnamon stick
3/4 pound (12 ounces) egg noodles, orzo, or fettuccine
Mizithra cheese, grated

Season chicken with salt and pepper. Place chicken in a deep ovenproof pan with cover. Add diced tomatoes, garlic, olive oil and cinnamon stick. Cover and bake in a preheated 425 degree oven for 45 minutes to 1 hour. Meanwhile, cook noodles and drain. When chicken is ready, remove from pan. Add noodles to the sauce. Mix well, cover and return to the oven for another 15 minutes. Season to taste. Sprinkle with mizithra cheese.

~ Roula
Tsirimiagos

One day when I did not have much time,
I created this recipe. Very tasty.

Lemon-Garlic Chicken
Kotopoulo sto Fourno

1 (2½ to 4 pound) chicken, cut up
⅓ to ½ cup olive oil
Juice of one lemon
1 teaspoon salt
6 garlic cloves, crushed
¼ teaspoon black pepper
2 teaspoons oregano, dried
Lemon zest (optional)
10 Kalamata olives, sliced (optional)

Combine all ingredients and pour over chicken. Marinate
½ hour or overnight if desired. Roast in a preheated 375 degree
oven 30 minutes. Turn chicken over and baste with marinade.
Bake 35 minutes longer. Transfer chicken to serving platter
and sprinkle with lemon zest and sliced Kalamata olives,
if desired.

~Sophia
Theoharis

Serves: 6

All ingredients except chicken
can be adjusted to taste—
how typically Greek!

Κότα με Φέτα

Chicken with Feta
Kota me Feta

3 tablespoons olive oil
1 chicken, cut up or individual parts as preferred
3 medium onions, peeled and sliced
2 garlic cloves, minced
1 (15-ounce) can plum tomatoes or
   1 1/2 pounds fresh tomatoes, peeled and seeded
Salt and pepper to taste
1 teaspoon oregano, dried
1/2 pound feta cheese, cut in paper-thin slices

Cooked orzo, rice or noodles

Heat 2 tablespoons of the olive oil in a heavy skillet. Add the chicken pieces and cook on each side over medium heat for 10 minutes or until browned. Remove chicken to a plate and add the onions to the skillet, adding the remaining tablespoon of oil, if necessary. Cook for 15 minutes, stirring constantly, until the onions are soft and browned, adding garlic the last 5 minutes. Stir the tomatoes into the onion and return the chicken pieces to the pan. Season with salt, pepper and oregano. Cover and simmer over medium heat for 30 minutes. Totally cover the chicken pieces in the pan with feta cheese. Cover and continue cooking 10 minutes longer. Serve over rice, orzo or noodles.

~Georgia Vareldzis

Serves: 4 to 6

I have prepared chicken this way for years. The feta was a later addition for one of my cooking classes.

Tomato Chicken with Rice in Egg-Lemon Sauce
Kota Kokinisti me Rizi Avgolemono

1 large onion, diced
1/4 cup oil
1 whole chicken (4 pounds), cut into smaller pieces
1 (8-ounce) can tomato sauce
1 teaspoon salt
Pepper to taste
5 cups water or chicken broth
2 cups rice

Egg-Lemon Sauce (Avgolemono):
2 eggs, separated
Juice of 1 1/2 lemons

In a large skillet, brown the diced onion in oil. Add chicken parts and brown on both sides. Add tomato sauce, salt, pepper and 1 cup broth (or water). Cook chicken for 15 minutes. Add remaining broth (or water). Bring to a simmer and add rice. Cover and cook 20 minutes longer until liquid is absorbed.

Egg-Lemon Sauce (Avgolemono): In a bowl, beat 2 egg whites until frothy. Add 2 egg yolks and continue to beat until well blended. Add juice of 1 1/2 lemons. With the stove turned off, add the egg-lemon sauce to the cooked chicken very slowly, stirring constantly.

Serves: 4 to 6

Presvytera
Effy
Stephanopoulos

Chicken Pilaf
Pilafi me Kotopoulo

3 tablespoons olive oil
1 medium onion, chopped
4 garlic cloves, minced
8 chicken thighs (skinless, with bone)
1 (4-ounce) can mushrooms
1 (8-ounce) can tomato sauce
1/2 cup white wine
1 teaspoon oregano, dried
1 tablespoon parsley, dried
Salt and pepper to taste
2 cups uncooked rice
4 1/2 cups water

1/4 cup (1/2 stick) butter, browned*

In a sauté pan over medium-high heat, sauté onion and garlic in olive oil until translucent. Add the chicken thighs and mushrooms and brown lightly. Add the tomato sauce, white wine, oregano, parsley, salt and pepper. Simmer about 30 minutes; then add 2 cups rice and 4 1/2 cups water. Bring to a boil then lower heat to simmer. Cover and cook for 25 minutes. Transfer to a serving platter and pour browned butter over the top.

~Katharine
Antonis
Melcher

* If you want to make this a lowfat meal, just add juice from 1/2 lemon, instead of butter.

Serves: 4

This recipe was passed down from my grandmother Katharine Tsngarris, to my mother Helen Tsngarris Antonis and then to me.

Lemon Chicken Breasts with Artichokes
Kotopoulo Lemonato me Aginares

8 whole chicken breasts, boned
1 to 1 1/2 cups (2 to 3 sticks) butter
4 garlic cloves, chopped
Salt and pepper to taste
Flour as needed (approximately 2 to 3 cups)
3 eggs, well beaten
Juice of 2 lemons
2 (14-ounce) cans artichoke hearts, halved, save juice
1/2 cup capers (optional)

Parsley for garnish

Separate chicken breasts into halves or quarters and remove all visible fat. Using a mallet, pound chicken until 1/2 inch thick.

In a bowl, have ready the flour, salt and pepper. Dredge the chicken pieces into the beaten eggs then the flour.

In a large frying pan melt 3 tablespoons butter and add 1/2 teaspoon of the garlic. When butter is bubbling, sauté chicken pieces approximately 3 to 4 minutes on each side. Continue this process until all chicken pieces are lightly browned, adding garlic and butter as needed.

Transfer cooked chicken to a baking dish. At this point you can refrigerate. Thirty minutes before serving, melt one stick of butter. Add 1 tablespoon of chopped garlic and sauté for 1 minute. Add juice of lemons and artichoke hearts, then gently stir. Add capers, then pour entire mixture over chicken. Place in a preheated 300 degree oven for approximately 20 minutes. Garnish with parsley.

~Christine Rulli

Serves: 8

This recipe was prepared by a friend I was visiting in New Jersey. It is easy to prepare and has become one of our family favorites. Even the kids like it.

Κοτόπουλο Κοκκινιστό με Μπάμιες

Chicken and Okra in Tomato Sauce
Kotopoulo Kokinisto me Bamyes

1 medium yellow onion, chopped
1 clove garlic, minced
1 pound boneless chicken breasts, washed
1 (10-ounce) package frozen okra
1 (14 1/2-ounce) can stewed tomatoes
1 (5 1/2-ounce) can tomato juice, a little more if necessary
1/4 cup white wine
1/3 cup olive oil
Salt and pepper to taste
Oregano to taste
1/2 cup (1 stick) butter
1/4 cup Parmesan cheese, grated

~Ellen
Demas Belesin

In a 9 x 13 inch pan, layer onions, garlic, chicken and okra. Pour stewed tomatoes and tomato juice over layers. Add the wine and drizzle olive oil over layers. Sprinkle with salt, pepper and oregano to taste. Slice butter over top. Place in oven and sprinkle with Parmesan cheese during the last 10 minutes of baking. Bake in a preheated 350 degree oven for 1 1/2 to 2 hours.

Serves: 6 to 8

In memory of my mother,
Anna Stratikos Demas.

Κότα ή Φασιανός σε Φύλλο

Chicken or Pheasant in Phyllo Pastry
Kota i Fassianos se Filo

2 tablespoons onion, chopped
1 garlic clove, crushed
1/4 cup (1/2 stick) butter
1 1/2 cups mushrooms, sliced and divided
1/2 cup whipping cream
4 chicken breasts, boned, skinned and
    cut into small pieces
Salt and pepper to taste

Phyllo dough
1/2 cup (1 stick) melted butter

In a sauté pan over medium-high heat, sauté onion and garlic in 2 tablespoons butter for 1 minute. Add 1/2 cup of the mushrooms and sauté for 3 minutes. Place in a blender or food processor with whipping cream and purée.

In a large frying pan, melt 2 tablespoons butter and sauté chicken until done. Remove and drain in a colander. Add remaining 1 cup mushrooms to same pan and sauté for 2 minutes. Mix chicken with puréed mixture, sautéed mushrooms and salt and pepper. Cool and refrigerate. Place a sheet of phyllo on working surface and brush well with melted butter. Place second sheet on top and brush with butter, also. Fold over in half. Brush only the exposed border. Place a small amount of mixture lengthwise on phyllo, leaving a border. Fold in bottom edge of pastry, then sides, then over again. Place on a greased baking sheet. Brush with melted butter. Bake in a preheated 425 degree oven 15 to 20 minutes until golden brown.

These can be made a day ahead and refrigerated. Bring to room temperature before baking.

~Kiki
Skordahl

Serves: 4 to 6

This is a recipe I developed myself as an adaptation for phyllo use. Makes a nice presentation. My husband is a pheasant hunter. I prepare pheasant this way often for guests.

Κοτόπουλο με Μπάμιες

Chicken with Okra
Kotopoulo me Bamyes

1 1/2 pounds fresh okra
3/4 cup vinegar
1/2 cup olive oil, divided
1 medium-size roasting chicken, cut up
1 large onion, chopped
3 garlic cloves, chopped
1 cup water
3 to 4 tomatoes, chopped
Salt and pepper

Wash and carefully trim okra, but not too close to the top.
Sprinkle well with vinegar and let stand for 30 minutes. Wash
and drain okra. Place part of the oil in a frying pan and sauté
for a few minutes. Set aside. Cut chicken into serving size pieces
and brown in remaining oil. Add chopped onion and garlic, and
continue to brown. Place the chicken parts, onions and okra in a
roasting pan; add water and tomatoes and season to taste. Roast
in a preheated 375 degree oven for 30 to 40 minutes.

~Angeliki
Anasis

Serves: 6

Γέμιση για Γαλοπούλα της Καίτης

Katy's Turkey Stuffing
Yemisi yia Galopoula tis Ketis

1 cup raisins, soaked in warm water
1 medium apple, peeled, quartered and sliced thin
1 cup roasted or canned chestnuts, coarsely chopped
1 pound lean ground beef
2 tablespoons butter or oil
1 medium onion, chopped fine
2 stalks celery, sliced thin
1 teaspoon salt
1/8 teaspoon pepper
2 (6.2-ounce) boxes long grain and wild rice mix
1 tablespoon mint, dried
1 tablespoon parsley, dried
1/2 to 1 teaspoon cinnamon
3 1/2 to 4 cups chicken or turkey broth

Combine the apple and chestnuts and set aside.

In a heavy skillet, over medium heat brown the ground beef.
Drain off fat and add butter or oil. Add onion and celery, and
sauté until onion is translucent. Add salt, pepper, and rice mix,
and sauté 1 to 2 minutes. Add seasoning packet ingredients,
mint, parsley and cinnamon, and stir. Add raisins, apple,
chestnuts and broth. Stir well and quickly bring to a boil.
Stir again. Cover; reduce heat and simmer 20 to 25 minutes
or until liquid is absorbed.

Note: Chopped chicken livers may be substituted for the beef.
Pine nuts may be substituted for the chestnuts. This recipe may
be prepared the night before and reheated in a 300 degree oven.

~ Katy Vokos

Serves: 12

*In memory of my mom, Christina Delistraty
Calabro, from whom this recipe came.
Through the years I've added to and
changed it as offered here.*

Λαγός Κοκκινιστός

Rabbit in Tomato Sauce
Lagos Kokinistos

1 rabbit, cut up
1 cup vinegar
Salt and pepper
1 cup olive oil
1 cup tomato sauce
1 tablespoon tomato paste
1 head garlic
2 to 3 bay leaves
3 to 6 whole cloves
Juice of 2 to 3 lemons

Place rabbit in a bowl and pour over the vinegar. Marinate 3 to 4 hours. Drain rabbit and season with salt and pepper. In a large frying pan, heat oil and sauté the rabbit until golden brown. Transfer the pieces to a stockpot. Stir in tomato sauce, tomato paste, garlic, bay leaves and cloves and cook until rabbit is tender. Add the lemon juice and serve with french fried potatoes or rice and a robust wine.

~Stamo
Linardatos

Serves: 6

My mother used to make this for us when we were young. It is my favorite meal.

Seafood

Contents

Broiled Fish with ☦
Roasted Tomato Chutney
Psari Psito me Saltsa Tsatni

Chutney:
5 Roma tomatoes, cut in 1 inch chunks
1 medium red onion cut in 1 inch pieces
1/4 cup extra virgin olive oil plus 1 tablespoon
1/4 cup raisins
1/4 cup hot Port or Mavrodaphne wine
2 tablespoons toasted pine nuts

4 (5 to 6 ounce pieces) of Chilean Sea Bass, Halibut,
    Red Snapper or Rainbow Trout
Sea salt to taste
Pepper to taste
Flour
2 tablespoons fresh oregano, chopped (optional)

To make the chutney, toss the tomato and cut onion with one
tablespoon of the oil. Arrange one layer deep on a baking sheet
and bake in a preheated 450 degree oven for about 15 to 20
minutes until brown and crisp on the edges. Remove from oven.

Steep the raisins in the hot wine. Add chutney mixture, 1/4 cup
of the olive oil and pine nuts.

Season the fish with salt and pepper. Place in a broiling pan and
broil about 4 minutes per side for each inch of thickness. Top
with chutney mixture and oregano.

*~Berbati
Restaurant*

Serves: 4

$\Psi\acute{\alpha}\rho\iota$ στο Φούρνο

Baked Halibut
Psari sto Fourno

8 (8-ounce) halibut fillets
2 cups (4 sticks) melted butter
Juice of 3 freshly squeezed lemons
1 teaspoon salt
Dash of pepper
Tarragon, dried, to taste

Wash the halibut and salt both sides. Spray a baking pan with
cooking spray and arrange fillets in a single layer. Cover and
bake the fish in a preheated 350 degree oven for 20 minutes.
Melt butter. Add rest of the ingredients and whip together with
a wire whisk. Pour lemon butter mixture over the cooked fish
and bake another 5 minutes. Transfer fish to serving platter.
Pour sauce into small individual side dishes for dipping.

~Saki and
John Tzantarmas,
New Copper
Penny
Restaurant

Serves: 8

Ψάρι Πλακί

Baked Fish in Tomato Sauce ☦
Psari Plaki

8 (8-ounce) salmon or halibut fillets
Salt

Sauce:
5 onions, sliced
$1/2$ cup olive oil
1 whole head of garlic, chopped
$1/4$ celery stalk, chopped
2 tablespoons tomato paste
2 tablespoons chicken base
1 (8-ounce) can diced tomatoes
1 small bunch fresh parsley, chopped
4 cups water

Wash fish and salt both sides. Place in a pan sprayed with cooking spray and bake covered in a preheated 350 degree oven for 20 minutes.

In a saucepan, boil all the sauce ingredients together and simmer until thickened. Pour sauce over top of the cooked fish and return to the oven. Bake 10 minutes longer.

Note: Fish may be kept at a very low heat covered for an hour before serving.

Serves: 8

~Saki and
John Tzantarmas,
New Copper
Penny
Restaurant

Ψάρι αλά Σπετσιώτα

Baked Fish with Bread Crumbs ☦
and Tomatoes
Psari ala Spetsiota

2 pounds firm white fish fillets or steaks
6 tablespoons olive oil, divided
1 tablespoon fresh lemon juice
Salt and freshly ground pepper to taste
2 cups peeled, seeded and chopped tomatoes
    or 1 (14 1/2-ounce) can stewed tomatoes, drained
1/2 cup dry white wine
4 garlic cloves, finely minced
1 tablespoon sugar or honey
4 tablespoons chopped fresh flat-leaf (Italian) parsley
1 teaspoon dried oregano or ground cinnamon (optional)
1 cup fine dried bread crumbs

In a large enough baking dish, arrange the fish in a single layer.
In a small bowl, whisk together 2 tablespoons of the oil, lemon
juice, salt and pepper and pour over the fish. Let stand for about
30 minutes at room temperature.

In a saucepan over medium heat, combine the tomatoes, garlic,
wine, sugar or honey, parsley and the oregano or cinnamon.
Bring to a simmer and cook for about 10 minutes. Season to
taste with salt and pepper.

Pour the tomato sauce evenly over the fish. Scatter the bread
crumbs evenly over the top. Drizzle with the remaining
4 tablespoons oil. Bake in a preheated 400 degree oven about
~Diane   15 minutes until the fish is cooked through and bread crumbs
Kondos   are golden brown. Serve immediately.

Serves: 4 to 6

*Named for the island of Spetsai, this dish is very easy
to prepare and very tasty. The elements are simple:
impeccably fresh fish, flavorful vine-ripened tomatoes
and good quality bread crumbs. You may serve
it hot or cold.*

Salmon Baked in Tomato Sauce
Solomos Plaki

3 pounds salmon
Salt and pepper to taste
5 tablespoons olive oil
2 tablespoons butter
1 1/2 cups onion, chopped
2 garlic cloves, minced
1 stalk celery, chopped
2 large carrots, chopped
1/2 cup fresh parsley, chopped
2 fresh tomatoes, chopped
1 (8-ounce) can tomato sauce

Season salmon with salt and pepper. Place in large baking
dish and set aside. In a large skillet sauté onions in oil and
butter until translucent; add garlic, celery, carrots, and parsley.
Cook until vegetables are tender. Add fresh tomatoes and
tomato sauce and continue to cook for 10 minutes. Pour
mixture over salmon.

~Michael
Nicholas
Diamond

Bake in a preheated 350 degree oven 45 minutes.

Serves: 4

*Fresh salmon from my annual Alaskan
fishing trip makes this recipe even better.*

Camp Angelos Barbecued ☦
Chinook Salmon
Solomos sta Karvouna ala Camp Angelos

1 (10-pound) Chinook salmon filet
Salt and pepper to taste
Lemon wedges for garnish

Place filet skin side down on center of 1 sheet (24 x 30 inch) aluminum foil. Season with salt and pepper. Fold foil over fish, sealing edges completely. Turn salmon over and place on second sheet of foil and wrap again to completely enclose. Place on barbecue grill skin side up for 10 minutes then turn over gently and continue to cook for 10 minutes longer. Salmon should flake easily when done. Serve with lemon wedges.

~Gus
Kriara

Serves: 20

This flavorful salmon was first served at Camp Angelos to over 300 Native Americans representing the Columbia River Inter-Tribal Fish Commission. It has become very popular and often requested by many of the organizations that frequent the camp.

Ψάρι στο Φούρνο αλά Κυπαρίσσι

Baked Fish (a la Kyparissi) ✝
Psari sto Fourno ala Kiparissi

2 to 3 pounds fish (halibut, cod, etc.)
Salt and pepper to taste
Juice of 1 lemon
2 to 4 tablespoons olive oil
3 garlic cloves, minced
1 teaspoon oregano, dried
1 tablespoon fresh parsley, chopped
1/2 cup white wine
2 large tomatoes, sliced
Dry bread crumbs

Wash fish, then sprinkle with salt, pepper and lemon juice. Place in a baking dish. Combine the next five ingredients and pour over fish. Place the sliced tomatoes over the top and sprinkle with the bread crumbs.

Bake in a preheated 375 degree oven for 45 minutes. Serve with white rice and tossed green salad.

~ Helen
Tsngarris Antonis

Serves: 5 to 6

This recipe was a favorite of my mother's, Katharine Tsngarris, who was born in Kyparissi, Greece.

Μαρίδες Τηγανιτές

Pan-Fried Smelt ☦

Marithes Tiganites

36 to 42 medium sea-smelt 5 to 6 inch long
Olive oil to fry fish
3 cups flour
Salt and freshly ground pepper to taste
1/4 cup granulated garlic

2 lemons, cut in half

Remove the guts and wash the smelt under cold running water. Removing the heads is optional, but we prefer to keep the heads on.

In a large bowl mix the flour, salt, pepper and garlic. Add the smelt and toss to coat evenly.

Heat a heavy-duty sauté or frying pan over medium-high heat. Add enough oil to cover the bottom, 1 inch deep, and heat to a frying temperature of 375 degrees. Put in 12 smelt, one at a time, and fry for 4 minutes until the bottom sides are golden-brown. Turn the fish over and fry until the other sides are golden-brown. Remove to paper towels to drain, and continue to fry the rest of the smelt. Strain the oil after each batch is cooked using a cheesecloth. Add more oil if needed, bringing the temperature up before adding the fish.

Remove to a serving platter and squeeze the lemons over the fish. Serve with a Greek salad or boiled vegetables with olive oil-lemon sauce. Suggested wine: a good Retsina.

~George Papas

Chef's note: If the fish are small, we prefer to eat the bones and heads when they are fried to a crispy consistency.

Serves: 4 to 6

From the book:
Papas' Art of Traditional Greek Cooking

Fried Calamari ☦
Kalamarakia Tiganita

2 pounds calamari, smallest possible
   (preferably 4 to 6 inches long), cleaned
Salt to taste
Flour (as needed)

Oil, for frying
Lemon wedges

Cut calamari into 1 inch pieces, leaving tentacles on head
as one piece. Put in strainer and wash thoroughly under
tepid water. While calamari are in the strainer, add salt.
Toss to distribute salt evenly. Put the strainer over a bowl
and refrigerate for approximately 30 minutes. Remove
calamari from the refrigerator. Coat each piece with flour.
Pan fry for 3 to 4 minutes or until golden brown. Serve
with lemon wedges.

~Alexis
Restaurant

Serves: 8

Καλαμάρια Γεμιστά

Stuffed Squid ✝
Kalamaria Yemista

18 squid, include tentacles
3 onions, chopped
3 garlic cloves, chopped
1/2 cup oil
Salt and pepper to taste
2 heaping tablespoons tomato paste
1 bay leaf, crumbled
1 cup converted rice
2 tablespoons fresh parsley, chopped
1 tablespoon fresh dill, chopped
2 cups vegetable broth

Wooden toothpicks to secure stuffed squid

Wash squid thoroughly and soak in water until ready to use.
Chop tentacles and set aside. In a large saucepan brown the
onions and garlic in oil. Add salt, pepper, tomato paste, bay
leaf, rice, parsley, dill and chopped tentacles. Add 1 cup of the
vegetable broth and cook this mixture until liquid is absorbed.
Cool mixture so that it is easy to handle. Dry the squid with
paper towels. Fill squid with this mixture about 3/4 full. Secure
with a toothpick. Place in oiled casserole dish and pour any
remaining stuffing on top. Add remaining vegetable broth and
~Meropi S.   correct seasoning. Cover and bake in a preheated 325 degree
Courogen   oven for about 20 minutes or until juices are absorbed.

Serves: 6

*I use cleaned squid which are large enough to
stuff. As I prepare this recipe, memories of
my mother's kitchen fill my mind. This was
one of our favorite Lenten meals.
For my mother, Maria Soulges.*

Καλαμάρια Γεμιστά

Stuffed Squid ✟
Kalamaria Yemista

3 pounds medium-size squid
1/2 cup olive oil
1 onion, finely chopped
1/2 cup fresh parsley, finely chopped
1 cup hot water
1 pound tomatoes, sliced
Salt and pepper to taste
1/2 cup pine nuts
1/2 cup rice
White wine
Juice of 1 lemon

Clean the squid, removing the small ink sac and intestines. Top
and chop the head finely. Heat 2 tablespoons oil in a saucepan
and fry the onions until golden. Add parsley, squid heads, water
and half the tomatoes. Season with salt and pepper. Cook over
low heat until soft. Add pine nuts and rice. Turn the heat off.
Fill the squid partially with the mixture leaving room for filling
to expand. Use toothpicks to close opening and secure the
filling. Heat oil in a frying pan; brown the stuffed squid until
golden. Transfer to a baking pan. Sprinkle with the white wine,
lemon juice, the rest of the tomatoes and the fried oil. Bake in
a preheated 350 degree oven for 45 minutes.

Serves: 6

~Ted and
John Papas,
Greek Cusina
Restaurant

Octopus with Macaroni ✟
Htapothi me Makaronia

4 pounds octopus
2 medium size onions, chopped fine
1 1/2 cups olive oil
1 cup white wine
5 tomatoes, chopped
Salt and pepper to taste
Water
1 1/2 pounds macaroni

Wash octopus and cut into 3-inch pieces. On top of stove, in a heavy-bottom pan cook octopus over medium-high heat, until juices are absorbed. Add onions and oil, and simmer until onions are soft. Add the wine and the chopped tomatoes. Add salt and pepper and 1 cup of water; bring to a boil. When octopus is half-way done, add some more water and the macaroni. Cook until the macaroni is done.

~Thanasi
Kosmas

Χταπόδι με Ρύζι

Octopus with Rice ✝
Htapothi me Rizi

2 pounds octopus, cleaned
1 medium onion, grated
2 tablespoons oil
1 (14 1/2-ounce) can stewed tomatoes
4 1/2 to 5 cups water
1 1/2 cups rice

In a large pot, boil octopus until tender (about 30 minutes). Discard water and cut octopus into 1/2 inch pieces. Sauté onion and octopus in oil. Add tomatoes and water; bring to a boil. Season with salt and pepper. Add rice and cook uncovered, over medium low heat, for 20 to 30 minutes or until rice is done. Stir frequently.

Variation: Scallops may be substituted for the octopus. Do not boil scallops before sautéing with onion. Reduce water to 4 cups.

Serves: 6

~Vassie
Stoumbos

Octopus Stew
Htapothi Yiahni

4 pounds octopus
1 cup olive oil
1/2 cup wine vinegar
3 pounds boiling onions, peeled and chopped
6 garlic cloves, chopped
1 cup red wine
1 (16-ounce) can crushed tomatoes
8 to 10 whole peppercorns
3 to 4 bay leaves
2 whole cloves
Salt to taste

With a knife, slit open the head of the octopus. Remove the ink sac and all of the internal organs. Remove the teeth from the bottom end and remove the eyes. Wash and clean the octopus, making sure no sand remains. Cut into 2 to 3 inch long pieces.

Place in a pot without water; simmer until the octopus has absorbed most of its juices. Add oil and vinegar and stir. Next add onions, garlic, red wine, tomatoes, peppercorns, bay leaves and cloves. Add salt to taste, if needed. Cook slowly on low heat until the liquid is absorbed and octopus and onions are fully cooked.

~Angeliki Anasis

Serves: 8 to 10

Crab Pilaf
Pilafi me Kavouri

1 whole crab (in shell)
1 cup onion, chopped
2 garlic cloves, chopped
3 tablespoons olive oil
1 (14 1/2-ounce) can chopped tomatoes
1/4 cup fresh parsley, chopped
1 1/2 cups rice
3 cups water
Salt and pepper to taste

Wash crab in shell; take off back and clean thoroughly. Crack and break into bite-sized pieces. Using a small cocktail fork, remove crab from shell.

In a large pot, sauté the onions and garlic in olive oil. Add tomatoes, parsley, rice and brown with cracked crab pieces. Add water, salt and pepper. Bring to a boil, reduce heat. Cover and simmer for 20 to 25 minutes.

~Elaine A.
Haralampus

Serves: 4

This was one recipe my mother made when we lived in Seaside. We had fresh crab there. In memory of Athanasia Haralampus.

Πιλάφι με Θαλασσινά

Clam or Shrimp Pilaf ✝
Pilafi me Thalassina

¹/4 cup olive oil
1 garlic clove, minced
1 medium onion, chopped fine
¹/4 cup pine nuts
2 cups long grain rice
1 (16-ounce) can stewed tomatoes
3 cups water
¹/4 cup currants
Salt and pepper to taste
1 pound minced clams or 1 pound small shrimp meat

In a saucepan sauté garlic, onion and pine nuts in oil for about
5 minutes. Add rice and stir to coat with oil. Add tomatoes,
water, currants, salt and pepper. Bring to a boil, lower heat
to simmer and add clams or shrimp. Partially cover and cook
20 minutes until rice is tender. Stir frequently to keep from
sticking to bottom of the pan; add a little more water if needed.
When the rice is done, stir lightly with a fork. Remove from heat
and allow to sit covered for 5 to 10 minutes before serving.

~Georgia
Vareldzis

Note: Orzo can be substituted for rice. The proportions are
the same. Canned minced clams can be used if fresh are
not available.

Serves: 6 to 8

*Another favorite Lenten dish.
Sometimes we eat it just
because we love it.*

Clam or Shrimp Pilaf ☦
Pilafi me Thalassina

1 tablespoon vegetable oil
1 tablespoon margarine
1 onion, chopped
1 (16-ounce) can crushed tomatoes, drained
1 (8-ounce) can mushrooms drained,
   or use fresh mushrooms
1 to 2 cans chopped clams or shrimp, drained,
   but reserve liquid
2 cups converted rice, uncooked

In a heavy saucepan, heat oil and margarine. Add onion and
sauté until translucent. Add tomatoes, mushrooms, clams and
rice. Add reserved liquid and water to equal 3 cups. Cover and
simmer for 25 minutes or until all liquid is absorbed.

Note: If using shrimp, add shrimp after rice is cooked and stir
in to heat throughly.

~Kathy
Phoutrides

Serves: 6

*This recipe comes from Yiayia Betty.
We eat this a lot during Lent!*

Γαρίδες Τηγανιτές με Σκόρδο

Garlic Shrimp
Garithes Tiganites me Skortho

Olive oil
1/4 cup (1/2 stick) butter
1 medium onion, chopped
1/2 large head garlic, minced
1 tablespoon fresh basil, chopped
1 tablespoon fresh rosemary, finely chopped
1 teaspoon coarsely ground pepper
2 pounds medium shrimp, shelled, deveined
    and butterflied
1 cup dry white wine
1/2 cup fresh parsley, chopped

Parmesan cheese, grated
Parsley sprigs and lemon wedges for garnish

Pour olive oil to 1/8 inch depth in a large skillet. Add butter, melt over medium heat. Add onion and garlic and sauté until translucent. Add basil, rosemary, pepper and shrimp. Cook 1 minute longer. Add wine and parsley; salt to taste. Continue cooking until shrimp curl and are pink in color.

~Ann Mehas

To serve, sprinkle with grated, Parmesan cheese. Garnish with fresh parsley sprigs and lemon wedges.

Serves: 6

Everyone that has tasted this recipe loves it. I believe it is a winner. You can add more or less garlic. This is excellent over rice pilaf.

Skillet Jumbo Shrimp ☦
Garithes sto Tigani

2 tablespoons olive oil
1 medium onion, diced
2 garlic cloves, minced
1/2 red pepper, diced
1/2 green pepper, diced
2 stalks celery, diced
Salt and pepper to taste
1 tablespoon honey
1/2 cup orange juice
Juice from 1/2 lemon
1 apple, diced
1/2 cup white wine
1 tablespoon cornstarch mixed with water to make a paste
1 pound jumbo shrimp, cleaned and deveined

Heat oil in a skillet. Add onion, garlic, red and green peppers and celery and sauté. Season with salt and pepper. Combine honey, orange juice and lemon juice, Stir in apple and add to mixture. Simmer for 10 to 15 minutes. Add wine.

Add to the dissolved cornstarch mixture and stir until sauce thickens. Add shrimp and cook until shrimp is pink. Serve over white rice.

Note: Sauce should be medium consistency. Use water to dilute if necessary.

Serves: 4

~Tony
Gianopoulos

Πίλαφι με Θαλασσινά για Πολλούς

Seafood Pilaf for a Crowd
Pilafi me Thalassina yia Polous

1 pound margarine
1 cup olive oil
6 pounds converted rice
4 large yellow onions, chopped
1 (#10) can crushed tomatoes
4 (#5) cans chopped clams, drained
   (reserve 12 cups of juice)
1 (#10) can sliced mushrooms

2 (5 pound) bags cooked shrimp

~Chefs:
Betty Phoutrides
and Helen
Buhler
~Sous Chefs:
Aristides
Phoutrides and
Jerry Buhler

In a large pot, sauté onions in oil and margarine. Add clams and mushrooms to onions and sauté. Add crushed tomatoes and simmer for a few minutes. Add rice to pan and mix well. Add clam juice and boiling water and simmer until almost done. Add thawed shrimp a few minutes before rice is completely cooked.

Serves: 60

Traditionally served at Holy Trinity Greek Orthodox Church, Portland, Oregon following one of the six Wednesday evening pre-sanctified liturgies during the "Great Lenten" fast preceding Easter.

Spinach Rice with Shrimp
Spanakorizo me Garithes

2 bunches fresh spinach, washed, dried and chopped
2 to 4 tablespoons olive oil
1 large onion, minced
2 garlic cloves, minced
2 teaspoons parsley, chopped
2 teaspoons oregano, dried
1 cup uncooked rice
1 (8-ounce) can tomato sauce
2 cups chicken broth
Salt and pepper to taste
1 pound large shrimp, cleaned
$^1/_4$ cup ($^1/_2$ stick) butter
Feta cheese, crumbled (optional)

Wash and dry the spinach and cut into small pieces; set aside.
In a sauté pan over medium-high heat, sauté the onions, garlic,
parsley, and oregano in the olive oil. Add rice and slightly
brown all ingredients. Add tomato sauce and chicken broth
and bring to a boil; salt and pepper to taste. Add the spinach
and cook for 15 minutes. Add the shrimp and cook an
additional 5 minutes.

In another saucepan brown butter and pour over shrimp.
Place in serving dish and sprinkle with crumbled feta cheese
if desired.

~Helen
Tsngarris
Antonis

Note: To cut fat grams, eliminate the butter and the cheese.
This recipe is just as flavorful without them.

Serves: 6

*This recipe was a family favorite of mine and my sister's
when we were young. We now make it for our families.
We also use it many times while fasting by simply
eliminating the chicken broth and the oil and
making the fasting substitutions.*

Φετουτσίνι με Γαρίδες και Σπανάκι

Shrimp and Spinach over Fettucine
Fetoutsini me Garithes ke Spanaki

1 (16-ounce) package fettucine
1/8 cup olive oil
4 garlic cloves, chopped
4 green onions, chopped
1 1/2 pounds shrimp, cleaned and deveined
5 Roma tomatoes, chopped
1 bag baby spinach, cleaned
1 pound feta cheese, crumbled
Salt and pepper to taste

Boil fettucine according to package directions while preparing the shrimp. Drain well, place on a deep platter and keep warm.

In a large skillet heat olive oil over medium heat and sauté garlic for about 1 minute. Do not brown. Add green onions; cook about 1 minute longer. Add shrimp and cook until entirely pink. Add tomatoes, cook about 1 minute then add spinach until wilted. Do not overcook. Immediately add the feta cheese, salt and pepper to taste. Remove from heat. Spoon spinach mixture over top of pasta.

~ Presvytera
Stephanie
Buhler Paris

Serves: 8 to 10

Father Paul and I have enjoyed this
wonderful recipe given to us from our
dear friend, Peter Philips of
Oakland, California.

Egg
Dishes

Contents

∽ EGG DISHES ∽

Potato Omelet
Patates me Avga Fourtalia

Butter or olive oil
6 to 8 medium potatoes, peeled and cut in small pieces
1 small onion, chopped
2 large sausages, fully cooked
4 large eggs
Fresh mint to taste, chopped
1/4 teaspoon salt
Pepper to taste

In a large oven proof skillet, heat butter or oil over medium-high heat. Add potatoes and onions, and cook until done adding butter or oil as needed. Add cooked sausage.

In a bowl, beat eggs; add mint, salt and pepper, and pour over potatoes. Put skillet in preheated 325 degree oven and bake until the eggs are firm.

~Mina
Tiniakos

Note: Recipe may be doubled or tripled. Substitute bacon, ham, or links for sausage.

Serves: 4

This is one of our favorite recipes prepared for a Sunday brunch. It originated in Andros, Greece.

Πατάτες με Αυγά Φουρταλιά

Potato Omelet
Patates me Avga Fourtalia

8 tablespoons butter or olive oil
6 medium potatoes, peeled and cut in round slices
12 eggs
1/2 cup milk or half and half
Salt and pepper to taste
Oregano (optional)
1 cup Parmesan cheese, shredded (optional)

Heat 4 tablespoons butter or olive oil in a large (12 x14 inch) oven-proof skillet. Sauté the potato slices until cooked through and begin to brown. Stir frequently and add butter or oil as needed to prevent scorching.

While potatoes are cooking, beat eggs and milk together and add the salt, pepper and oregano to taste. If using cheese, sprinkle on top of the potatoes, then pour the egg mixture over the cheese. Place the skillet in a preheated 350 degree oven for 5 minutes or until the eggs are set. Remove from the oven and cool for a few minutes. Run a knife around the edge of the pan and place a serving plate over the top. Invert and carefully remove pan from the Fourtalia. Cut in wedges like a pie and serve.

~Areti
Vlahakis and   For variations, other ingredients may be added such as onions,
Vasiliki Vlahakis   mushrooms, peppers, zucchini, tomatoes, bacon or sausage.

Serves: 6 to 10

Areti Vlahakis came from Kohilou, Andros, Greece and with her she brought this village recipe. The dish is one that the women depended on for an all-around meal or one to serve when company arrived unexpectedly. The meal is complete when served with bread, salad and beverage.

Potatoes with Eggs
Patates me Avga

4 to 5 potatoes, cut in french fry strips
Oil
3 to 4 eggs, beaten
1/2 cup feta cheese, crumbled
5 garlic cloves, minced
Oregano

In a skillet, fry potatoes in oil. Remove potatoes with a slotted spoon and set aside. Drain any excess oil, leaving about 2 tablespoons. Return fried potatoes to skillet and reduce the heat. Add eggs, feta cheese, and garlic. Cook until eggs are done. Remove to a serving platter. Sprinkle with oregano.

~Martha
Athanasakis

Καγιανάς

Tomatoes in Scrambled Eggs
Kayianas

4 small tomatoes
2 tablespoons olive oil
4 eggs, slightly beaten
Salt and pepper to taste
Feta cheese to taste, crumbled (optional)

Place tomatoes in scalding water for 2 to 3 minutes. Peel skin from tomatoes with a paring knife. Cut tomatoes into small pieces. Place them in a non-stick frying pan and allow to simmer over medium heat, stirring occasionally, until all the juice has evaporated. Pour olive oil over tomatoes and simmer for approximately 1 minute. Pour eggs and feta, if desired, over the tomatoes; add salt and pepper. Stir with a wooden spoon until tomatoes are cooked to desired consistency.

~Voula
Bakouros

Στραπατσάδα

Tomatoes and Scrambled Eggs
Strapatsatha

4 small firm tomatoes
1 small onion, finely minced
2 tablespoons butter
1/2 teaspoon sweet basil, dried
4 large eggs
Salt and pepper to taste

Place tomatoes in scalding water for a few minutes. Peel skin with a paring knife. Cut tomatoes into small pieces. Sauté onion in butter until golden. Add tomatoes and sweet basil and simmer 15 minutes. Beat eggs lightly in a bowl with salt and pepper. Pour eggs over ingredients in pan and stir with a fork until they are the consistency desired. Serve immediately.

Eggs should be on the soft side rather than firm, but the dish will be even better if the eggs are cooked to the consistency which suits your palate.

~Jeanette
Michas

Serves: 2

My Yiayia didn't like plain old boiled, scrambled or fried eggs as a main dish. She was particularly fond of eggs with vegetables. She did not use anything but fresh vegetables in her egg dishes. She had a large garden in back of her home in Baker, Oregon and, of course, had plenty of vegetables and fruit. Once I tried canned okra when okra was out of season, and the result was horrible.

Sweets

Contents

⌒ COOKIES ⌒

⌒ SWEETS ⌒

⌒ PASTRIES & PHYLLO ⌒

Μελομακάρονα

Honey-Dipped Cookies
Melomakarona

1 cup (2 sticks) butter, room temperature
2 cups vegetable oil
1 cup powdered sugar
1/2 teaspoon cinnamon
3/4 cup of orange juice
8 cups flour
Walnuts, finely ground

Syrup:
2 cups honey
1 cup water

With an electric mixer, beat butter and oil with sugar for
30 minutes on low speed. Add orange juice and continue
beating for another 30 minutes. Add enough flour to make a
soft dough that holds its shape. Knead it well. Take a small
amount of dough in hand and form into a 3-inch oval shape.
The correct amount of flour is very important (too soft a dough
will spread and too much dough may toughen the cookie). Put
on a greased cookie sheet and bake in a preheated 350 degree
oven for 45 minutes. Remove from cookie sheet and set aside
until cookies are partly cooled.

Syrup: In saucepan combine honey and water over medium
heat. Dip cookies in warmed syrup allowing them to soak for
2 to 3 minutes. Sprinkle with ground walnuts.

~Anastasia
Mallos

Yield: 40

Μελομακάρονα

Orange-Honey Crescents ☦
Melomakarona

1 1/2 cups vegetable oil
6 tablespoons frozen orange juice (from concentrate)
1/3 cup sugar
1 1/2 teaspoons orange peel, grated
3 1/2 cups sifted all-purpose flour
3/4 teaspoon baking powder
3/4 teaspoon baking soda
1/4 teaspoon salt
1 teaspoon cinnamon
1/4 teaspoon cloves
1/4 teaspoon nutmeg
3/4 cup pecans, chopped

3/4 cup honey
3 tablespoons orange juice (from concentrate)

1/2 cup pecans, finely chopped

In a mixing bowl combine oil, orange juice, sugar and orange peel. Sift together all dry ingredients and spices. Add to first mixture. Stir in chopped pecans. Chill dough. Shape into crescents and place on a cookie sheet. Bake in a preheated 350 degree oven approximately 15 minutes.

Combine honey and remaining orange juice. Heat. Drizzle over crescents, which have been cooled. Sprinkle with chopped pecans. This is an easy recipe and keeps well.

~Virginia Calley

Yield: 3 1/2 dozen.

My mother-in-law, Anna Calley's recipe from Smyrna, Turkey.

Μελομακάρονα

Orange-Honey Crescents
Melomakarona

1 cup (2 sticks) unsalted butter, room temperature
2 cups vegetable oil
2 tablespoons vegetable shortening
1 cup powdered sugar
2 eggs
1/2 cup orange juice
1/2 teaspoon baking soda
1/3 cup orange-flavored liquor (may substitute lemon juice)
1/2 teaspoon cloves
1/2 teaspoon cinnamon
1/2 teaspoon nutmeg
1 teaspoon salt
4-5 cups flour

Syrup:
2 cups honey
1/2 cup water

Walnuts, finely chopped

In a large mixing bowl, beat butter, shortening and oil slowly. Keep beating while adding the sugar and eggs. Beat well and add orange juice. Dissolve baking soda in liquor or lemon juice. Add to mixture. Add spices, salt and flour and beat well. Keep adding flour to make a soft dough. Bake 1 cookie to test; if it spreads out, add a little more flour. Dough will get stiffer as it sets, but must be soft enough to handle. Take about a tablespoon size piece of dough and make into an almond shape. Place cookies on baking sheet and bake in a preheated 350 degree oven for 30 minutes or until light brown.

When cookies have cooled bring honey and water to a boil to make syrup. Dip cookies in the honey syrup until they are thoroughly soaked. Sprinkle with walnuts.

Ann Mehas

Yield: 80 cookies.

This was my mother-in-law's, Christine Mehas, recipe. She felt this was the best because when cookies were dipped in the syrup, they did not crumble or break.

Μελομακάρονα

Honey-Dipped Cookies
Melomakarona

2 cups (4 sticks) unsalted butter, room temperature
4 egg yolks
1 cup milk
2 tablespoons sugar
2 heaping teaspoons baking powder
5 to 6 cups sifted flour (approximately)

Honey for dipping after cookies are baked
1 cup walnuts, finely chopped

In a mixing bowl, beat the butter until creamy. Add the egg
yolks, milk and sugar. Mix thoroughly. Add the baking powder
and flour. Mix by hand at this point. Add enough flour until
batter becomes a soft dough and firm enough to shape into
an oval cookie.

Once the cookie is shaped lightly press the cookie on a fine
grater to make a fine indentation. Bake on a greased cookie
sheet in a preheated 300 degree oven for 25 to 50 minutes.
Cool the melomakarona and then dip in warm honey for a
few minutes on each side. Remove and sprinkle with walnuts.

Hints: You may want to dilute the honey with homemade syrup
like you make for baklava. You do not need to dip the cookies in
honey the same day you bake; it is best to dip the cookies the
day before you plan to serve them.

~ Joan Liapes

Yield: 48 cookies.

*This was a favorite recipe of my mother,
Evanthia Liapes, who prepared this dessert
every St. Demetrios and St. Basil's day
to celebrate my father and uncle's
respective name days.*

Μελομακάρονα

Honey-Dipped Cookies
Melomakarona

2 cups vegetable oil
1/2 cup (1 stick) butter, melted
1/2 cup sugar
1/2 cup orange juice
5 to 6 cups sifted flour
3 teaspoons baking powder
1/4 cup warm water
3/4 cup walnuts, finely chopped
1/2 teaspoon cinnamon
1/4 teaspoon ground cloves

Syrup:
1 pound honey
1/2 cup water

1/2 cup walnuts, finely chopped

In a large bowl, combine oil, butter and sugar. Stir in orange juice and flour until smooth. Quickly mix baking powder with warm water and stir into dough at once. Stir in 3/4 cup walnuts, cinnamon and cloves. Shape dough into ovals, about 3 x 1 x 1/2 inch. Place on ungreased baking sheet. Bake in a preheated 350 degree oven for 20 to 25 minutes. Let stand 5 minutes. Remove to wire rack. (At this time cookies can be frozen in an airtight container until ready to use.) Thaw completely and dip in syrup just before ready to serve.

Syrup: In a saucepan over medium heat, combine honey and water. Dip cookies, drain and place on platter. Sprinkle walnuts on top.

~Angeline
(Jennie) Kanas

Note: For a buffet table, cookies can be made smaller.

Yield: 50 to 60

This has proved to be an excellent dessert for any occasion.

Honey-Dipped Cookies
Melomakarona

2 cups (4 sticks) unsalted butter
1 cup vegetable oil
3 egg yolks
1 cup orange juice
1 cup sugar
6 cups cake flour (approximately)
1 teaspoon baking powder
1/2 teaspoon baking soda
Walnuts, halves or coarsely chopped
Additional walnuts, finely ground (for topping)

Syrup:
2 cups water
1 cinnamon stick
1 1/2 cups sugar
1 cup honey

In a mixing bowl, cream butter until light and fluffy. Add oil
slowly, blending well. Add egg yolks one at a time, beating well
after each addition. Add orange juice gradually; stir until well
mixed. Add sugar gradually and mix well until dissolved. Sift
flour, baking powder and soda together. Add enough flour
mixture to the creamed butter to make a soft dough that is not
sticky. Take a walnut-sized piece of dough and flatten in palm
of hand. Place a small amount of coarsely chopped nuts or a
walnut piece in the center of the flattened dough and fold over
to enclose. Shape into an oval. Make an indentation with a fork
(to hold nuts). Bake in a preheated 375 degree oven 25 minutes
until golden brown.

To make syrup, combine all ingredients. Boil for 5 minutes.
Cool syrup. Dip warm cookies in the syrup. Sprinkle with
finely ground nuts.

~Carolyn
Damis

*In memory of Virginia J. Damis. My personal
favorite of the Greek sweets made by my
mother-in-law, Virginia Damis.*

Honey-Dipped Cookies ☦
Melomakarona

2 cups (4 sticks) margarine, room temperature
2 cups vegetable oil
3 heaping tablespoons sugar
5 pounds flour (approximately)
4 heaping teaspoons baking powder
2 cups orange juice
1 heaping teaspoon baking soda
2 to 3 heaping tablespoons cinnamon
1/2 teaspoon nutmeg
1/4 teaspoon ground cloves
2 small packages walnuts, finely ground

Syrup:
2 cups water
1 cinnamon stick
1 1/2 cups sugar
1 cup honey

In a large mixing bowl, beat margarine for 1 to 2 minutes on
low speed. Add oil, scraping the sides occasionally. Add sugar
and beat until creamy and fluffy. Meanwhile, sift the flour into
a large bowl. In a separate bowl add baking soda to orange
juice and stir. (This will cause a bubbling up action.) Hold the
soda/orange juice bowl over the margarine mixture (which
should still be mixing on low speed) and let the bubbles spill
out into the mixer bowl. Continue to stir the orange juice
mixture and slowly add it to the margarine and sugar. Slowly
add 1 cup flour into the mixing bowl, then baking powder,
cinnamon, nutmeg, cloves and half of the nuts. Gradually
add more flour, 1 heaping tablespoon at a time until it starts
getting too thick for the mixer. Remove the dough by hand,
adding flour and kneading until it is soft, but not sticky.
Continue kneading for about 5 more minutes.

Syrup: Combine the first 3 ingredients in a medium saucepan;
boil for 15 minutes. Add honey and continue boiling for an
additional 5 minutes. Place syrup in the refrigerator while
completing the recipe.

(Optional) Cover dough with plastic and put aside while you drink a cup of coffee, eat a previously prepared pastry and visit.

Take a bit of dough about the size of a walnut, roll in hand and shape into an oval. Place on an ungreased cookie sheet about 1/2 inch apart as these cookies will not spread much. Bake in a 300 degree preheated oven for about 30 minutes. When done, they will be brown on the bottom and tan on the top.

Dip the hot cookies (6 to 8 at a time) in the cool honey mixture for 2 to 3 minutes, turning frequently. Return to cookie sheet and sprinkle lightly with the remaining ground walnuts and cinnamon.

~Vasiliki
Marandas

Optional shapes: Twists, "S", or donut shaped.

Yield: 4 to 5 dozen cookies.

Advice for cooking:
"You can learn or do anything
ifa you want."

Honey-Dipped Cookies ☦
Melomakarona

8 cups oil
2 cups sugar
2 tablespoons cinnamon
2 tablespoons nutmeg
2 teaspoons cloves
4 tablespoons baking powder
2 teaspoons baking soda
2 cups orange juice
16 cups flour

Syrup:
3/4 cup honey
3 tablespoons water
Cinnamon stick

Walnuts, finely chopped for topping

In a large bowl, combine all ingredients except flour and mix thoroughly. Add flour gradually. Form into oval or round shapes. Roll to about the size of a generous cigar about 2 to 2 1/2 inches long. Prick with fork and bake in a preheated 350 degree oven 20 minutes or until lightly browned. Remove from oven and cool cookies on a rack.

Syrup: In a saucepan over medium heat, combine honey, water and cinnamon stick. When cookies have cooled, dip in hot syrup. It is not necessary to leave these in the syrup long. Sprinkle with finely chopped walnuts.

Suggestion: Test bake one cookie to see if it flattens out while baking. If so, add 1/4 cup flour and test again.

~Pearl Pavlos

This recipe is from my hometown, Spokane.
We think it is the very best.
You can cut this recipe in half.

Μελομακάρονα

Honey-Dipped Cookies
Melomakarona

2 cups (4 sticks) butter, room temperature
1 cup oil
1 1/2 cups powdered sugar
4 rounded teaspoons baking powder
1/2 teaspoon cinnamon
8 to 9 cups flour
1 cup orange juice
Rind of one orange

Syrup:
2 cups honey
1 cup water

Walnuts, finely chopped

Beat butter and oil until smooth. Sift sugar, baking powder
and cinnamon with some of the flour. While still beating
butter, add the dry mixture. Add juice, rind and remainder
of flour until dough is easy to handle and can be made into
oval shapes. Place on cookie sheets and bake in a preheated
325 to 350 degree oven until golden. Remove from oven
and cool.

Syrup: In a saucepan, combine honey and water. Heat
to lukewarm.

While still warm, dip cookies in syrup allowing them to soak
for 2 to 3 minutes. Remove and place on platter. Sprinkle with
finely chopped walnuts.

~Sophia
Economus
Leventis

Serves: 4 dozen.

This is a recipe of Christina Economus, my mother.
She always made this from memory. One day as
we made these together, I wrote the recipe down.
These cookies are her grandchildren's favorites.

Filled Honey-Dipped Cookies
Finikia Yemista

1 cup (2 sticks) unsalted butter
1²/₃ cups sugar
1 teaspoon orange rind, grated
¹/₄ cup orange juice, freshly squeezed
2 tablespoons lemon juice, freshly squeezed
2 tablespoons Cognac
1 teaspoon vanilla
1 egg (optional)
4¹/₂ to 5¹/₂ cups flour
1 teaspoon baking powder
¹/₂ teaspoon baking soda

Filling:
3 cups walnuts, chopped fine
3 tablespoons sugar
1 teaspoon cinnamon
¹/₄ teaspoon ground cloves
3 tablespoons butter, melted
¹/₂ teaspoon nutmeg

Syrup:
³/₄ cup water
1 cup sugar
¹/₂ cup honey
Cinnamon stick
Several whole cloves

Almonds, chopped (enough to sprinkle over all cookies)
Dash of cinnamon

In a mixing bowl, cream butter with sugar. Add orange rind, orange and lemon juices, Cognac and vanilla. Add egg, if desired. Add 1 cup flour, baking powder and baking soda. Gradually add more flour until a smooth dough forms. Mix well.

In another bowl, mix walnuts with sugar, cinnamon, cloves, butter and nutmeg.

Pinch off dough into pieces about the size of a walnut. Insert 1 teaspoon of nut filling into center of dough. Form into oval shapes about 2¼ inches long. With fork tines, press on top of cookie, then place on cookie sheet. Bake in a preheated 350 degree oven for approximately 18 minutes, or until lightly browned. While cookies are cooling make syrup.

Syrup: Combine all syrup ingredients in a saucepan and bring to a boil. Cook until thickened. Dip cooled cookies in syrup. Sprinkle with almonds and a dash of cinnamon.

~Sophia Kondoleon

Yield: 50 cookies.

This family favorite has a rich history. The cookies were brought to the Ionian Islands by the ruling Venetians around the 15th century. Women of these islands pride themselves in baking the best Finikia in all of Greece.

Honey-Dipped Cookies
Finikia

1/4 cup (1/2 stick) unsalted butter, melted
1/4 cup (1/2 stick) margarine, melted
2 ounces corn oil
1/4 cup sugar
Dash of cognac

1/4 cup orange juice
1 teaspoon baking soda
2 tablespoons orange zest
3 cups flour
2 teaspoons baking powder
1/2 teaspoon ground cloves
1/2 teaspoon ground cinnamon

Syrup:
3/4 cup water
1/2 cup sugar
1 cup honey

Topping:
1/2 cup sugar
1 teaspoon cinnamon
1 cup walnuts, chopped

In a large bowl, combine the butter, margarine, and oil and mix well. Add sugar and cognac. Mix baking soda with orange juice and add to the mixture. Stir in the zest. In another bowl, sift together flour, baking powder, cloves and cinnamon. Gradually add flour mixture to the above ingredients. Mix well. Form into oval shapes. Place cookies on ungreased cookie sheet. Bake in a preheated 350 degree oven for 30 minutes or until slightly browned. Cool on a rack.

Syrup: In a saucepan over medium-high heat combine water, sugar and honey and bring to a boil. Boil approximately 3 minutes. Keep warm.

~Theodora Vlachos

In a smaller bowl, mix sugar, cinnamon and walnuts. When cookies are cool, dip in warm syrup and sprinkle with nut mixture.

Φοινίκια Γεμιστά

Filled Cookies
Finikia Yemista

1 cup (2 sticks) unsalted butter, room temperature
1 cup oil
1 cup sugar
3/4 cup orange juice
1 teaspoon grated orange rind
1 egg, well beaten
1 teaspoon baking soda
5 to 6 cups all purpose flour
1 cup nuts, ground for filling
1/2 teaspoon cinnamon
1/4 teaspoon nutmeg

Syrup:
2 cups honey
1/2 cup water
1/2 cinnamon stick
Whole cloves
Small piece of orange peel

In a mixing bowl, beat butter and oil together for 20 minutes. Add sugar and continue beating for another 10 minutes. Add juice, orange rind and egg and blend well. Mix baking soda with first cup of flour and add flour by hand until dough is the consistency of molded cookie dough. Test by rolling a small amount between your palms. It should not stick, or fall apart. Shape into ovals. Make an indentation in the center and add 1/2 teaspoon of the nut filling. Re-shape cookie to close the hole over the nuts. Bake in a preheated 375 degree oven about 20 minutes or until golden brown. Cool to room temperature.

Syrup: Heat ingredients over medium heat for 15 minutes. Strain. Dip cooled cookies in warm syrup and coat them completely. Drain and re-use the syrup.

Note: If you wish to freeze the cookies, do not dip them, but store and dip when you wish to serve them. The syrup will keep in a closed jar in the refrigerator.

~ Georgia
Vareldzis

Yield: approximately 55 cookies.

My mother, who was not Greek, learned to make these cookies from a koumbara of hers who was a wonderful cook and baker.

Cookie Twists
Koulourakia

2 cups (4 sticks) salted butter, room temperature
1 cup granulated sugar
2 cups powdered sugar
4 extra-large eggs
1/4 cup fresh orange juice
1/4 cup corn oil
1/4 cup milk
4 rounded teaspoons baking powder
7 to 8 cups flour
Sesame seeds

In a mixer cream butter until it is the consistency of mayonnaise. Add the sugars and beat until fluffy and well blended. Add eggs beating well. Gradually add the liquids and continue beating until well blended. Sift about 6 cups flour with baking powder. Gradually add flour mixture to butter mixture, until you can form long rolls without dough sticking to your hands. Fold rolls in half and braid cookies so that two "tails" are at one end. Roll in sesame seeds. Bake on an ungreased cookie sheet in a preheated 375 degree oven for 20 to 25 minutes or until slightly brown.

~Betty
Phoutrides

Note: This recipe can be made in a food processor.

Yield: approximately 100 cookies.

This recipe came to me years ago from the late Kalliope Lambros. It became the recipe for the Philoptochos Circles for use in all the coffee socials.

Melt-in-Your-Mouth Cookies
Koulourakia

2 cups (4 sticks) unsalted butter, melted
6 eggs, separated
2 cups sugar
3 teaspoons vanilla
1 tablespoon whiskey or Scotch
6 teaspoons baking powder
6½ to 7 cups flour

2 egg whites
Sesame seeds

In a saucepan, over medium-high heat, melt butter, then cool.
Beat butter for 15 minutes. Beat 1 cup sugar with 6 egg yolks.
Set aside. In a mixing bowl, beat egg whites until stiff, then
add remainder of sugar. Fold egg whites into egg yolks until
thoroughly mixed. Add vanilla and whiskey. Slowly add flour
and knead gently until dough is easy to form. Break off a piece
of dough and roll in the palm of your hands to make a "thicker
than pencil" sized rope about 4 to 5 inches long. Then braid it,
make an "S" or an "8" shape, or be creative and make your own
design. Brush cookies with egg whites and sprinkle with sesame
seeds. Arrange on a greased, heavy duty cookie sheet. Bake in
a preheated 350 degree oven for 20 to 25 minutes or until
lightly browned. When completely cooled, store in an air-tight
container. They keep for a very long time and require no
refrigeration.

~ Katherine
Vlahos Lockie

Yield: 6 dozen

*"A handful of this and a pinch of that"... this recipe comes to
the family of Marina Vlahos via her neighbor Jenny who,
to our good fortune, had the patience and good nature to
measure every handful and pinch. Thanks, Jenny!
We are forever in your debt!*

Cookie Twists
Koulouria

2 cups (4 sticks) butter, room temperature
12 egg yolks
2¼ cups sugar
1 teaspoon baking soda
1½ teaspoons vanilla
2¼ teaspoons baking powder
9 cups flour

1 egg yolk, beaten

In a mixing bowl, beat butter until creamy. In a separate bowl, beat egg yolks and sugar together. Slowly fold into whipped butter. Add baking soda and vanilla, beating slowly until blended. Sift baking powder into part of the flour. Add gradually to the butter mixture. Continue to add flour a little at a time until the dough no longer sticks to the sides of the bowl and the consistency is firm enough to shape.

Form or roll dough (about the size of an egg) into desired shapes, such as a wreath or twisted pencil. Place cookies on an ungreased cookie sheet. Brush the tops with beaten egg yolk. Bake in a preheated 350 degree oven until light brown, about 20 minutes.

~Kathy
Karabatsos

Yield: 3 dozen.

In memory of my mother, Angelika Psihogios, who made baking Greek pastries look effortless! Growing up, there were always Koulouria around for my after school snack. Later, all her grandchildren looked forward to Yiayia's Koulouria.

Cookie Twists
Koulourakia

1 cup (2 sticks) unsalted butter, room temperature
2 cups sugar
6 eggs
1/2 cup milk
4 teaspoons baking powder
8 to 9 cups flour, sifted
1/2 teaspoon cinnamon
1 teaspoon vanilla
1 teaspoon anise extract

2 egg yolks
1/3 cup sesame seeds (optional)

Cream butter until soft, add sugar and beat thoroughly. Add
6 eggs, then add milk. Combine 8 cups flour with baking
powder; gradually add to batter. Add cinnamon, vanilla
and anise.

Knead dough and add more flour if necessary to form a smooth,
firm dough (test by rolling in your hand: if firm and doesn't
stick, consistency is correct). Roll dough in the palm of your
hand into cylinders about 3 inches long and 1/2 inch in diameter.
Fold in half and shape them into linear braids that end with
two "tails."

Beat two egg yolks and brush on cookies. Dip in sesame
seeds if desired. Bake on greased cookie sheet in a preheated
350 degree oven for 15 minutes or until slightly brown.

~ Virginia
Rozos

Yield: about 5 dozen.

Orange-Flavored Cookie Twists ☦
Koulourakia Portokalion

2 cups olive oil
2 cups orange juice, freshly squeezed
1 1/2 cups sugar
2 teaspoons ground cinnamon
1 teaspoons ground cloves
Rind of 2 oranges
8 to 10 cups all purpose flour (may require more)
2 teaspoons baking powder
2 teaspoons baking soda

In a blender on medium speed, beat oil, orange juice, sugar, cinnamon, cloves and orange rind. In a large bowl mix well most of the flour with the baking powder. Pour half of blender mixture into flour mixture. Add baking soda to remaining blender mixture and blend for 1 more minute. Add to the flour and mix well to form a very soft dough. Add the rest of flour, as needed. Take walnut sized pieces and form ropes, twisting them twice. Place on ungreased baking sheets. Bake in a preheated 350 degree oven for 20 minutes or until lightly brown. Do not overcook.

~ Litsa
Dussin

Yield: 6 dozen.

No cholesterol, lenten cookie.

Κουλουράκια

Cookie Twists
Koulourakia

2 cups (4 sticks) unsalted butter, room temperature
4 cups sugar
1 dozen eggs
2 jiggers whiskey
1 cup milk
8 cups flour
9 teaspoons baking powder
1 teaspoon baking soda

Mix butter until creamy for about 20 minutes. Add sugar gradually, then beat in the eggs. Add whiskey and milk and mix well. Sift 1 cup flour with baking powder and soda. Add flour to butter mixture, enough to make stiff dough. Roll into long pieces and braid two pieces together to make twists, or use single long pieces to form rings. Bake in preheated 300 to 325 degree oven until light brown in color, about 15 minutes. Cool and store in tightly covered container.

~Michael
Anthis

This recipe is dedicated to my mother, Marge Karafotias Anthis.

Cookie Twists

2 cups (4 sticks) butter, room temperature
1/4 pound vegetable shortening
1/4 cup oil
1/2 cup orange juice (heat slightly)
3 eggs
2 1/2 heaping teaspoons baking powder
1/2 teaspoon baking soda
1 1/2 cups sugar
2 tablespoon vanilla
Cinnamon to taste
8 1/2 cups flour, sifted

1 egg, beaten for top

In a bowl cream butter, vegetable shortening and oil. Add orange juice, eggs, baking powder, baking soda, sugar, vanilla and cinnamon to taste. Add flour and knead. Scoop out a tablespoon of dough to make cookies. Place on an ungreased cookie sheet and brush with egg wash. Bake in a preheated 350 degree oven until golden brown. Remove from oven. Cool on wire rack.

~Tom and
Marie
Avgerakis

In memory of our mother, Mary Avgerakis.

Cookie Twists
Koulourakia

1 cup (2 sticks) unsalted butter, room temperature
1 cup sugar
3 eggs
1 teaspoon vanilla
4 cups flour
3 teaspoons baking powder

1 egg, beaten for top
Sesame seeds

In a mixer cream butter, beat in sugar gradually and cream well. Add one egg at a time and mix well after each addition. Add vanilla. Sift flour and baking powder together and gradually add two cups to the creamed mixture. Work in the remaining flour by hand until the dough is smooth and workable. Divide dough into 4 balls. Place in a bowl, cover and let stand approximately 20 to 30 minutes.

On a hard surface, work 1 ball with fingers of one hand and heel of the other hand to stretch and pull dough until it is smooth. Roll to approximately 1 inch thick and cut into walnut-sized pieces. Shape as desired into braids or "S" shapes. Place on greased cookie sheets. Beat egg with a little water to create a wash and brush each cookie. Sprinkle each cookie with sesame seeds.

Fill 2 cookie sheets. Place them both in a preheated 350 degree oven using both the upper and lower racks. Bake 14 minutes, then reverse pans in the oven. Bake an additional 10 to 11 minutes until lightly golden. Remove cookies and cool on racks.

~Theodora
Vlachos

Yield: 4 dozen.

Κουλούρια

Cookie Twists
Koulouria

7 1/2 cups flour
2 tablespoons baking powder
2 cups (4 sticks) butter or margarine
2 tablespoons vegetable shortening
1 1/2 cups sugar
1 teaspoon vanilla
5 eggs

1 egg, beaten, for top

In a large mixing bowl, sift flour together with baking powder.
In a separate bowl, cream butter, shortening, sugar and vanilla
together well. Add 5 eggs one at a time and continue mixing
until well blended. Gradually add liquid mixture into flour
mixture. Knead until well mixed. Roll into linear braids or
cylinders pinched into round circles. Beat one egg well and
lightly brush each cookie. Bake in a preheated 350 degree
oven until slightly brown, about 15 to 25 minutes.

~Martha
Athanasakis

Yield: 4 to 5 dozen.

*This recipe is from my beloved
mother-in-law Eugenia Athanasakis.
Submitted in her loving memory.*

Low-Cholesterol Cookie Twists ☦
Koulourakia Nistisima

1 cup vegetable oil
1 cup sugar
2 tablespoons shortening
1 cup orange juice
1 tablespoon orange peel, grated
1 teaspoon vanilla
1 teaspoon cinnamon
1/2 teaspoon ground cloves
1 teaspoon nutmeg
1 ounce cognac or whiskey
5 to 6 cups flour, sifted
3 teaspoons baking powder
1 teaspoon baking soda

Beat together oil, sugar and shortening until well-blended. Slowly add orange juice, vanilla, orange peel, cinnamon, cloves, nutmeg and cognac. Continue mixing well. Combine flour, baking powder and soda. Slowly add liquid mixture to flour mixture and knead until dough becomes soft. Form into desired shapes (braids, circles, "S" or "8," etc.). Bake in a preheated 350 degree oven for about 20 minutes or until slightly golden.

~Martha
Athanasakis

Yield: 4 to 5 dozen.

Κουλούρια

Cookie Twists
Koulouria

1 dozen eggs (reserve one egg for topping)
2 cups (4 sticks) butter
1 pound powdered sugar
3 teaspoons vanilla
10 teaspoons baking powder
1/2 cup milk
Flour

1 egg, beaten for top
Sesame seeds (optional)

Beat eggs well and set aside. Beat butter and sugar together
until creamy; add vanilla, baking powder and milk. Mix well.
Add the beaten eggs. Mix in flour by hand until dough is soft
but easy to handle. Take a walnut-sized piece of dough. Roll
into a 9-inch long piece. (Roll in sesame seeds if desired.) Fold
in half and twist. For another shape, roll the ends toward center
into an S-shape. Place on a greased cookie sheet. Brush with
beaten egg. Bake in a preheated 350 degree oven for 15 to
20 minutes, or until golden brown.

~Helen
Gianopoulos
Tzakis

*This is my Yiayia (Rose) Triandafili's
recipe. When she made them, she had
to hide them because my brothers and
I would eat so many.*

Παξιμάδια της Μαίρης

Mary's Twice-Baked Cookies
Paximathia tis Meris

2 cups (4 sticks) unsalted butter, room temperature
1 cup corn oil
6 eggs
2 1/2 cups sugar
1 1/2 teaspoons vanilla

1 box cake flour
2 cups white flour, pre-sifted
3 teaspoons baking powder
1 teaspoon baking soda

Cinnamon
2 cups powdered sugar

In a mixing bowl, cream first 5 ingredients. In another bowl, combine dry ingredients and then add to creamed mixture. Chill mixture for 1 hour or overnight. Divide mixture into 10 (9-ounce) balls. Shape each ball into a loaf. Place on a cookie sheet. Bake in a preheated 375 degree oven 20 minutes. Remove from oven. Slice up to 23 cookies from each loaf. Lay cookies on their sides. Return to oven. Brown lightly. Remove from oven. Sprinkle with powdered sugar and cinnamon.

Anastasia Boudoures Gianopoulos

Yield: 8 dozen.

This is similar to a koulouria recipe, however, to save time, my mom Mary would bake in loaves instead of twisting the cookies. It was a favorite among her lady friends.

Greek Dunking Cookies
Paximathia

1 cup (2 sticks) margarine
1 1/2 cups sugar
3 eggs
1/8 cup bourbon or liquor
2 teaspoons vanilla
1 teaspoon salt
5 teaspoons baking powder
5 cups flour
3/4 cup walnuts, finely chopped

Egg wash (1 egg slightly beaten with dash water)

In a mixing bowl, cream margarine and sugar. Add eggs
and beat well. Add bourbon, vanilla and salt. Mix well.
Sift 1 teaspoon baking powder to 1 cup of flour and add
to margarine mixture. Repeat this 4 more times with the
remaining 4 cups of flour and 4 teaspoons baking powder.
Add chopped walnuts to mixture. Mix dough with hands until
thoroughly mixed.

Divide the dough into 4 equal rolls approximately 2 1/2 inches
wide and 16 inches long. Press 4 rolls into 11 x 16 inch pan,
leaving a small space between each flattened roll. Slice each
of the 4 rolls diagonally into approximately 20 1/2-inch cookies.
Brush with egg wash. Bake in a preheated 375 degree oven 20
minutes. Remove from oven and slice each cookie immediately.
Remove from pan and lay each cookie on one side. Bake again
until slightly browned (approximately 10 minutes). Pay close
attention so they do not burn. Cool. Eat and enjoy!

~ Paula
Dudunake
Diamond

Yield: 80 cookies.

*My mom and her sister, "Thetsa Helen," learned this recipe
from their mom. They made these often to serve with
coffee or milk — to dunk and enjoy! They're similar
to biscotti — not too sweet, just right.*

Nona's Cookies
Biskota tis Nonas

2 cups (4 sticks) butter, room temperature
1¼ cups of sugar
2 egg yolks, separated, reserve egg whites
2 teaspoons vanilla
4½ to 5 cups flour, sifted
1 teaspoon water
Sesame seeds

In a mixing bowl, beat butter until creamy. Slowly add the sugar and continue to beat. Add egg yolks one at a time and the 2 teaspoons vanilla, beating until mixture is very creamy. Change mixer setting to low and add 2½ cups of sifted flour (adding ½ cup at a time). Remove the bowl from the mixer and add the remainder of the flour, ⅓ cup at a time. The mixture will seem a little soft. Cover with plastic wrap and refrigerate for a couple of hours to firm up the dough.

When ready to bake, scoop out dough, 1 tablespoon at a time. Roll into a ball and press it down onto an ungreased cookie sheet. To the reserved egg whites, add 1 tablespoon of water. Brush this over the cookies and sprinkle with sesame seeds. Bake in a preheated 350 degree oven for 20 minutes.

~ Mimi
Palumbis

This recipe is a family favorite of
ours handed down by my
mother Maria Jatos.
My kids love it!

Μπισκότα Γεμιστά με Χουρμά

Date Cookies
Biskota Yemista me Hourma

1 tablespoon sugar
1 package yeast
1 1/2 cups water, lukewarm
5 cups all-purpose flour
1 1/2 teaspoons ground cloves
2/3 cup vegetable shortening, melted
1/3 cup oil
1/2 cup milk
1/2 water

Filling:
1 (10-ounce) container dates, pitted
4 tablespoons (1/4 stick) unsalted butter, room temperature
2 teaspoons ground cinnamon
1 teaspoon ground cloves

Powdered sugar

In a 1 quart measuring cup, melt 1 package yeast and 1 tablespoon sugar in 1 1/2 cups lukewarm water. Let stand 10 minutes until bubbly or until double in size. In the meantime, melt the vegetable shortening and oil in a saucepan over low heat. In a large bowl, combine flour and yeast mixture kneading into a ball. It will be smooth in texture, not sticky.

Filling: In a meat grinder, grind the dates (mixture will resemble ground meat). If you do not have a meat grinder, you can process the dates in a food processor. Add a little flour into the food processor before adding the dates to prevent them from sticking to the mixing bowl. Empty into a bowl and add the softened butter, cinnamon and cloves, stirring well to combine.

Now you are ready to prepare the cookies. With a rolling pin, roll out the dough fairly thin. Using a round cookie cutter cut as many rounds as you can. Using a spoon, place some of the date mixture into the center of each round and roll into a cylinder and press firmly so that it does not open. Place cookies on ungreased cookie sheet, seam side down, and bake in a preheated 350 degree oven 15 to 20 minutes or until lightly browned. Remove from oven and cool. Sprinkle with powdered sugar.

Yield: 45 to 60

~Karen Henkhaus for Armine Megurian

My mother has made these cookies all my life. Now my children enjoy their grandmother's baking in much the same manner; we can't get enough!

A CELEBRATION OF FOOD, FAITH & FAMILY

Despina's Almond Cookies
Amigthalota tis Despinas

2 pounds almonds, blanched, peeled, and finely ground
2 cups sugar
2 heaping tablespoons semolina
1 teaspoon almond extract (optional)
Orange flower water (in a spray bottle)

Confectioners sugar

In a large bowl, combine almonds, sugar, semolina and almond extact. Knead for approximately 3 minutes. Shape 1 tablespoon of dough into an oval shape.

On a greased cookie sheet that has been sprinkled with a small amount of semolina, place cookies close together. Bake in a preheated 350 degree oven for 25 minutes or until golden brown.

Remove cookies from oven. Without removing them from the cookie sheet, spray generously with orange flower water.

~Evangelos
Fasilis
Allow to cool and then roll in confectioners sugar.

Yield: 3 dozen.

Each time we leave Greece, a box of these delights is in our suitcase. This is Despina's way of sending a part of herself along.

Almond-Filled Phyllo Triangles
Trigona

2 sheets Phyllo dough

Filling:
2 cups sugar
1 cup water
Juice from 1/2 lemon
3 cups almonds, ground
1 drop Bergamot* oil, optional

Syrup:
6 cups sugar
3 cups water
Juice from 1 lemon
2 strips rind from lemon

For filling: In a saucepan, combine sugar, water and lemon juice and boil for 5 minutes. When cool, add almonds and a drop of Bergamot flavoring. Set aside and prepare syrup.

Syrup: In a saucepan, combine sugar and water and boil for 1 hour until syrupy. Add lemon juice and lemon rind and boil for 10 more minutes.

While syrup is cooking, cut phyllo into 2 1/2 inch strips. Butter one sheet of phyllo dough. Lay another sheet on top and butter the second sheet. Place one heaping teaspoon filling on each strip and fold into triangles. Place on baking sheet and bake in a preheated 300 degree oven for 15 to 20 minutes or until lightly golden in color. Remove and let cool. Dip trigona (several at a time) in warm syrup. Remove to wire rack to drain.

*Can be found in some pharmacy sections.

~Anastasia
Mallos

Καтάδες

Nut-Filled Butter Cookies
Katathes

Filling:
2 cups walnuts, chopped
3/4 cup toasted sesame seeds, chopped
1/2 teaspoon nutmeg
1 teaspoon cinnamon
1/4 teaspoon cloves
5 tablespoons butter, melted
7 tablespoons honey

Cookie Dough:
2 cups (4 sticks) butter, room temperature
2 cups corn oil
1 1/2 cups granulated sugar
1 teaspoon baking soda
4 tablespoons baking powder
1 1/2 cups water
Juice of one lemon
6-8 cups flour or enough to form a soft dough
Zest of one lemon

Powdered sugar
Lemon blossom water

To make filling, mix all filling ingredients together in a medium bowl and set aside.

To make dough: In a large bowl, beat together butter, oil and sugar. Add baking soda. Dilute baking powder in the water, add lemon juice and immediately add to butter mixture. Beat well. Add enough flour to create a soft dough. Add lemon zest and knead dough. To make each cookie, take a small piece of dough about the size of a walnut, and flatten it. Place 1/2 teaspoon of filling in the center of the dough. Pinch the edges of the dough together to form a seam (to secure the filling and create an oval shape). Place on cookie sheet with seam side down. Bake in a preheated 350 degree oven on center rack for 15 minutes or until golden. Remove from oven and let cool a few minutes.

Sprinkle powdered sugar onto a large piece of white butcher paper. Remove cookies from the cookie sheet and place them on the butcher paper. Sprinkle top of cookies with lemon blossom water, then sift more powdered sugar to completely cover. Allow cookies to cool completely (overnight), then store in airtight container.

~Angeliki Anasis

Yield: 10 dozen.

Παστέλι Ανδριώτικο

Sesame Seed Honey Bars ☦
Pasteli Anthriotiko

2 cups honey
1 cup sugar
3 cups walnuts, chopped
2 cups sesame seeds
1/4 cup plain bread crumbs
Oil or sesame oil
1/2 cup sesame seeds for sprinkling on outside

In a saucepan over medium high heat, combine honey and sugar and bring to a boil, stirring to dissolve the sugar. Boil until syrup thickens (use a candy thermometer to 270° to 275°) stirring constantly. Remove from heat and add the walnuts, the 2 cups sesame seeds, and bread crumbs.

Brush a 9 x 13 inch oven proof baking dish with oil or sesame oil. Sprinkle the 1/4 cup sesame seeds on the bottom of the pan. Spread the hot mixture on the sesame seeds until the mixture is even (smoothing it with a damp spatula). Sprinkle the rest (1/4 cup) of the sesame seeds on top. Cool slightly, then cut into 1-inch squares.

~Chrysiis D. Rigas

Yield: 55 to 60 pieces.

Grabee Sugar Cookies

2 cups (4 sticks) butter, clarified
1 1/2 cups sugar
4 1/2 cups flour

~ Jeannette Lucas & Bill Bitar

In a saucepan, clarify the butter and let cool. Cover and let set overnight at room temperature. Add sugar and flour. Mix with hands until ingredients are well blended. Scoop little balls and work between the palm of both hands; insert a hole in the middle of each cookie. Bake in a preheated 300 degree oven for 20 minutes on an ungreased cookie sheet. Do not remove cookies from the cookie sheet until the next day.

Recipe in memory of our beloved mother, Mrs. Margaret A. Bitar, who was famous for her Grabee.

Κουραμπιέδες

Powdered Sugar Butter Cookies
Kourabiethes

2 cups (4 sticks) unsalted butter, room temperature
2 egg yolks
1 box powdered sugar, divided
1 teaspoon baking powder
1/2 jigger of whiskey
5 cups flour
1 cup almonds, finely ground

~ Sophia Kriara

In a mixer, beat butter until light and fluffy. Add egg yolks to butter. Gradually add 1/2 cup powdered sugar and beat together until creamy. Add baking powder and whiskey. Slowly add half of the flour and blend thoroughly. Knead in remainder of flour by hand. Add almonds to batter and mix thoroughly. Break off small amount of dough and work in hands until soft and pliable. Form about 50 cookies into desired shape. Bake in a preheated 350 degree oven for 20 minutes or until slightly browned. Remove from oven and sift powdered sugar generously over hot kourabiethes. Remove from pan when completely cooled.

Yield: 50

Powdered Sugar Butter Cookies ✝
Kourabiethes

3 cups olive oil
1 cup powdered sugar
Juice of 2 lemons
1 cup brandy or ouzo
1 teaspoon vanilla (optional)
1 tablespoon baking soda
1 tablespoon baking powder
7 to 8 cups flour
1 cup almonds, roasted, slivered

Ouzo in a spray bottle
Powdered sugar for topping

In a bowl, beat oil, powdered sugar, lemon juice, brandy, and vanilla until well-beaten. Mix in baking soda, then baking powder mixed together with a little flour. Slowly add rest of the flour to make a soft, but not sticky dough. Add the almonds and mix into dough.

Take a small amount of dough and shape into 2 inch half moons. Place on cookie sheets at least 1 inch apart. Bake in a preheated 350 degree oven about 30 minutes. Remove from baking sheet onto flat surface. Spray lightly with ouzo, then sift powdered sugar generously over cookies to completely cover.

~Antigone
Konkoumanos

Yield: 60

Powdered Sugar Butter Cookies
Kourabiethes

2 cups (4 sticks) unsalted sweet butter, melted
1 cup powdered sugar (approximately)
2 egg yolks
Juice of one orange
4 to 6 cups flour
Powdered sugar for topping

Melt butter over low heat. Remove from heat and skim off top. Let
stand 3 to 5 minutes. Pour slowly into bowl and leave whey particles.
Put bowl in refrigerator and let thicken, about 1 hour. In a mixer, beat
chilled butter at low speed for 45 minutes. Increase speed slightly and
slowly add the sugar. Beat 15 minutes. Add the egg yolks and beat
15 minutes. Add orange juice and beat 15 minutes longer. Slowly blend
in flour. Remove beaters and use hands to knead dough lightly. Take
a small amount of dough and roll into cylinders, then braid into shape.
Bake in a preheated 375 degree oven for 20 minutes. Remove from
oven. Wait 5 minutes, then with a spatula remove cookies carefully to
~Nick a surface lined with waxed or parchment paper. Sift powdered sugar
Vanikiotis heavily over cookies. Cool completely before storing.

Powdered Sugar Butter Cookies
Kourabiethes

2 cups (4 sticks) unsalted butter, melted
1/4 cup powdered sugar
1 egg yolk
2 teaspoons vanilla
5 cups cake flour
Powdered sugar for the top
Whole cloves

Refrigerate butter to a soft consistency. Beat at medium speed until
very light and creamy, about 15 minutes. Add powdered sugar, egg yolk
and vanilla, beating thoroughly after each addition. Add flour a little at
a time until a soft dough is formed. Form into a small round ball. Top
with a whole clove placed in the center of each cookie and bake on
ungreased cookie sheets in a preheated 350 degree oven for 20 to 25
minutes. Sift powdered sugar onto a plate. Place warm cookies on the
~Elaine A. plate and generously sift powdered sugar on top while still warm. Cool
Haralampus completely and store in air-tight container. Can be frozen.

Mother always put a clove in the center. In memory of Athansia Haralampus.

Powdered Sugar Butter Cookies
Kourabiethes

2 cups (4 sticks) unsalted butter, room temperature
2 cups powdered sugar
2 eggs
2 teaspoons baking powder
2 teaspoons vanilla
3/4 cup milk
1 cup nuts, chopped
4 to 6 cups flour

Beat butter and sugar about 15 minutes. Add eggs and continue beating for 5 minutes. Add baking powder, vanilla, milk and nuts. Work in flour with hands until you have a soft dough. Take dough and shape into desired shape. Place on ungreased cookie sheets and bake in a preheated 350 degree oven about 15 minutes or until very lightly colored. Cool. Then roll in powdered sugar. Sift additional sugar on top.

~Helen
Gianopoulos
Tzakis

My American friends call these "choke cookies." They say you should give out instructions with them. Don't breathe in as you are taking a bite.

Quince ☦
Kithoni

8 cups quince, peeled and cut into small french fry pieces
4 cups sugar
3/4 cup water
2 leaves scented geranium
2 tablespoons lemon juice

Put quince, sugar and water in large pot. Mix well and cook over high heat for 5 minutes, stirring occasionally. Turn heat off and let stand until completely cooled, about 4 hours. Cook again for 5 to 10 minutes until color is dark orange. Add geranium leaves and lemon juice the last 5 minutes of cooking. Remove from heat and put in sterilized jars and lids.

~Georgia
Belesin

Yield: 5 cups.

A recipe from my village Karies. In Greece it is served as a welcoming dessert. Quince is a golden yellow fruit with fuzzy skin, apple-shaped and fragrant. May also be used as a jam.

Cottage Cheese Pie

1 cup cottage cheese
2 tablespoons butter, room temperature
2 eggs
2 tablespoons heavy cream
1/2 teaspoon salt
3/4 cup sugar
2 tablespoons flour
1 cup milk
1 teaspoon vanilla, or juice and rind (zest) of 1 lemon

1 pie crust

In a bowl mash cottage cheese, cream and butter with a fork. In a separate bowl, whisk eggs with lemon juice. Beat thoroughly. Add lemon rind then stir into cottage cheese mixture. Pour into pastry-lined pie plate. Bake in a preheated 300 degree oven for 30 to 35 minutes. Cool.

~Anastasia
Mallos

Serves: 6 to 8

Greek Coffee ✝
Kafes

¼ cup water
1 heaping teaspoon powdered Greek coffee
1 heaping teaspoon sugar

Bring water to boil and remove from flame. Add coffee and
sugar. Do not stir! Return to flame. The instant it begins to
'swell' remove from flame let it boil over. Return to flame
and remove 2 more times. Pour into demitasse and serve
immediately. Since sugar is a matter of taste, you may use
more or less or none at all. I like my coffee 'metrion' (medium).

~Jeanette
Michas

Serves: 1

There isn't a town in Greece today that doesn't boast a
Kaffenion (coffee house) where men gather to sip coffee
during card games, bull sessions or the heated
arguments. Greeks consider this coffee
successfully brewed only when kamaki (a creamy
foam or bubbles) remains on top of the liquid
after it has been poured.

"Hrimata" (money) is what the recipient of such a cup
always says, because Greek superstition says that
when one sips kamaki, he will receive an unexpected
sum of money. If you know of someone who can tell
your fortune, you will be delighted in all
the things that will happen to you.

Yiayia's "Loukous"
Loukoumathes

1 yeast cake
1 1/2 cups warm water
1 3/4 cups warm milk
1/2 teaspoon salt
4 1/2 cups flour, sifted

1 1/2 quarts vegetable oil, heated very hot in large pan
   for stove top or you can use a deep fryer

In a large mixing bowl dissolve yeast in warm water. Add warm milk and salt. Add sifted flour. Mix until "ploppy" and sticky. (It's easier to mix by hand so remember to wash hands thoroughly and remove jewelry!) Cover and set aside in a warm place to rise. When dough has risen to double in size (or more) it is ready to deep fry.

To use the traditional way of spooning each loukoumatha into the very hot oil use the following method: wash hands. Put left hand in the dough mixture (do not punch down) and gather some dough. Squeeze the mixture to ooze out of left hand between thumb and forefinger. With spoon in right hand, scrape off a walnut-size ball of dough from left hand and drop dough in hot oil, being careful not to touch hot oil. Deep-fry several balls of dough at a time, being careful they do not touch. Fry until golden brown and cooked all the way through. With slotted spoon, remove loukoumathes onto platter. Before serving cover with warm honey and sprinkle with cinnamon. Keep warm, if desired, by placing in oven on low heat.

~Fifi
Thomas
Psihogios

Serves: 10

Our family has always gathered together every New Year's Eve. It is our tradition to eat loukoumathes right after we usher in the New Year. The first thing we share to eat in the New Year is sweets, so that our year will be filled with sweetness. The recipe is from a relative who had a zaharoplastio (sweet shop) in Athens.

Mama's Pumpkin Pie
Kolokithopita

4 pounds fresh pumpkin, peeled and coarsely grated
1 1/2 cups raisins
2 cups walnuts
1 teaspoon salt
2 1/2 cups brown sugar
1/2 teaspoon cinnamon
3/4 teaspoon nutmeg

3/4 pound phyllo dough
1 1/2 cups (3 sticks) butter, melted

Syrup:
4 cups sugar
3 cups water
1 cinnamon stick

Drain pumpkin in colander overnight. Squeeze, drain well and combine with raisins, walnuts, salt, brown sugar, cinnamon and nutmeg. In a buttered 11 x 14 inch pan, layer 7 phyllo sheets, buttering each sheet. Pour filling over top phyllo. Cover filling with the remaining phyllo sheets, buttering each one. Score the top few layers of phyllo into serving sized pieces. Bake in a preheated 350 degree oven for about 45 minutes until golden brown and crispy.

Syrup: Combine syrup ingredients in a saucepan, bring to a boil and simmer for 25 minutes. Pour cooled syrup over hot pie and allow to cool before cutting.

~Evangelos
Fasilis

Στριφτά

Nut-Filled Pastries
Strifta

Filling:
1 1/2 cups walnuts, finely ground
1/2 cup sugar
1/2 cup sesame seeds, toasted and crushed
1/2 teaspoon ground cinnamon
1/4 teaspoon ground cloves

Pastry Dough:
1 cup (2 sticks) butter, clarified and cooled
1 cup vegetable oil
1 cup orange juice, freshly squeezed
2 teaspoons baking powder
6 to 6 1/8 cups all-purpose flour, sifted

Syrup:
1 1/2 cups water
1 1/2 cups sugar
1 cup honey
1 to 2 strips of lemon peel or
    1 to 2 thin slices of lemon with peel

Topping:
2 to 2 1/4 cups walnuts, finely ground
1/2 to 1 teaspoon cinnamon

In a small bowl mix together the ground walnuts, sugar, crushed sesame seeds, cinnamon and cloves and set aside.

In an electric mixer, beat the clarified butter until light in color, about 8 minutes. Gradually add the vegetable oil and the orange juice. Beat 10 minutes. Put the baking powder in the first cup of flour and add it to the butter mixture. Continue beating the mixture as you gradually add the remaining flour. When the dough pulls away from the sides of the mixing bowl, take it out of the bowl and knead by hand for a few minutes. The dough should be soft and smooth. Put the dough back into the mixing bowl and keep it covered with a dishtowel. To form the strifta, take a small amount of the dough, about the size of a walnut, and pat it into a circle, 3 inches in diameter and 1/16 inch thick. Place 1 teaspoon filling near the center of the dough on the side closest to you. Then take the closest section of dough, fold it over the filling and continue to roll up completely. The edge of the dough should be at the bottom. Place the strifta on an ungreased cookie sheet and bake in a preheated 350 degree oven 18 to 28 minutes until light golden in color. Put the baked strifta in a large baking pan.

Syrup: In a saucepan bring the water, sugar, and lemon to a rolling boil. Reduce heat slightly and boil gently for 15 minutes. Add the honey and cook for another 3 to 4 minutes. Discard the lemon peel. Dip 5 to 6 strifta at a time into the hot syrup. Remove with a slotted spoon to a plate. Then transfer to a large sheet of wax paper or cookie sheet. Immediately sprinkle the strifta generously with the walnut-cinnamon topping while they are still warm. Continue dipping and sprinkling until all are completed. When cool, serve or store in a tightly covered container.

Notes: In order to save time, you may grind the walnuts on the day before baking. Cover and set aside. Also, clarify the butter. Keep it refrigerated. On the day of baking, allow the clarified butter to stand at room temperature for 30 minutes before using.

Frozen orange juice may be substituted for freshly squeezed and almonds may be substituted for walnuts.

~Fotini J.
Rumpakis

Yield: 4 1/2 dozen.

This fragrant and delicious pastry makes an exquisite dessert. It is a favorite of my family and a frequently requested recipe. Your friends will give you rave reviews, so make sure you serve plenty, as they will quickly disappear.

Πάστα Φλώρα

Shortbread with Apricot Filling
Pasta Flora

2 cups (4 sticks) unsalted butter, room temperature
1/2 cup sugar
1/2 cup half & half
2 egg yolks, separated
2 teaspoons vanilla
2 teaspoons baking powder
1 quart apricot preserves
3 or more cups flour

2 egg whites, slightly beaten

In a mixer, blend butter until smooth. Add sugar, half and half, egg yolks, vanilla and baking powder. Pour mixture into a large bowl. Gradually by hand, work in flour until you have a soft dough. Line the bottom of a 17 x 11 1/2 inch pan with 2/3 of the dough and spread it up the sides with a rolling pin. Spread with fruit preserves. With the remaining dough, roll out strips of pencil thickness and arrange them 1 inch apart diagonally to form a lattice topping. Brush lattice strips with beaten egg whites. Bake in a preheated 350 degree oven about 35 to 40 minutes until pastry is golden brown. Preserves should be bubbling. Cool, then cut in desired squares. Freezes very well in an air-tight container.

~Eleni
Nicholson

Substitutions: Milk for half & half. Also, may use quince preserves.

Yield: 52 (2-inch) squares

My family has used this recipe for years on all holidays and special occasions. It's not only delicious, but also colorful. I now make it for our Greek Festival, and it has become quite popular.

Shortbread with Quince Filling
Pasta Flora

1/3 pound butter, room temperature
1 1/4 cups sugar
4 eggs (reserve 2 egg whites for top)
3 or more cups flour
3 1/2 rounded teaspoons baking powder
1 tablespoon vanilla
1 1/2 quarts of canned quince strips, drained
Dash of lemon juice

Blanched almond halves

In a mixing bowl beat melted butter until creamy and then add sugar, eggs and baking powder. Beat well. Add vanilla and gradually add enough flour to form a soft, moist dough. Add dash of lemon juice to quince. Spread dough in an 18 x 12 inch cookie sheet. Spread quince over dough. Lay diagonal strips of dough over top of quince. Brush with egg whites. Arrange almond halves decoratively. Bake in a preheated 350 degree oven 30 to 35 minutes.

Substitute: Part shortening for 1/2 of the butter (optional).

Yield: 30

~Virginia
Langus

Phyllo and Nut-Layered Pastry for a Festival

Baklava yia Paniyiri

Syrup:
15 cups water
25 pounds sugar
4 oranges
1/16 crate of lemons

Cinnamon-Sugar mixture:
3 cups sugar
3 heaping teaspoons cinnamon
4 1/2 cups walnuts, finely-chopped

25 pounds butter, melted
27 pounds phyllo dough

Syrup: Put 15 cups of water and 25 pounds of sugar into a very large stockpot. Bring to a boil. Quarter the rinds from 4 oranges, and add them to the water. Maintain a low boil for about 30 to 40 minutes, until you can lift a spoonful of syrup 1 foot above the syrup surface and see a continuous unbroken stream. Meanwhile, squeeze lemons and strain the juice to produce 1 cup of strained lemon juice; add to syrup. Allow syrup to cool about 2 hours, then store in cooler.

Combine sugar and cinnamon and mix well. Add nuts to 5 well rounded tablespoons of cinnamon-sugar mixture. Mix well.

Butter an 11 x 18 inch baking pan. Layer 10 sheets of phyllo, brushing each layer with melted butter. Sprinkle the 10th layer with some nut mixture (enough to cover phyllo). Add three more layers of phyllo, buttering each layer, and sprinkle the top layer with nut mixture. Continue adding 3 buttered phyllo layers and a nut mixture layer alternating until the entire nut mixture is used up. Cut the baklava into pieces, and run the knife around the inside perimeter of the pan.

Bake the baklava in a preheated 300 degree convection oven, using a low fan setting. Rotate the pans 180 degrees every 15 minutes. Baklava is done when you place a knife between the cut pieces and hear a crunchy sound ("crutsi-crutsi"), about 1 1/2 hours.

Carefully pour 1 batch of cold syrup over the warm baklava, ensuring you soak the cut areas and the perimeter. Do not cover.

Buyer's lists for total ingredients for 16 batches (215 pans)
    432 pounds phyllo dough
    400 pounds butter
    270 pounds walnuts
    450 pounds sugar
    1 gallon cinnamon
    1 crate oranges
    1 crate lemons

~Betty and
Aristides
Phoutrides

This recipe is broken down into one batch, which yields approximately 13 pans. This way each work party can work on one batch. Listed at the end is the buyer's list for the total ingredients required to make 215 pans or 16 batches. To control quality, schedule 3 days for work parties to make and bake the Baklava (about 5 batches or 71 pans per day).

In memory of Anna Stratikos Demas, who for many years co-chaired this project.

Phyllo, Chocolate & Nut-Layered Pastry
Chocolate Baklava

1 pound phyllo dough
2 cups (4 sticks) unsalted butter, melted

Filling:
5 cups walnuts, chopped
1 1/2 teaspoons cinnamon
1 (8 ounce) chocolate bar, grated

Syrup:
1 cup water
1 cup sugar
Choose one of the following, per your preference:
  1/4 cup honey and 3/4 cup corn syrup,
  or 1 cup honey, or 1 cup corn syrup
1 teaspoon lemon juice
Cinnamon stick

Topping:
1 (6-ounce package) semi-sweet chocolate morsels

Filling: In a bowl, mix walnuts, cinnamon and chocolate.
(Be sure to use a spoon all the time or your hands will be a
chocolate mess!)

Butter the bottom of an 11 x 18 inch pan. Place a layer of phyllo
in the pan and brush it with butter. Repeat with 5 more sheets.
Generously spread some of the walnut mixture on top of the
5th sheet. Continue to layer phyllo sheets and brush with butter.
Sprinkle the cinnamon-nut mixture over each layer until there
are 6 sheets left and all the walnut mixture is used up. Top with
remaining 6 sheets. Cut into diamond shapes or squares, then cut
squares diagonally to make triangle shapes. Bake in a pre-heated
350 degree oven approximately 1 hour, or until golden.

Syrup: While choclava is baking, prepare syrup. In a saucepan
combine water, sugar, honey and lemon juice and bring to boil.
Keep syrup warm.

*I made up this recipe Christmas of 1978. When I moved to Utah in 1984, I
saw a recipe contest sponsored by a walnut company. Someone told me to enter my
recipe but I never did because I thought it was not original enough. Guess who
won? A lady from back East whose choclava was not even as choclatey as mine!*

Topping: In a double-boiler over low heat, melt semi-sweet chocolate bar. Keep warm. When choclava and syrup are still warm (but not hot) pour syrup over choclava. When choclava is cool, drizzle warm chocolate on top.

~Helen Gianopoulos-Tzakis

Μπακλαβάς

Phyllo and Nut-Layered Pastry
Baklava

1 cup almonds, coarsely chopped
1 cup walnuts, coarsely chopped
I teaspoon cinnamon
1/2 teaspoon ground cloves
1 teaspoon sugar
2 teaspoons brandy

2 pounds phyllo dough, reserve 15 sheets for top
2 cups (4 sticks) butter, melted

Syrup:
3 cups sugar
2 1/2 cups water
1/2 cup corn syrup
1/2 cup honey
1/2 lemon wedge

Syrup: Combine all ingredients except honey and boil for about 10 minutes. Slowly add honey and simmer on low heat an additional 3 minutes. Squeeze lemon juice into syrup and let cool.

Combine almonds, walnuts, cinnamon, cloves, sugar and brandy. Use a baking pan about the size of the phyllo sheets. Layer 15 sheets of phyllo on bottom of pan. Brush each sheet well with melted butter. Sprinkle with 1/3 the nut mixture, then cover with 3 more phyllo sheets. Repeat 2 more times and finish with the reserved phyllo sheets, brushing each with butter. Let butter firm up, about 20 minutes, then cut into triangles. Bake in a preheated 300 degree oven for about 1 1/2 hours. Pour cooled syrup evenly over the hot baklava.

~Antigone Konkoumanos

Almond Torte "Copenhagen"
Kopenhayi

Crust:
1/2 cup (1 stick) unsalted butter, room temperature
1 1/2 cups powdered sugar, sifted
2 egg yolks, separated (reserve whites for filling)
1 teaspoon vanilla
1 3/4 cup flour
1 teaspoon baking powder
Dash of salt
1/4 cup apricot preserves

Filling:
4 whole eggs, room temperature
2 reserved egg whites, room temperature
1 cup powdered sugar, sifted
2 tablespoons brandy
Pinch of grated nutmeg
1 1/2 cups blanched almonds, finely ground
1 cup farina

Topping:
4 to 6 sheets phyllo dough
1/4 cup (1/2 stick) unsalted butter, melted, clarified

Syrup:
1 cup water
1 cup sugar
1 tablespoon lemon juice
2 tablespoons brandy

Crust: In a mixer cream butter until very light. Add sugar gradually, alternating with egg yolks. Add vanilla. Mix in flour sifted with the baking powder and salt. Knead by hand just enough to blend dough evenly. Spread in the bottom of a buttered 9 x 13 inch pan and bake in a preheated 350 degree oven about 8 minutes. Remove from oven and set aside. Spread with preserves after it has cooled awhile.

Filling: In a mixer beat eggs and egg whites on high until volume has tripled (about 10 minutes.) Gradually add powdered sugar and beat about 5 minutes more. Add brandy and nutmeg. Stop machine and fold in by hand the nuts and the farina. Do this quickly to avoid reducing the volume of the egg mixture. Pour over the apricot preserves and the cookie crust in the pan.

Topping: Place phyllo sheets one by one over the top of the egg/nut batter. Brush each one with butter and fold over any

FLAVOR IT GREEK !

excess dough. Score through the phyllo layer to cut diamond shapes. Bake in a preheated 325 degree oven about 45 minutes or until golden brown. Remove from oven to cool.

Syrup: In a saucepan, over medium high heat, combine water, sugar and lemon juice. Bring to a boil, reduce heat and simmer for 10 minutes. Add the brandy. Pour the hot syrup over the cooled pastry. Allow to set several hours before serving.

~Maria
K. Boyer

Κανταΐφι

Nut-Filled Shredded Phyllo
Kadaifi

1 pound kataifi pastry (shredded phyllo dough)
2 cups (4 sticks) unsalted butter, melted
2 pounds chopped walnuts
    (or 1 pound chopped walnuts and
    1 pound ground almonds)
2 teaspoons cinnamon
Rind of 1 orange

Syrup:
2 1/2 cups sugar
3 cups water
Juice of 1/2 lemon

Combine the syrup ingredients in a medium saucepan and heat to boil for about 20 minutes, until slightly thickened. Cool while making pastry.

Spread half of the shredded pastry dough evenly in a 9 x 13 inch greased baking pan. Spoon about half of the melted butter over this evenly. In a separate bowl, mix together the chopped walnuts, cinnamon and orange rind. Spread this mixture over the buttered kataifi. Spread remaining shredded pastry over the nut mixture and pour remaining butter over the entire pastry. Bake in a preheated 300 degree oven for 45 minutes. Remove from oven and pour cooled syrup over. Let stand until cool, then cut into rectangles. Wrap tightly to keep moist. (For smaller pieces, make sure the kadaife is wrapped tightly and the syrup is thick.)

~Presvytera
Spiridoula
Tsigas and
Presvytera
Eleni Tsigas

Yield: 15 to 20

Δίπλες

Fried Honey-Dipped Pastries
Thiples

5 large eggs
1 3/4 flour or enough to form a soft dough
Vegetable oil for frying

Syrup:
3 cups sugar
1 1/2 cups water
1/2 cup honey

Walnuts, finely chopped
Cinnamon

Beat eggs and mix in enough flour for a soft dough. Turn out onto a table and begin to knead, adding flour until dough becomes stretchy and does not stick to the table. Cut in half and shape into 2 balls, Set 1 ball aside and cover with a damp towel. Roll out the other very thinly.

In a large skillet heat 2 to 3 inches oil on medium-high heat. Cut out a dollar-size rectangle of dough. Pick it up and stretch it out until translucent. Drop into the hot oil. Work quickly with 2 forks to immediately straighten and flatten out the strip of dough on the surface of the oil, turn it over and gently fold over 3 or 4 times to shape a cylindrical roll. Lift it out while still pale in color. This process takes only about 10 to 15 seconds. Set thipla on a tray and continue cutting and frying dough pieces until dough is used up. Replenish the oil occasionally as you work. Repeat process with second ball of dough. Pastry is ready to be dipped into hot syrup or diluted honey, but it may be dipped a day or two later.

Georgia Katchis as recorded by Maria K. Boyer

Syrup: In a small saucepan, bring to a boil and gently simmer the sugar, water and honey about 15 minutes for a thin syrup. Quickly dip in each thipla and lift out to drain briefly before setting on wax paper. Sprinkle thiples while still hot with chopped walnuts and cinnamon.

Thiples were my mother Georgia Katchis' specialty for celebrations. There was no more impressive dish on the pastry table than her glistening and golden pyramid of thiples.

Fried Honey-Dipped Pastries
Thiples

6 large eggs
1 tablespoon vegetable oil
1 teaspoon salt
1 teaspoon orange juice
1 teaspoon vanilla
2 cups flour, or enough to form a soft dough

Vegetable oil for deep frying

3 cups sugar
2 cups water
1 cup honey

Cinnamon
Walnuts, chopped

Beat eggs together with vegetable oil until light and fluffy. Add salt, orange juice and vanilla. Gradually mix in enough flour to make a soft dough that does not stick to hands. Take a section of dough and roll out paper thin on a working surface sprinkled with flour. Cut dough 2 inches wide and desired length to shape into bows or knots.

Syrup: In a small saucepan bring to a boil the sugar and water. Simmer over low heat about 15 minutes to make a thin syrup. Add honey. Keep warm while frying thiples.

~Constantine
N. Deleganes

Heat oil in a large frying pan or deep fryer. With 2 forks, drop strips in hot oil and quickly form into desired shapes. Using a slotted spoon, dip thiples individually in the warm syrup. Lift out to drain and set on a waxed paper surface. While still hot, sprinkle with cinnamon and chopped nuts. Serve at room temperature.

Yield: approximately 3 dozen

Γαλατόπιτα

Milk Pudding
Galatopita

4 eggs (add one more for richer pita)
1 quart milk
Dash of salt (optional)
1 cup sugar
1/2 cup farina (Cream of Wheat)
2 to 3 tablespoons butter
Cinnamon

Butter a 9 x 13 inch baking pan. In a bowl, beat eggs well and set aside. In a 3 quart saucepan, bring milk, salt and sugar to a boil. Slowly pour in farina, stirring constantly until mixture thickens. Remove from heat. Stir in butter. Add eggs to hot mixture. Pour mixture into baking pan. Bake in a preheated 350 degree oven for 30 minutes or until pita is brown. When ready to serve, sprinkle with cinnamon and cut diagonally into diamond shapes. Serve warm or cool.

~Mari Lou
Psihogios
Diamond

This is a simple dessert or snack that is a lot like Galatobouriko, but without the phyllo and syrup. It's especially nutritious for an after-school snack on a cold day, and very simple to make.

Κρέμα

Farina Pudding ☦
Krema

5 cups water
1 to 1 1/2 cups sugar
1 cup farina (Cream of Wheat)
Pinch vanilla powder or 1 teaspoon vanilla
Cinnamon

Mix water and sugar together in a medium saucepan. Boil for
one minute. Stir in farina until it thickens, about two minutes.
Remove from heat and add vanilla. Stir mixture well. Pour into
an 8 x 8 inch dish or individual bowls. Sprinkle with cinnamon.
Let cool, then refrigerate overnight. Cut into pieces and serve.

~Roula
Tsirimiagos

This is my favorite. It's quick and easy!

Μουσταλευριά

Grape-Must Pudding ☦
Moustalevria

8 cups must
1 cup fine farina (Cream of Wheat)
1/2 cup sugar

Almonds, thinly sliced or walnuts, finely chopped
Sesame seeds
Cinnamon

Strain the must and place it in a large pot and bring it to a boil.
Skim off the froth that may collect on the surface and from the
sides of the pan. Remove pot from the heat and add the farina
gradually, stirring constantly with a wooden spoon. Add the
sugar and return the pot to the burner. Simmer over low heat
until it becomes a creamy pudding.

Serve on a round platter and garnish with the nuts and a
sprinkling of sesame seeds and cinnamon.

~Athina
Galanopoulos

Custard-Filled Pastry in Syrup
Galaktoboureko

Custard:
2 quarts milk
1 cup sugar
1 cup Cream of Rice
1 tablespoon vanilla
8 eggs

1 cup (2 sticks) butter, melted
1 pound phyllo dough

Syrup:
2 cups sugar
2 cups water
Juice from 1 lemon

Custard: In a 4 quart saucepan over medium low heat, combine milk, sugar and Cream of Rice. Cook, stirring constantly with a wooden spoon. When thickened, stir in vanilla and set aside to cool. Beat eggs until thick and fluffy. Pour slowly into cooled mixture, stirring constantly with wooden spoon. Mix well.

Butter a 10 x 15 inch baking pan. Line pan with 1 sheet of phyllo (let phyllo overlap the sides). Brush the phyllo with butter. Repeat for a total of 10 sheets. Pour cooled custard over top sheet, then fold overlapped phyllo sheets over the top. Cover with remaining phyllo sheets, brushing each with butter. Cut through the top few sheets with a serrated knife into lengthwise strips. (Do not cut all the way as custard will seep through) Bake in a preheated 350 degree oven for 1 hour, then lower heat to 250 degrees and bake 1/2 hour longer.

Syrup (prepare while baking custard): In a saucepan over medium-high heat, combine sugar and water and bring to a boil. Reduce heat and simmer covered 40 to 45 minutes. Remove syrup from heat and add lemon juice. Let cool.

~Helen
Lampus

When cooled, cut into diamond squares and pour syrup evenly over Galaktoboureko.

Serves: 12

This is my mother's recipe, Panagula Maletis. She made it for us for holidays and special days. My children loved it.

Custard-Filled Pastry in Syrup
Galaktoboureko

Custard:
9 eggs
2 cups sugar
1 cup farina (Cream of Wheat)
2 quarts milk
2 teaspoons vanilla
1 1/2 cups (3 sticks) unsalted butter, melted
1 pound phyllo dough

Syrup:
1 1/2 cups water
3 cups sugar
Small piece lemon peel

Custard: In a bowl, beat eggs and sugar well; add farina.
In a large saucepan, over medium-high heat, bring milk
to a boil. Slowly add egg mixture and stir constantly until
mixture boils again. Add vanilla and boil until mixture
thickens, then remove from heat and cool. Stir occasionally
so crust will not form.

Butter a 17 x 18 inch pan. Place first layer of phyllo in pan and
brush with butter. Prepare 10 sheets of phyllo in this manner.
Top with warm custard. Place 10 more sheets of phyllo on top
of custard, buttering each sheet. Trim phyllo to edge of pan.
Fold edges neatly inside pan. With a sharp knife, cut into
diagonal serving pieces. Bake in a preheated 350 degree oven
for 30 to 40 minutes. When custard is removed from oven,
let it cool.

Syrup: Bring syrup ingredients to a boil and simmer until
thickened. Cool slightly. Pour over custard.

~Rene
Contakos

Serves: 10

This is YiaYia's recipe!

Μπουγάτσα

Custard-Filled Pastry
Bougatsa

2 cups (4 sticks) unsalted, melted and clarified
   butter for brushing phyllo
1 (1 pound) package phyllo dough

Custard:
9 cups milk
2 1/4 cups sugar
1 1/2 cups (3 sticks) butter, for custard
1 1/2 tablespoons vanilla
3/4 cup farina (Cream of Wheat)
3/4 cup Cream of Rice
9 eggs

Topping:
1/3 cup honey or syrup
Powdered sugar
Cinnamon

Custard: In a saucepan over low heat, bring milk, sugar, 1 1/2 cups
butter and vanilla to a near boil. While stirring constantly to
prevent lumping. Gradually add Cream of Wheat and Cream of
Rice. Continue to stir until thick. Empty mixture into a bowl,
and set aside to cool.

Meanwhile, butter an 11 x 18 inch pan. Place a layer of phyllo
and brush with melted butter. Continue in the same manner
until half of the phyllo sheets are used. Immediately wrap the
remaining phyllo in plastic to prevent drying.

In the meantime, beat the eggs. Gradually add to the cooled
custard mixture and mix well. Pour the mixture into the pan.
Lay the reserved phyllo sheets in the same manner. Cut into
6 equal lengthwise strips. Sprinkle lightly with water.

Bake in a preheated 325 degree oven for 45 minutes on bottom
rack. Allow to cool, then cut into diamond or square shapes.
Pour honey or syrup sparingly over top layer of phyllo to
~Angeliki   produce a sticky surface, then sprinkle with powdered sugar
Anasis   and cinnamon.

Serves: 40

Custard Torte
Ekmek

Elite Toast or other brand

Syrup:
3 cups water
2 cups sugar
1 tablespoon whiskey
1 cinnamon stick

Custard:
3 eggs, slightly beaten
3 cups milk
6 tablespoons cornstarch
3/4 cup sugar
1 teaspoon butter
1 teaspoon vanilla

Topping:
2 envelopes whipped topping mix
1 cup milk
Cinnamon

Syrup: In a saucepan over medium high heat cook water, sugar and cinnamon stick until it comes to a boil. Remove from heat and add whiskey.

In a 9 x 13 inch pan, arrange a layer of toast. Pour the warm syrup over the toast. Sprinkle with cinnamon.

Custard: In a 2 quart saucepan, thoroughly mix milk, cornstarch, eggs and sugar. Stir over medium heat until it thickens. Remove from heat and add butter and vanilla. Cool slightly. Cover with plastic wrap and gently press onto custard. Continue to cool for 15 minutes. When cool, spread the custard over the toast. Cover and refrigerate 3 hours.

Topping: Beat topping mix in milk until thick (about 5 minutes). Remove custard from refrigerator. spread with whipped topping and sprinkle with cinnamon. Cover and refrigerate for 15 hours.

~Roula
Tsirimiagos

This tastes better the following day.

Rice Pudding
Rizogalo

3 1/2 cups water
10 tablespoons rice
6 cups whole milk
1 1/2 cups sugar

1/2 cup sugar
4 egg yolks
3/4 cup milk
5 heaping tablespoons cornstarch

Cinnamon

In a saucepan over medium high heat, add rice to boiling water and cook over medium heat until water is absorbed and rice is overcooked (soft but not mushy), about 15 to 18 minutes. (It may be necessary to add more water.) Add whole milk and 1 1/2 cups sugar to cooked rice and cook over low heat until milk is hot.

In a bowl, whisk together the egg yolks and 1/2 cup sugar until smooth.

~Presvytera
Effy
Stephanopoulos

In another bowl dissolve cornstarch in milk and stir until smooth. Combine with egg yolk mixture and stir well. Add slowly to hot milk and rice mixture, stirring until thickened. Pour into a serving dish and sprinkle with cinnamon.

Serves: 4 to 6

Rice Pudding
Rizogalo

2 to 4 eggs, separated
3 cups milk
3 teaspoons vanilla
3/4 cup sugar
2 cups rice

In a saucepan over medium-high heat cook 2 cups rice in
4 cups water. Bring to a boil then reduce heat and simmer for
20 minutes. In a bowl beat egg yolks with 2 tablespoons milk.
Add remaining milk and 2 teaspoons vanilla. Set aside.

In another bowl, beat egg whites until frothy, add 1/3 cup sugar
and 1 teaspoon vanilla. Gently fold into egg yolks, then combine
with the rice-milk mixture. To serve, pour in a large bowl and
sprinkle top with cinnamon. Enjoy!

~Michael
Anthis

*Some very fond memories of my mother are
connected to this recipe; she would often make
it for me. I know she would have enjoyed
sharing this with others. I dedicate it to
her memory. Marge Karafotias Anthis
. . . forever remembered.*

Κρέμα Λεμονιού

Lemon Crema for Fruit
Krema Lemonion

3/4 cup sugar
2 teaspoons cornstarch
1 cup evaporated milk
1/2 cup water
2 egg yolks, beaten
2 tablespoons lemon juice
1 teaspoon lemon rind

Combine sugar and cornstarch in a small saucepan. Gradually stir in the milk, water and egg yolks. Cook over medium-low heat for 15 minutes, stirring constantly. Cook until mixture comes to a boil and thickens. Cool slightly. Add lemon juice and lemon rind and stir well.

Serve warm in individual bowls or chilled over mixed, freshly cut fruit.

~ Petroula
Koukoumanos

Note: If the sauce doesn't thicken enough, mix 1 teaspoon cornstarch with 2 to 3 tablespoons milk and add it to the sauce. If sauce gets too thick, add a little more milk.

Serves: 3

Golden Farina Molded Dessert
Halva

1 cup olive oil or butter
2 cups regular farina (Cream of Wheat)
4 cups water
3 cups sugar
1 teaspoon vanilla
1 cinnamon stick
1/2 cup roasted almonds (optional)

Cinnamon

Heat the oil or butter in a large pot until it just starts to
smoke lightly. Add the farina, lowering the heat and stirring
constantly with a wooden spoon so that it starts to turn to
a light brown color.

Syrup: Meanwhile in a saucepan, bring the water, sugar, vanilla
and cinnamon to a simmer just long enough for the sugar
to dissolve. Remove cinnamon stick.

Once the farina has browned, reduce heat and gradually add
the syrup to the pan. (Proceed carefully as it will splatter). Stir
over low heat until the mixture forms a mass and does not cling
to the sides of the pan. You may add the almonds as it starts to
thicken. The halva is now done. Pour at once into a mold and
allow it to cool. Unmold and sprinkle with cinnamon.

~Koula
Fkiaras

Serves: 12

*A traditional sweet from Velvento
Kozanis of Western Macedonia – a
favorite dessert of my grandmother
and of my mother.*

Yiayia Pauline's Baked Farina
Halva Fournou

1 dozen eggs
1 cup sugar
1 teaspoon vanilla
1 cup (2 sticks) butter, melted and cooled
1 cup (8 ounces) regular farina (Cream of Wheat)
1 cup walnuts, ground
1 cup flour, sifted
4 heaping teaspoons baking powder
1/2 teaspoon nutmeg
1/2 teaspoon cloves
1/2 teaspoon cinnamon

Syrup:
2 cups sugar
1 cup water
1 teaspoon vanilla
1 teaspoon lemon juice
1/2 teaspoon cinnamon

In a mixing bowl beat eggs until thick and creamy. Add sugar, vanilla, cooled butter, farina and walnuts. Combine flour, baking powder, nutmeg, cloves and cinnamon. Add to the mixture. Pour into a greased a 9 x 13 inch pan and bake in a preheated 350 degree oven 30 to 35 minutes or until cake tests done.

Syrup: While cake is baking, in a saucepan over medium-high heat, bring the sugar, water, vanilla, lemon juice and cinnamon to a boil. Boil for 6 minutes. Slowly pour hot syrup over hot cake. Cool and cut into diamond-shaped pieces. Can be frozen.

~Bessie Lekas

Serves: 12

Back in the 1950's, the ladies of Everett, Washington, took turns hosting their monthly Women's Hellenic Club meetings/luncheons. This was a favorite of my mother's desserts. I always enjoyed coming home from school and joining the ladies.

Χαλβάς

Golden Farina Dessert
Halva

Syrup:
8 cups water
3 1/2 cups sugar
1 stick cinnamon
6 to 7 whole cloves
1 slice orange
1 slice lemon

1 cup (2 sticks) butter
2 cups regular farina (Cream of Wheat)
1/2 cup almonds, slivered
1/2 cup pine nuts

Walnuts, finely chopped
Cinnamon to taste

Syrup: Combine syrup ingredients and bring to a boil, then lower heat and simmer for 45 minutes. Keep warm.

In a large heavy bottom saucepan, melt butter. Stir in farina and continue stirring until the mixture reaches an oak-brown color (approximately 45 minutes). Add almonds and pine nuts and stir for another 10 to 15 minutes. Do not leave unattended! Pour the syrup gradually into the halva mixture, stirring constantly. Remove from heat and cover for about 5 minutes, allowing the farina to rise. Return the mixture to low heat and stir while the syrup is being absorbed. Place in a 9 x 13 inch baking dish. Allow to cool.

Sprinkle walnuts and cinnamon over the halva. Cut into squares.

~Mary
Dariotis Martin

Serves: 30

This recipe was introduced to Portland by my mother, Soteria Dariotis, when she first came to America.

Χαλβάς Μαρμαρινό

Farina "Marmarino"
Halva Marmarino

Syrup:
7 cups water
4 cups sugar
1 lemon, cut into slices
1 cinnamon stick

Halva:
2 cups (4 sticks) butter, room temperature
2 teaspoons baking powder
2 tablespoons sugar
1 cup orange juice
2 pounds walnuts, chopped
Flour as needed to make a soft dough
50 half or whole blanched almonds

Syrup: In a saucepan, over medium high heat, combine water, sugar, lemon and cinnamon stick. Bring to a boil and cook until thickened. Set aside to cool.

Halva: Cream butter until light and fluffy. Add baking powder, sugar and orange juice. Mix well. Add walnuts to creamed mixture, stir and blend well. Add about 1 cup of flour at a time, mixing with hands until dough is soft. Put into a buttered 10 x 14 inch pan. Cut into diamond shaped pieces. Place a blanched almond on each piece. Bake in a preheated 350 degree oven for 30 to 40 minutes, until golden brown.

~George
Varkados

Remove lemon slices and pour syrup over halva (may not be necessary to use all the syrup). Leave in pan until the next day. To serve, place in cupcake liners.

Yield: about 150.

This is an old family favorite of more than 50 years. Prepare this one day ahead of serving. Enjoy!

Χαλβάς της Δώρας

Dora's Molded Farina Dessert
Halva tis Thoras

Syrup:
3 cups sugar
4 cups water
1 cinnamon stick

Halva:
1 cup (2 sticks) butter
2 cups farina (Cream of Wheat)
1 cup almonds, blanched and chopped
2 teaspoons cinnamon

Syrup: In a saucepan over medium high heat, bring the sugar, water and cinnamon stick to a boil. Reduce heat and simmer for 10 to 15 minutes. Set aside.

In another saucepan melt the butter slowly (do not let it burn). Add the farina, almonds and 1 teaspoon of cinnamon. (The key is not to burn this but work as fast as you can while you are constantly stirring.) Add the cooled syrup and bring to a soft boil (again while stirring). Cover the saucepan and turn the heat down to low until the syrup is absorbed. Take the lid off and stir very well. Take a spoon and pat it down. Turn the heat down to simmer and leave the mixture covered for 15 minutes. Take the lid off and press it down again. Turn the heat off and leave the pot on the stove until it cools down.

When the mixture is cool, scoop it out and press into a mold. Sprinkle with the remainder of the cinnamon and let it cool completely. Take out of the mold and enjoy!

Note: Pecans may be substituted for the almonds.

~Mimi
Palumbis

Stove-Top Farina
Halva Koutalion

1 (14 oz.) box regular farina (Cream of Wheat)
1 cup (2 sticks) unsalted butter
2¹/₂ cups sugar
1 cup unblanched almonds or pistachios
3 cups water, very hot (to boiling point)

Cinnamon

In a large saucepan over medium low heat, melt butter without letting it brown. Stir in farina and continue to stir over very low heat. Add sugar and continue cooking for about 20 minutes stirring constantly. Continue to stir and take care not to burn. Add nuts and slowly stir in hot water. Continue to cook stirring until mixture holds its shape. Spoon into cupcake liners and sprinkle with cinnamon.

Meropi S. Courogen   If you use margarine instead of butter it makes a wonderful lenten sweet.

Serves: 20

This halva is made in a pan on top of the stove, cooked until golden brown. It is divided into portions using a large spoon (koutali) and put into paper cups.

Golden Farina Diamonds
Halva

1 cup (2 sticks) butter
2 cups white farina (not instant or quick
  cooking Cream of Wheat)

Syrup:
3 cups sugar
4 cups water
1/3 whole orange

1 cup walnuts or blanched almonds, chopped
Ground cinnamon
Whole blanched almonds or walnut halves

Melt butter over low heat in a non-stick frying pan; gradually add farina, and brown until the color of peanut butter. Keep stirring to avoid scorching. The heat may be increased.

Syrup: In a 4 quart saucepan combine sugar and water and the 1/3 orange. Bring to a boil for about 5 minutes, then remove the orange. Stir farina and butter mixture into the syrup and add nuts. Turn the heat down until it thickens. (The heat may be increased but the mixture needs to be watched carefully.) When thick enough (consistency should resemble thick cooked cereal), spoon onto a large serving platter. Sprinkle the top with cinnamon and decorate with the larger nuts. When completely cooled, cut into diamond shapes, similar to baklava.

~Mary Aspros and Elisa Aspros

Yield: 25 servings.

In loving memory of Georgia Karussos, submitted by her daughter-in-law, Mary Aspros, and her granddaughter, Elisa Aspros. On many special occasions Georgia would take a beautiful platter of halva to the homes of friends and relatives.

Κέικ με Μήλα

Applesauce Cake ☦
Keik me Mila

4 cups flour
4 teaspoons baking soda
1 1/2 teaspoons salt
2 cups sugar
1 teaspoon cinnamon
1 teaspoon allspice
1 teaspoon cloves
1 teaspoon nutmeg
1 cup (2 sticks) margarine
3 cups applesauce
1 1/2 cups chopped nuts
1 1/2 cups raisins

Sift dry ingredients together. In a saucepan, melt margarine and applesauce together. Add applesauce mixture to the sifted dry ingredients. Fold in the nuts and raisins. Spread batter into a buttered 9 x 13 inch pan. Bake in a preheated 350 degree oven for one hour. Check cake at 45 minutes; may be done and not require the full hour.

~Pearl
Pavlos

Serves: 20 to 24

This recipe is from Kassie Brannion. She was a member of our Priscilla Circle. She now lives on Mercer Island, Washington. Great Lenten cake, nice and moist. Great for picnics, travels well, no frosting and no eggs.

Ouzo Cake
Keik Ouzou

2 boxes lemon cake mix
2 small boxes instant lemon pudding mix
8 eggs
1 1/2 cups water
1 cup oil
1/2 cup ouzo liquor
2 cups walnuts, crushed

Syrup:
2 cups sugar
2 cups water
2 cinnamon sticks
1 teaspoon whole cloves
2 cups honey
3 tablespoons ouzo

Powdered sugar (optional)

In a mixing bowl, combine the first 6 ingredients until completely mixed. Sprinkle walnuts on bottom of greased 11 x 15 inch rectangular baking pan. Pour the prepared cake mixture over walnuts. Bake in preheated 350 degree oven for approximately 30 minutes. When cake is done, remove from oven to cool. Prick holes with a large fork to bottom of cake.

Syrup: While cake is baking, prepare syrup by slowly boiling the sugar, water, cinnamon and cloves together for 1 hour. Then add 2 cups honey and 3 tablespoons ouzo to sugar mixture. Pour hot syrup over cooled cake. Cut into serving-size pieces. Invert each piece and serve with the nut mixture on top. Sift powdered sugar on top if desired. Enjoy!

~Karen
Dudunake

Serves: 35

My Aunt June makes this for many church events in my home town of Pocatello, Idaho. It's delicious, the ouzo makes it Greek, and it's very easy.

Κέικ με Σταφίδες του Φτωχού

"Poor Man's" Fruitcake ☦
Keik me Stafithes tou Ftohou

1 cup water
1 cup sugar
1 cup raisins
1/2 cup vegetable shortening
1 teaspoon cinnamon
1/2 teaspoon ground cloves
Dash of salt

2 cups flour
1 teaspoon baking powder
Scant teaspoon baking soda

In a saucepan, bring first seven ingredients to a boil. Remove from heat and cool to lukewarm. Add flour, baking powder and baking soda. Mix well and transfer to a 9 x 9 inch greased and floured square pan. Bake in a preheated 350 degree oven for 45 minutes.

Amalia Gianopoulos

Serves: 9 to 16

This recipe was passed down to me by my mother and to her by her mother and probably before that. This is a nice Lenten sweet.

Mocha-Graham Cracker Torte
Tourta Moka

2 cups (4 sticks) unsalted butter, room temperature
1 pound powdered sugar
3 eggs, separated
1/3 cup prepared Greek coffee, medium sweet
    (metrion), cooled
1 1/2 cups prepared cocoa, cooled
1/3 cup ouzo
1/4 cup whiskey
1/3 cup milk
2 pounds graham crackers

2 cups walnuts, finely chopped

In a mixer, beat the butter and sugar together until creamy. Add
the egg yolks, one at a time, alternating with portions of the
Greek coffee. Set aside. In a separate bowl, beat the egg whites
to a meringue-like stiffness. Gently fold in the butter and egg
yolk mixture with a spatula.

In a narrow glass baking dish, combine the cocoa, ouzo,
whiskey and milk. Dip the crackers in the liquid one by one and
lay enough to cover a round cake plate or serving platter in a
single layer. Spread some of the egg mixture on top and sprinkle
with some of the chopped nuts. Continue to build up layers in
this fashion until all the graham crackers are used. Usually this
results in six layers. Reserve enough of the mixture to frost the
torte and cover all of the crackers completely. Sprinkle with nuts
and refrigerate for two hours before serving.

~Anastasia
Kondilis

Serves: 25 to 30

Καρυδόπιτα

Walnut Cake
Karithopita

4 cups powdered sugar
4 cups biscuit mix
4 cups walnuts, finely chopped
2 cups corn oil
2 cups milk
3 teaspoons baking powder
1 teaspoon cinnamon
1 tablespoon orange extract
1 tablespoon vanilla extract

12 eggs, separated

Syrup:
3 cups water
3 cups sugar
1/2 cup honey

Chopped walnuts (enough to cover baked dessert)
Maraschino cherries, cut in half (optional)

In a large bowl, combine first 9 ingredients and mix well.
Set aside.

Beat the egg whites in a mixer until stiff. Add the yolks and mix
until fairly well mixed. Add the eggs to the walnut mixture and
mix thoroughly. Pour into a 17 x 11 1/2 x 2 1/2 inch baking pan.
Place the pan in a preheated 350 degree oven, and bake for
approximately 30 to 45 minutes until golden brown.

Syrup: Combine water, sugar and honey. Boil about 15 minutes,
until thick. Remove syrup from heat, set aside and let cool.

Pour the cooled syrup over the baked karithopita. (Syrup will
be absorbed). Top with chopped walnuts. When cool, cut
diagonally into strips to form diamond shapes.

~Anne
Chimiklis
Pavlos

Note: For a nice touch during the holidays, top each piece with
half a maraschino cherry.

Yield: about 4 dozen.

*This is another great recipe from my mother-in-law. She
liked easy no-fail recipes and this is one. Keeps very well.*

Καρυδόπιτα

Walnut Cake
Karithopita

1 dozen eggs, separated
1 cup granulated sugar
3 heaping teaspoons baking powder
1 teaspoon cinnamon
3 tablespoons whiskey
1/2 cup (1 stick) butter or margarine, melted
2 cups (1 pound) walnuts, finely chopped
1 box (2 cups) rusk, crushed
1/2 cup (1 stick) butter or margarine, melted

Syrup:
2 cups water
2 cups sugar
1 teaspoon lemon juice

In a mixer, beat egg whites until stiff, set aside. In separate large bowl, beat yolks until creamy, gradually add sugar. Continue to beat and add baking powder, cinnamon, whiskey and melted butter. Mix well. Add nuts and rusk, then gently fold in beaten egg whites.

In preheated 300 degree oven, place the second stick of butter in a 9x13 inch pan to melt. When it has melted remove from oven and pour in cake mixture. "Swirl" the melted butter through with a knife or rubber spatula. Return to oven and bake for 1 hour. While the cake is hot, score into diamonds, marking the pattern for the deeper cuts you will make after it cools.

Syrup: While cake is baking, bring water to a boil, add sugar and lemon juice, stirring constantly. Reduce heat and let mixture boil until consistency is slightly thickened. Pour cooled syrup mixture over the cake and cover with foil. Cut the cake after it has cooled.

~Presvytera
Eleni Tsigas

Serves: 20 to 24

This recipe is a popular one in my family, having been passed down from my Yiayia Despina Samaras to all four of her daughters and their children. I knew it was especially good when I presented a pan of it to my new in-laws and received requests for the recipe.

Καρυδόπιτα

Walnut Cake
Karithopita

Syrup:
4 cups sugar
5 cups water
1/2 lemon, juiced

2 1/2 cups walnuts, finely chopped
2 1/2 cups zwieback, crumbled
14 eggs, separated
2 cups sugar
2 teaspoons vanilla

Maraschino cherries to decorate

Syrup: In a saucepan, combine water, sugar and lemon. Bring to a boil for about 15 minutes. Keep warm on stove.

Grease an 11 x 16 inch baking pan. Chop walnuts and crumble zwieback. Mix together and set aside.

In a mixing bowl, beat egg yolks with sugar for about 15 minutes until mixture becomes smooth and creamy. Add vanilla. Set aside. In a separate bowl, beat egg whites until stiff peaks form. Fold the yolk/sugar mixture into the egg whites.

Quickly fold zwieback-walnut mixture into eggs, then pour mixture into the prepared pan. Immediately place in a preheated 375 degree oven and bake for 25 to 30 minutes, until golden brown. Remove from oven. While the cake is warm, pour over the warm syrup.

~Joan
Liapes

The next day, cut diagonally into diamond-shaped pieces. Decorate each piece with a maraschino cherry.

Yield: about 4 dozen.

This was a favorite recipe of my Aunt Nota Marcoules, who prepared a pan of Karithopita every St. Basil's and St. Demetrios' day to celebrate my uncle and father's respective name days.

Κέικ με Γιαούρτι

Yogurt Cake
Keik me Yiaourti

1/2 cup (1 stick) butter, room temperature
2 1/2 cups sugar
5 eggs
5 cups flour
2 teaspoons baking powder
1 teaspoon baking soda
2 1/2 cups plain yogurt
Juice of 2 oranges
1 teaspoon vanilla
1/2 cup almonds, chopped

Syrup:
3 1/2 cups sugar
4 cups water
1 tablespoon lemon juice

Butter and lightly flour a 14 1/2 x 10 1/2 inch baking pan. In a mixing bowl cream together butter and sugar. Add eggs one at a time, beating well after each addition. Sift together the flour, baking powder and baking soda. Add flour alternating with yogurt and orange juice, mixing thoroughly. Add vanilla and almonds. Bake in a preheated 350 degree oven 45 to 50 minutes. Insert knife in center to test; if done it should come out clean.

Syrup: In a saucepan over medium high heat combine sugar, water and lemon juice. Bring to a boil. Reduce heat and simmer for 25 to 30 minutes until thick. Pour syrup over cooled cake.

~Presvytera
Effy
Stephanopoulos

Serves: 35 to 50

Τούρτα Σοκολάτας

Chocolate Torte
Tourta Sokolatas

3 eggs, separated
1 1/2 cups (3 sticks) unsalted butter
1 1/2 cups super-fine granulated sugar
4 tablespoons cocoa powder
3 tablespoons milk

1 egg
1/2 to 3/4 cups milk
1 tablespoon cognac (optional)
2 dozen lady fingers

2 cups (1 pint) whipping cream
Dash of powdered or finely granulated sugar
Small jar maraschino cherries
Slivered almonds (enough to cover entire surface)

Separate 3 eggs into two mixing bowls. Beat egg whites until stiff. Set aside. Beat yolks. In a separate bowl, beat butter, sugar, cocoa and milk until very smooth (about 5 minutes). Fold in egg yolks until well blended. Then gently fold in egg whites.

In a small bowl, mix one egg, milk and cognac. One-by-one, dip a lady finger in the mixture and place it in a shallow 9 inch round glass baking dish until completely lined. Sprinkle half the cocoa mixture over the lady fingers. Add another layer of dipped lady fingers. Now add another layer of cocoa mixture.

In another bowl, whip the cream with a little sugar. Using an ice cream scoop, place scoops of cream around the periphery of the dish, and one scoop in the middle. Place a maraschino cherry in the middle of each scoop. Sprinkle the entire surface of the dish with slivered almonds.

~ Kathy
Papachristopoulos

Serves: 8 to 10

In the mid-1800's, my father-in-law was a doctor in Greece. He went out into the villages on horseback to care for his patients, and sometimes they would pay for his services with food, chickens, etc. Often when he liked the food, he would ask for the recipe. This is one of those recipes. When we lived in Greece, my mother-in-law always made this for me on my birthday.

Farina Cake in Syrup
Ravani

7 eggs
1 cup sugar
1 cup flour
1 cup instant enriched farina
1 teaspoon baking powder
1 teaspoon vanilla
1 teaspoon orange peel, grated

Syrup:
3 cups sugar
4 cups water
1/2 cup fresh squeezed orange juice
Orange rind
1 teaspoon liquid vanilla

Beat the eggs and the sugar very well until they reach the consistency of a meringue. Gradually beat in the remaining ingredients. Pour the batter into a greased and floured 9 x 13 inch baking pan and bake in a preheated 350 degree oven 25 minutes. Remove cake from oven and set aside to cool in the pan.

Syrup: In a saucepan, over medium-high heat, bring the syrup ingredients to a boil and simmer for 12 minutes. After the cake has cooled, pour the hot syrup over the cake and allow to set for several hours before serving.

Serves: 30

~Koula
Fkiaras

A very easy, light dessert from Northern Greece and especially in northern Western Macedonia, which is famed for Revani.

Saint Fanourios Torte
Fanouropita

1 1/2 cups fresh orange juice
1/2 cup cream sherry
2 tablespoons butter
1 cup golden raisins
1 cup sugar
1 teaspoon salt
1 tablespoon cinnamon
2 tablespoons brandy or rum

2 cups sifted flour
1 1/2 teaspoons baking powder
1/2 teaspoon baking soda

3/4 cup walnuts, chopped

In a medium saucepan, combine the first 8 ingredients. Bring to a boil; simmer for 10 minutes, stirring often. Remove from heat; cool. Mix together next 3 ingredients; stir into cooled mixture. Blend until smooth. Add nuts and mix well. Pour into a greased 8 inch cake pan or loaf pan.

Bake in a preheated 325 degree oven for 1 hour 15 minutes, or until cake tests done.

~ Sophia
Kondoleon

Keeps well when cooled cake is tightly wrapped.

Serves: 10

*Our family tradition honors Saint Fanourios
by baking this moist and flavorful cake
for his feast day, on August 27th.*

Faith
&
Tradition

Contents

~ FAITH & TRADITION ~

~Faith and Tradition

A soup, a sweet, a serving of fish – ordinary foods may take on divine importance in a Greek kitchen. In our lives as Orthodox Christians, we Greeks infuse our "daily bread" with a profound, yet matter-of-fact connection to God. Certain foods figure in the sacramental rituals of the Church and in the year's prescribed feasts and fasts. Alongside the joys and struggles of life, other culinary customs relating an awareness of Christ among us also evolved. Life, death, mercy and salvation; wheat, olives and meat – the earthly and the theological are naturally linked as Greeks eat, commemorate and celebrate.

Some things we don't eat, but only sometimes.

Two days of the week mark occasions of "fasting," an abstinence from meat, dairy products, eggs and fish: Friday for the day of Christ's crucifixion and Wednesday for His betrayal. Other fasts occur in anticipation of great feasts: for Easter, Holy Week and the 40 days preceding it called "Great" Lent; Advent, the 40 days before Christmas; the days of August until the August 15th feast of Mary; and a lent of varying duration for the Holy Apostles in late June. We follow Jesus' example when we fast. Fasting provides a lighter, less indulgent diet for a clearer mind, facilitating prayer during these periods intended for penance and contemplation of the feasts to come. In practice, degrees of strictness in abstinence may vary according to special considerations such as travel, age or illness. On a few stricter fast days, the custom also rules out olive oil and wine. Fasting requires will power and fortifies us for resistance to temptation. It also helps us appreciate God's gift of all foods. Sacrifices through fasting free up resources we may donate to the needy.

Preparation for Holy Communion requires that we neither eat nor drink anything from bedtime the night before liturgy, or for the preceding eight hours before an evening service. All baptized children in the Orthodox Church participate fully in the sacrament of communion even from infancy. Starting at about seven years of age they learn to observe this fast along with the older members of the family.

The feast is greatest after the greatest fast.

Easter, the Feast of Feasts following the many weeks of meatless, spare fare, is first celebrated in the wee hours following the midnight Resurrection service with the cracking of eggs dyed red and a jubilant and simultaneous proclamation, "Christ is risen"! The faithful, now hungry for all the foods they had given up, gather at middle-of-the-night suppers. Rather than eating the lamb slaughtered especially for Easter and reserved for the holiday dinner, they enjoy bowls of *mayiritsa,* a rich soup made of the animal's organ meats, laced with egg-lemon sauce and spring herbs.

Bread makes a supreme offering.

The most vital mystery of the Church, Holy Communion, cannot take place without a lay person's baked offering. *Liturgy,* a Greek word, refers to the "people's work" of worship. Central to this work is the baking of *Prosphoro,* the "offering" bread for the altar: a parishioner prepares a round loaf of bread, imprinting a design on the rising dough with a special carved stamp. This design guides the priest as he cuts out a small cube from the center to be consecrated as the Body of Christ. He places it on the paten. Smaller shapes commemorating His mother Mary and other saints are also cut out and placed with it. Alongside are sections cut out commemorating deceased and living loved ones of the family offering the bread.

A sweeter, richer bread, *Artoklassia,* baked in five round loaves, is for a special service commemorating Christ's feeding of the multitude. It is offered by a family in thanksgiving for blessings received and for their health, and is shared with all who are gathered.

We make a little Heaven in a bowl of wheat.

Jesus gave special significance to kernels of wheat when He used them to illustrate the promise of eternal life. He told of how they bear fruit after their burial and "death." When our loved ones die, we continue to pray for them through memorial services offered 40 days after a death, again at six months, on the first anniversary and at special "Saturday of Souls" liturgies on the Church calendar. Again, we begin preparation for these memorials in our kitchens by making *koliva,* a dish of boiled wheat enhanced with raisins, sesame, nuts and sugar. The mixture is shaped into a white sugary mound, decorated with the initials of the deceased and with a cross. It is placed on a lace-trimmed tray before the altar. Over the koliva, priest and congregation chant special prayers for life everlasting. Koliva represents both resurrection and the sweets of Heaven. Servings are distributed to anyone in attendance. Each person accepts and shares this special confection as a gesture that they have forgiven the deceased for any offenses, and uttering the expression "God forgive them."

Not just desserts, sweets mean celebration.

Pastries and confections don't follow meals in Greek homes. They function instead as special treats in observance of a happy occasion: it may be a grand Easter banquet or a wedding, or an event so simple as the arrival of a visitor to the home. Just as the requisite cake appears at a birthday party in America, Greeks serve sweets on "namedays." Traditionally the anniversary of one's own birth is not celebrated as it is now in the states, but the feast of the saint whose name he or she bears: Those named John or Joanne would celebrate on St. John's day, January 7; Helens and Constantines on May 21, etc. Invitations are not required to visit with a wish for *"hronia polla"*–"many years" of happy returns of the day. The celebrating friend is expected to be receiving and treating the guests. They arrive bearing not presents, but sweets they have prepared for the occasion.

More than mere symbols, more than quaint customs, the guidance of Scripture has made the *nature of food itself* an integral part of our daily devotions. Unconsciously, we are inspired in preparing it and our gift is the fuller appreciation and enjoyment of it. The result is a flavor truly Greek.

Easter Bread
Tsourekia

1 cup milk
1 cup granulated sugar plus 1 teaspoon (for the yeast)
1/2 cup (1 stick) unsalted butter
1/8 teaspoon mahlep, crushed
1/2 cup warm water
3 tablespoons active dry yeast
5 to 6 cups all purpose flour
2 eggs, beaten
Grated rind of 1 lemon
1/8 teaspoon mastiha, crushed

4 to 6 hard boiled eggs, dyed red, optional

1 egg plus 1 egg yolk
Sesame seeds
Slivered almonds (optional)

Heat oven to the lowest setting and turn off. Bring the milk,
sugar, butter and mahlep to a boil (until a "skin" forms). Cool
to lukewarm. In a large measuring cup stir the yeast and
1 teaspoon sugar into the warm water and allow to sit until
foamy (mixture will rise a bit). Add the 1/4 cup flour and allow to
foam again. Stir the two beaten eggs, lemon rind and mastiha
into lukewarm milk mixture, then add to the yeast mix and stir
to blend.

Use a food processor with a capacity to 8 cups flour. Place 5 1/2
cups flour in the work bowl fitted with the dough blade. Have
extra flour to add by tablespoons if dough is too sticky. With the
machine running, slowly pour the liquid mixture through the
feed tube until the dough gathers into a ball and cleans the
bowl. Add a little flour if dough is too sticky. Allow the dough
to knead; run for 30 to 40 more seconds.

Place the dough in a gallon size zip lock bag. Squeeze out all
the air and close. Set the bag in the warmed oven on a pot
holder so the plastic will not touch the metal shelf. Leave in

the bag until the dough doubles in size, about 1 hour. Open the bag, punch down, reseal and allow to rise again until doubled, about 45 minutes.

Remove the dough from the bag, punch down again and form into two braided loaves or one large ring loaf. If you are using the red eggs, insert them into the dough now so they are halfway concealed. Place the loaves or ring on greased or parchment lined cookie sheets. Cover with oiled plastic wrap and allow to double in size.

Beat the egg and extra yolk and gently brush the entire surface of the loaf. Sprinkle with sesame seeds or slivered almonds, if desired. Bake in a preheated 350 degree oven for 30 to 40 minutes until the crust is dark brown and shiny. Cool on a rack.

Note: If using an electric mixer, place all liquids in the bowl. Attach the paddle and add half the flour while the machine is running to form a batter. Now attach the dough hook and continue running the machine, adding flour a little at a time until the dough forms into a ball. Continue kneading for 3 to 4 minutes. The dough should clean the sides of the bowl and not be sticky.

~Georgia
Vareldzis

Traditionally baked for Easter and decorated on top with red eggs. This recipe was given to me by a dear friend and I have adapted it for use in the food processor.

Easter Bread
Tsourekia

2 cups milk, scalded
1 1/2 cups (3 sticks) butter
1 1/2 cups sugar
1 1/2 cakes yeast or 1 1/2 packages fast action dry yeast
3 eggs, beaten
1/2 teaspoon salt
2 1/2 to 3 pounds unbleached flour

Almonds or sesame seeds (optional)

Mix hot milk, butter and sugar in a large saucepan until butter and sugar are dissolved. Add yeast and dissolve. (Ideal temperature for the liquids is about 120 degrees.) Add eggs and mix. Slowly add in the flour and salt. Mix by hand until enough flour is taken up to make a smooth, non-sticky, yet soft, dough. Knead dough well until smooth and satiny (10 to 15 minutes). Cover and let rise in a warm place (80 to 85 degrees). After rising, divide dough and make any shape you desire. Let rise in buttered pans until volume doubles. Brush with beaten eggs. If desired, sprinkle with almonds or sesame seeds. Bake in a preheated 350 degree oven 30 to 40 minutes until golden brown.

~Diane
Jonganatos Cook

Yield: 3 large loaves.

This particular recipe has been given to many, many people. It's my mother's best. Not too sweet, but very tasty. I prefer to use no flavorings.

Greek Easter Bread
Tsourekia

3 packages yeast *
1/2 cup lukewarm water
1 cup warm milk
1 teaspoon sugar
10 to 11 cups flour

6 eggs
1 1/2 cups sugar
Grated rind from 1 large or 2 medium lemons

1 cup (2 sticks) butter, melted

Topping:
1 egg, beaten
Dyed red eggs, optional

In a large bowl, dissolve yeast in lukewarm water. Add milk,
1 teaspoon sugar and 2 cups flour. Stir batter, cover and set
in a warm place for about 1 hour. Beat the eggs, sugar and
lemon rind over hot water until warm. Stir mixture into batter.
Add remaining flour and butter alternately until the dough
is moderately stiff. Knead on floured surface for about 8 to
10 minutes until smooth and elastic. Place in a large, covered
bowl and brush surface with melted butter. Cover with a
cloth and let rise in a warm place until doubled in size (about
2 hours). Punch down and let rest for 10 minutes. Cut dough
into 3 sections and braid or shape each section into desired
shape. Let the loaves rise until doubled (about 1 hour).

Before baking, brush with beaten egg and sprinkle with sesame
seeds or almonds, or press in one or more dyed red eggs. Bake
in preheated 350 degree oven 25 to 30 minutes.

*If you use quick rising yeast, cut all rising times in half.

Yield: 3 loaves.

~Presvytera
Barbara Retelas

New Year's Bread
Vassilopita Vorioipirotiki

Homemade phyllo* dough:
4 cups flour
4 tablespoons (1/4 stick) unsalted butter, melted
Warm water
Cornstarch

Filling:
4 cups water
2 tablespoons (1/4 stick) plus 1/2 cup (1 stick) butter
1/4 pound feta, crumbled
1 cup bulghur
2 eggs
2 cups milk, scalded and cooled
Dash salt, optional
Egg wash
Coin wrapped in foil

1 egg beaten with a little milk for top

Homemade phyllo dough: In a bowl, combine flour, butter and water and mix. Knead until dough has an elastic consistency. Divide into 6 parts and roll each one with a small amount of cornstarch using a Kalamidi until the dough is very thin and slightly larger than the size of the baking pan. In a preheated 300 degree oven, brown two sheets phyllo, checking often to prevent burning. Remove and set aside while preparing filling.

Filling: In a saucepan boil water, add 1/4 stick butter, return to boil. Add feta, return to boil and add bulghur. Return to a gentle boil. Cover and cook until the mixture absorbs the water. Remove from heat and set aside. To the bulghur mixture, add 1 stick butter and 1 egg. Mix well. Add milk gradually until mixture reaches a consistency that is easy to spread. Add salt, if desired.

To assemble: Butter a 14 inch round, deep-sided stainless steel pan. Place 4 sheets of unbaked phyllo in the pan allowing excess dough to hang over the sides. Top with 1 sheet of baked phyllo. The baked phyllo should be placed to fit inside the pan exactly. Brush this layer with melted butter. Spread half of the bulghur mixture over the phyllo. Place the other baked phyllo sheet over and spread the remaining bulghur on top, spreading to the edges of the pan. Roll and tuck excess dough to form a built up edge. Insert the foil-covered coin in the rolled edge now so that it is not visible.

Pour the egg wash over the top of the pita and spread to the edges. Bake in a preheated 400 degree oven 30 to 40 minutes until golden brown. Serve with honey.

*Frozen, pre-made phyllo can be used

~Effie Gadinas

This pita is quite different from what most people think of when they hear Vassilopita. It is a very old family recipe and very traditional from the area around Northern Epirus in Northwestern Greece. The region is very mountainous and villagers use only ingredients available to them during the deep winter months.

Saint Basil's Bread
Vassilopita

1/2 cup warm water
2 packages active dry yeast
1 cup milk
2/3 cup (1 stick plus 2 tablespoons) butter
1 3/4 cup sugar
6 eggs
3 teaspoons grated lemon peel
6 teaspoons grated orange peel
1 teaspoon salt
7 to 8 cups unsifted flour
Silver coin wrapped in foil
1 or 2 packages blanched almonds
1 to 2 egg yolks mixed with 1 tablespoon water

Sprinkle the yeast into the warm water and stir briefly; let it stand until dissolved. In a saucepan heat milk and butter together until butter melts. Place in a mixing bowl. Add sugar and let cool to luke-warm while grating the lemon and orange peels. Add eggs, one at a time, beat until smooth; add yeast mixture. Stir in orange and lemon peel and salt. Slowly add 4 cups of the flour. Beat for 5 minutes using a heavy duty electric mixer or wooden spoon.

Turn dough out onto a heavily floured board and knead gradually adding the remaining 3 to 4 cups flour until smooth and no longer sticky (approximately 5 to 10 minutes).

Place dough in a bowl greased with vegetable oil; lightly grease the top of the dough. Cover with plastic wrap then a kitchen towel and let rise in a warm place until doubled, approximately 1 1/4 to 1 1/2 hours.

Turn dough out on lightly floured board and knead lightly. Wash, dry and wrap a silver coin (i.e., quarter) in foil and place in the dough. Divide dough; shape one into a large (11 inch) round loaf, and one into a small (6 inch) round loaf. Cover and let rise 1 hour until doubled. Arrange almonds on top in the shape of a cross or the numbers of the new year; press in firmly.

~Sarah
Spathas

Bake in a preheated 350 degree oven for 30 minutes. Carefully brush with egg yolk and water mixture and bake an additional 10 to15 minutes until golden brown.

Every January of the 15 years my husband and I have been married, I have tried a different recipe for Vassilopita. Some were disasters! This is my favorite so far...a slightly sweet bread with a hint of lemon and orange.

Saint Basil's Bread
Vassilopita

1 cup (2 sticks) butter, room temperature
2 cups sugar
6 eggs, separated
1 whiskey glass cognac
3/4 cup orange juice
1 orange peel grated (about 1 1/2 tablespoons)
5 cups flour
3 teaspoon baking powder

Gold-wrapped coin

In a bowl, beat butter until creamy. Add sugar and egg yolks.
Beat well. Add Cognac, orange juice and grated peel, and
continue mixing. Add baking powder to flour and sift into butter
mixture. Stir until mixed. In a separate bowl, beat egg whites
until stiff. Fold into creamed mixture. Fold in the foil-wrapped
coin. Pour into a 9 or 10 inch springform pan. Bake in a
preheated 350 degree oven 55 to 60 minutes. Test with cake
tester or long toothpick in center to be sure it is done. Remove
pan from oven.

Let set 10 to 15 minutes before inverting onto serving platter.

~Anne
Chimiklis Pavlos

Serves: 12 to 18

This recipe is from my mother-in-law.
It is a very good no fail recipe.

Tangerine Buttermilk Bread
Vassilopita

Peel from 3 tangerines, chopped
1 cup (2 sticks) unsalted butter, room temperature
2 cups sugar
4 large eggs, room temperature
2¹/2 cups flour
¹/2 teaspoon baking soda
1 teaspoon baking powder
¹/2 teaspoon salt
³/4 cup buttermilk

In food processor, finely grind tangerine peel. With motor running, add sugar and blend well.

In an electric mixer, cream butter. Add sugar-tangerine mixture (from the food processor) a little at a time, and beat until light and fluffy. Add eggs, one at a time and blend thoroughly after each.

Sift flour, soda, baking powder and salt together. Add to creamed mixture, alternating with buttermilk. Mix until just blended. Pour into a greased and floured 10 inch bundt pan. Bake in a preheated 350 degree oven 50 to 60 minutes or until done. Cool in pan 10 minutes. Turn out on wire rack to cool completely.

~Helen
Kallimanis
Buhler

One of our family's favorites. Enjoy!

Βασιλόπιτα με Φύλλο

Phyllo Vassilopita
Vassilopita me Filo

2 pounds phyllo dough (reserve 4 sheets for top of pita)
1 1/2 to 2 pounds unsalted butter, melted, keep warm

Filling:
2 pounds finely ground walnuts
2 cups sugar
3/4 teaspoon cloves

Decorations for top:
1 egg white, beaten
1 teaspoon cinnamon
Scant 1/2 teaspoon cloves
Almonds, blanched and split
Sesame seeds

Brush a large circular or 11 x 15 inch rectangular pan with melted butter. Layer 4 to 5 phyllo sheets, each brushed with melted butter. Combine walnuts, sugar and cloves. Sprinkle some of filling mixture on top of the phyllo. Add remaining phyllo, 1 sheet at a time, brushing each with melted butter and then sprinkling each with a light layer of filling. For the next 3 phyllo sheets (reserved for the top), brush each with melted butter. Top with the 4th reserved sheet and brush with the slightly beaten egg white.

Mix the cinnamon and cloves in a small dish. Make dots with your finger here and there on top of the pita. Decorate top with split almonds by placing them around the cinnamon dots to form a flower. Note: It takes 6 split almonds to make each flower. Sprinkle the top of the pita with sesame seeds. Bake in a preheated 350 degree oven for 15 minutes. Reduce heat to 325 degrees and bake 40 to 45 minutes longer. Watch carefully as it may get a little too brown. If necessary, cover loosely with foil. If the pita turns too brown before time, lower oven temperature to 300 degrees.

~Kathleen
Hallis

Serves: 18 to 21

This is a special family recipe made especially for New Year's Day. For religious holidays, you can form a cross in the center of the pita using the split almonds. Once the top has been decorated, sprinkle it with sesame seeds.

New Year's Cake
Vassilopita

1 cup (2 sticks) unsalted butter, room temperature
1 1/2 cups sugar
Rind of one lemon or orange
5 large eggs, separated
3/4 cup milk
3 cups flour
1 tablespoon baking powder

Coin wrapped in foil

Whole almonds
Powdered sugar

In an electric mixer, cream butter until it turns white, about
15 minutes. Add sugar gradually and beat until fluffy. Add rind.
Beat in egg yolks one at a time. Continue until mixture is well
blended. Beat egg whites separately until stiff and set aside. Mix
baking powder with flour and add alternately with the milk.
Scrape bowl frequently with spatula to make sure flour is well
blended. Fold beaten egg whites carefully into the batter. Pour
into the prepared pan and spread evenly. Push foil wrapped coin
into the batter so it disappears, being careful not to push it all
the way to the bottom, or it will show through. Make a cross
on top with the almonds. Bake in a preheated 350 degree oven
for 40 to 45 minutes until center of cake springs back when
touched lightly, or check with a cake tester. Cool in the pan for
15 minutes. Carefully invert cake and place on a rack. Turn it
upright, cool completely and dust with powdered sugar.

~Georgia
Vareldzis

*My husband's family lived in the Middle East
for many years. This Vassilopita is made like a
pound cake, rather than a yeast bread and is
the traditional Vassilopita from his family.*

Bread for Artoklassia
Artos yia Artoklassia

1 1/2 quarts or more lukewarm milk
9 cakes yeast
4 cups (8 sticks) butter, melted
1/2 cup vegetable shortening
5 cups sugar
1 dozen eggs, beaten
1 teaspoon mastika
4 ounces orange juice and grated rind
3 drops anise
10 pounds all-purpose flour

Scald milk and cool to lukewarm. In a bowl, dissolve yeast in the milk. Add the melted butter and shortening. Add beaten eggs, mastiha, orange juice, grated rind and anise flavoring. Sift the flour and add a little at a time until a soft dough has formed. Knead well. Cover and let rise. Punch down, knead and let rise again. Shape in pans. (Use 10-inch round pans, 2 inches deep.) Let rise again.

Brush with egg yolk. Bake in a preheated 350 degree oven for about 1 hour.

~Submitted
by Aristides
Phoutrides

This excellent sweet bread was developed in the 1960's through the efforts of Aspasia Phoutrides Pulakis who, together with a local baker, created the recipe for the blessing of the five loaves of bread.

Bread for Artoklassia
Artos yia Artoklassia

2 tablespoons salt
1/4 pound fresh yeast
6 cups warm water
10 pounds flour (approximately)
3 cups sugar
1 dozen eggs
3 tablespoons anise seed
3 pounds margarine, melted and cooled

Melt the yeast and salt in the warm water. Add enough flour
to make a soft dough. Let this dough rise in a warm place.
After dough has risen, punch it down and add sugar, eggs,
anise seed and margarine. Add more flour to make a thick
dough. Put dough in a warm oven (warmed and then turned
off) to rise. When doubled in size, remove pans from oven and
knead dough until smooth. Repeat 3 times. Divide the dough
into 5 parts. Knead each part and shape into 5 round loaves.
Put into greased 10-inch springform pans. Let them rise to
double in a warm place.

~Athena Bake in a preheated 350 degree oven for 1 hour. Cool,
Kekrides then sift confectioners sugar over each loaf and sprinkle
with cinnamon.

Yield: 5 loaves.

*Bread for the service of the Five Loaves.
Holy Trinity has enjoyed Athena Kekrides'
excellent sweet bread for Artoklassia for over
20 years. The bread she makes for the church
service requires 30 pounds of flour. This is
a smaller version, but just as delicious!*

Μαγειρίτσα

Easter Soup
Mayiritsa

Heart, liver and intestines of lamb
1/2 cup olive oil
2 bunches green onion, chopped
1/2 cup fresh dill
2 Tablespoons tomato paste
2 cups water
Salt and pepper to taste

The intestines must be washed and cleaned very well. Use a thin
stick to turn them inside out when washing. It works well. Rub
with salt during this process. Heart and liver should be washed
well also. Place intestines, heart and liver in stockpot and cover
with water. Boil for 5 minutes. Rinse in cold water and cut into
small pieces. Return to a clean stockpot. Sauté pieces in oil for
a few minutes. Add onions, dill, tomato paste, water, salt and
pepper. Cook until tender and broth has very little liquid. Serve
with red dyed eggs, tsourekia and a salad.

~Georgia
Belesin

*This is a traditional Easter soup served
after Midnight Easter service.*

Μαγειρίτσα

Greek Easter Soup
Mayiritsa

3 pounds lamb with bone in (shoulder, shanks, or neck)
2 carrots, peeled and sliced
2 stalks celery, sliced
1 medium onion, quartered
3 bay leaves
3 quarts water
3 tablespoons margarine
1 bunch green onions, finely chopped
1/4 cup dill, finely chopped
1/2 cup fresh parsley, finely chopped
1/2 cup rice
4 to 5 egg yolks
Juice of 2 lemons
Salt and pepper to taste

Remove all fat from lamb. Place in a 4 quart pot and simmer
with carrots, celery, onion and bay leaves in 3 quarts of water
until tender, removing scum as it forms. Allow broth to cool.
Skim off fat and strain. Discard vegetables and bay leaves.
Remove meat from the bones and chop fine. In a pan, sauté
green onions in margarine. Add lamb, dill and parsley and sauté
again for 4 to 5 minutes. Return lamb and onion to broth and
bring to a boil. Add more water if needed. Stir in rice and
simmer for 20 minutes. Remove from heat.

Beat egg yolks until light. Blend in lemon juice. Gradually
blend in broth, beating constantly, until most of the broth is
used. Gradually pour the egg-lemon mixture back into the pot,
stirring well. Season to taste. Serve at once, with lemon wedges
on the side if desired.

~Vassie
Stoumbos

Serves: 10 to 12

*Traditionally, mayiritsa is made with the lungs, liver
and heart of a lamb. This recipe uses only lamb meat;
however, organs can be added if desired.*

Red Easter Eggs
Passhalina Avga

1 tablespoon red dye
3 tablespoons white vinegar
3 quarts water (tepid)
1 to 1 1/2 dozen eggs

Place all of the above ingredients into a large kettle. Put the eggs into the kettle and bring to a boil. Boil for 15 minutes. Remove the eggs individually and allow to cool. Then take a soft cloth soaked in vegetable oil and shine each egg. Check your kettle dye to see that it retains its strength if you wish to dye another 1 to 1 1/2 dozen eggs.

~Joan Liapes

Traditionally, Easter eggs are dyed on Holy Thursday or Holy Saturday.

Bread for Altar Offering
Litouryia (Prosforo)

1 package active or compressed yeast (fresh yeast is best)
5 cups bread flour plus 1 cup regular flour
2 1/2 cups warm water (about 115 degrees)
1 teaspoon salt

1 prosphoro seal

Dissolve the yeast in 1/2 cup water, cover and let stand for several minutes. In a large bowl combine the remaining water, salt and yeast mixture. Add a cup of flour at a time, kneading well after each addition. To keep the dough pliable and smooth add a little flour or water to your hands as needed. Continue kneading for about 15 minutes, until dough no longer sticks to hands. Cut off 1/2 the dough and set aside. Fit the remaining dough into a 9 inch round floured (but not greased) cake pan. Shape the smaller portion of dough into a round shape on a floured surface. Dip prosphoro seal in flour and press it down firmly in the center of the round. Remove the seal. Moisten the dough in the pan with a little water. Put the small round with seal markings on top. Cover and let rise for 45 minutes. Bake in a preheated 325 degree oven for 1 hour.

~Meropi S.
Courogen

NOTES: Use non-stick pans or line pan with parchment paper. After dough rises, prick around the imprint with a toothpick.

Prayer to be read when preparing prosphoro:
Dear Lord, this bread that we have baked represents each one of us in this family and in our congregation. We are offering ourselves to You, our very life, in humble obedience and total commitment to You. We place ourselves on Your holy altar through this bread to be used by You in any way that You feel will help enlarge Your Kingdom. Accept our gift that You will give us when You consecrate this bread and give it back to us as Your Precious Body.   Amen

Liturgy
means the common work of the people.
It is a blessing to prepare prosphoro
as a family and take it
to church as an offering
with a list of names
to be prayed for
"the living"
and
"the departed."

Memorial Wheat ✝
Koliva

2 pounds Sadaf wheat pelted
1 1/2 pounds walnuts, chopped
2 tablespoons fresh parsley, chopped
3 cups rusk, crumbled
1 pomegranate, harvest seed
2 boxes golden raisins
1 cup sesame seeds, toasted
1 pound powdered sugar
6 ounces slivered almonds, toasted and chopped
1 tablespoon cinnamon
Sprinkle of nutmeg
Yogurt almonds

Prepare the wheat on Saturday morning: Empty wheat into a large pot (approximately 10 inch diameter x 5 1/2 inches high) and soak for two hours. Boil the wheat for 2 to 3 minutes, drain and add fresh water, then boil for 2 to 3 minutes again. Drain again and put fresh water in pot to 1 inch from top of pot, bring to boil reduce heat to low and cook for 1 1/2 to 2 hours. **Do not stir.** The wheat is cooked when the kernels open up. When cooked, put in colander and rinse thoroughly with cold water. Put clean towels on the kitchen table. Squeeze the wheat with your hands to get the water out, then spread it thinly on the towels. Let dry 2 to 3 hours. Then place in refrigerator in a sealed plastic container.

Chop the walnuts and parsley, crumble the rusk, and harvest the pomegranate seeds. Separately place these ingredients in sealed, plastic containers in the refrigerator. Gather the remaining ingredients and keep handy for Sunday morning, along with a large bowl, some waxed paper and a 15 x 10 inch silver tray with handles. Place doilies on the tray and cover the doilies with aluminum foil.

Mix the Koliva on Sunday morning: In the large bowl, mix wheat with all remaining ingredients except half of the crumbled rusk (1 1/2 cups). Place the mixture in a mound on the tray, and sprinkle the mound with the rusk. Sift the powdered sugar over the mound. Place a sheet of waxed paper on top of the mound and smooth out the mound. Clean the tray around the edges, and decorate with yogurt almonds all the way around. Also with yogurt almonds, make a cross in the middle and make the initials of the departed on each side of the cross.

After the memorial service, carefully transfer the mound with all edible decorations into a large bowl. The mixture is called "sitari." Mix the sitari well to blend the layers of rusk and powdered sugar. Spoon into cups to serve.

—*Frances Stefanis, submitted by Nicolas Hanches*

A memorial service is traditionally offered in the Orthodox Church in remembrance of the departed 40 days after death and again one year after death. The offering of Koliva is an ancient custom and signifies that the dead will rise again, just as wheat, when in the earth, sprouts and bears fruit. The various sweets added to the Koliva signify that after Resurrection, life will be sweet and blissful. The parsley signifies the Green Path. The pomegranate seeds symbolize the refreshing of the soul, and the raisins symbolize that God is the vine and we are the branches.

My Aunt Frances Stefanis has been making Koliva for many years. She printed her recipe because she felt it was important that younger members of the church learn how to make Koliva. Aunt Frances is a member of Panagia Pantovasilissa Greek Orthodox Church in Lexington, Kentucky. For her congregation, she makes 2 pounds of Koliva.

Κόλλυβα

Memorial Wheat ☦

Koliva

3 pounds sitari, whole (whole wheat unpeeled)

1 cup flour (browned in pan)
1 1/2 pounds walnuts, chopped
1 1/2 pounds slivered almonds, lightly toasted
1 1/2 teaspoons salt
2 tablespoons ground cinnamon
2 cups sesame seeds, lightly toasted
1/4 cup fresh parsley, finely chopped

1 box white raisins
1 box dark raisins
2 boxes rusk, ground
1 to 2 pounds powdered sugar
White Jordan almonds (for cross and initials of deceased)

The preparation of Koliva begins three days before the
memorial service.

Late in the day of the 1st day, inspect wheat for foreign
matter. Wash in a strainer under warm running water.
Place in a large pot, cover with water and soak overnight.

On the morning of the 2nd day, drain wheat and cover with
fresh water. Add salt, bring to boil and then simmer for about
4 hours, until tender and wheat splits in two. Do not scorch.
Add water as needed. Place cooked wheat in a colander and
rinse under cold running water to remove starch. Drain
thoroughly. Air dry wheat 8 to 12 hours in a single layer
on double thickness linens placed on a large table.

On the morning of the service, in a large bowl, mix together
dried wheat, browned flour, walnuts, slivered almonds, raisins,
spices, sesame seeds and parsley. Line a large tray with waxed
paper and edge with paper doilies. Put the light and dark raisins
down first. Next, mound wheat mixture onto tray; pack and
shape well. Cover the whole mound with the zwieback (this is
what will keep the powdered sugar dry). Sift powdered sugar
over all at least 1/4 inch thick. Keep on pressing and patting it
down. Make a cross in the center of the mound using the
Jordan almonds. On either side of the cross, form initials of
the deceased using Jordan almonds. Other designs may be
added as desired.

*~Meropi S.
Courogen*

Yield: A large tray

In the Orthodox Church, Koliva is prepared in remembrance of the departed forty days after death, six months, one year and as often as a family desires after the first year. The family prepares and brings the Koliva to Church for the Mnimosinon (Memorial Service), where prayer for the repose of the souls of the departed are offered. Boiled wheat (Koliva) symbolizes the Resurrection. Just as wheat must be planted in the ground to take root and bring forth fruit, man is buried because of death, but with the promise that one day he too will be resurrected. The various sweets added to the Koliva signify that after Resurrection, life will be sweet and blissful. Yes, it is a time consuming process, but it gives you time, as a family, to talk about the loved one, work out grief and to pray.

Acknowledgements

The collective passion that impelled **Flavor It Greek! A Celebration of Food, Faith and Family** to completion was an extraordinary experience in and of itself. Our mission to produce a cookbook required the expertise of many and its success is a compliment to all those volunteers and financial donors who made this book possible.

COMPUTER AND RECIPE ASSISTANCE
Helen Antonis
Georgia Belesiu
Lena Brice
Leslie Buhler
Aneta Englund
JoAnne Finicle
Rhonda Gadinas
Katina Joannides
Sophia Kondoleon
Eleni Marschman
Kathy Molesa
Gail Morris
Lyn Pangares
Nancee Pangares
Tracey Pangares
George Papas
Kathy Phoutrides
Presvytera Effy
    Stephanopoulos
Anna Stratis

FUNDRAISING
Catherine Diamond
    Owen
Tasia Couris
Ann Kadlub and
    Koala Blue
Jim and Ann Mehas
Chrisoula Papas
Christine Rulli
    and Bambini's
    Children's Boutique
Paul Pavlos
Philoptochos Circles
    Makrina
    Martha
    Mary Magdalene
    Philothea
    Phoebe
    Priscilla
Holy Trinity Church
    Community

COOKBOOK REPRESENTATIVES
Angeliki Anasis
Angie Anast
Helen Antonis
Georgia Belesiu
Erin Christ
Tasia Couris
Meropi Courogen
Ann Davis
Christina Lingas Geist
Sylvia Handris
Todd Hinchliffe
Chrysi Kondilis
Sophia Kriara
Elaine Lampros
Helen Lampus
Kathleen Lee
Joan Liapes
Sophia Makris
Mary Maletis
Joanna Mason
Ann Mehas
Jeanette Michas
Mimi Palumbis
Katherine Pappas
Pearl Pavlos
Betty Phoutrides
Katy Vokos
Vasiliki Vlahakis

ABOUT THE ARTISTS

Frank and Victoria Colburn, a husband and wife artistic team, live in Lake Oswego, Oregon. Their mutual love for art, art history and their travels to Greece and Italy for study brought them together 20 years ago. Frank researched and studied for his Master's thesis in Salonica (Thessaloniki), Greece, where he specialized in Byzantine art history. He currently enjoys his career as a painter and muralist. Victoria studied art and art history in Italy and Greece. Through the years she has developed her artistic style, specializing in fabric painting and textile design.

Their collective talent created the divider pages and cover artwork for **Flavor It Greek! A Celebration of Food, Faith and Family.**

Donors

While vision, faith and volunteer power enabled us to assemble the cookbook, our sincere thanks goes to the following donors who contributed funds and in-kind services to produce **Flavor It Greek! A Celebration of Food, Faith and Family.** *

Benefactor ($ 15,000+)

THE DUSSIN FAMILY

Georgia Dariotis, Guss Dussin and Alice Pulos

In memory of their mother **Anastasia Dussin**–an outstanding example of a devoted mother, a creative and innovative cook and a dedicated participant in community activities.

Patrons ($ 5,000 - $ 14,999)

ASSOCIATION OF GREEK RESTAURANT OWNERS (A.G.R.O.)

A non-profit charitable corporation founded in 1995 whose primary objective is to support and fund Greek Orthodox and community-at-large youth activities. Funds are used for charitable, athletic, literary, educational and scientific programs. Annual donations to Doernbecher Children's Hospital are made by A.G.R.O.

SAKI AND DENYELE TZANTARMAS

JOHN TZANTARMAS AND NEW COPPER PENNY RESTAURANT/
PANTHEON BANQUET HALL (IN-KIND)

Sponsors ($ 1,000 - $ 4,999)

CAMP ANGELOS (AMERICAN HELLENIC EDUCATIONAL CENTER)

A non-profit corporation founded in 1977 to conduct and maintain a 96-acre property along the Sandy River in Corbett, Oregon. *Camp Angelos* serves the spiritual developmental and educational needs of all races, ages, creeds and cultures.

JIMMY DEMAS, ELLEN, JIM, THOMAS AND MATTHEW BELESIU

In memory of our beloved **Anna Stratikos Demas**

THE FAMILY OF VIOLET DIAMOND

Henry and Catherine Diamond Owen, Michael and Mari Lou P. Diamond and George N. and Paula D. Diamond

In memory of **Nicholas Diamond** and **The George Lewis Café** (1913 - 1963).

GEORGIA VARELDZIS

Donors

～ *Supporters ($500 - $999)*

THE WILLIAM F. BITAR FAMILY, DR. KEN & MARY KOREK,
KENT & JEANETTE LUCAS, THE DOUGLAS O'BRIEN FAMILY,
THE WHITNEY DAVIS FAMILY, MS. LISA LUCAS
> In loving memory of **Frank and Margaret Bitar**

JIMMY W. GEORGE, SUE GEORGE, KATHERINE PAPPAS, JULIE TICE
> In loving memory of **William and Julia George,**
> and **James and Anna Gann**

ANDY AND ANASTASIA GIANOPOULOS
> In loving memory of our mothers,
> **Mary Boudoures** and **Rose Gianopoulos**

ANGELO AND HELEN LAMPUS, GEORGE LAMPUS, JIM AND
DIANA LAMPUS, DEAN LAMPUS

JOAN LIAPES AND GEORGIA LIAPES
> In memory of our beloved sister, **Helene C. Anasis**

PETER AND FIFI PSIHOGIOS
> In memory of our beloved parents,
> **George and Angeliki Psihogios**, and **Gus and Mary Thomas**.

～ *Friends (up to $ 499)*

ALEXIS FOODS (IN-KIND)
CATHY AMEN
JOHN ANASIS
GUS AND HELEN ANTONIS
BILL AND VEVEE ASPROS
GEORGIA BELESIU
MR. AND MRS. ROBERT BITAR
ANASTASIA BUCHANAN
JERRY AND HELEN BUHLER
PETER CORVALLIS
PETER CORVALLIS PRODUCTIONS
  (IN-KIND)
BASILIOS AND MEROPI COUROGEN
MRS. PETER DEMAS
JACKIE SPATHAS DICKINSON

GLORIA DROUGAS
PAUL AND BETH DUDUNAKE TRUST
  MICHAEL DUDUNAKIS
  KENNETH DUDUNAKIS
  KAREN DUDUNAKE
  PAULA DUDUNAKE DIAMOND
ANETA ENGLUND
PETER AND RHONDA GADINAS
JAMES AND GEORGIA GEORGE
ANTHONY GIANOPOULOS
NICHOLAS GIANOPOULOS
GRETCHEN GOEKJIAN
BILL GRANT
JOANNE KRIARA GREWE
KALLIOPI HARRISON

continued . . .

Donors

Friends (up to $499) ~

continued . . .

STEPHANIE JEWELL
  COOL TEMPTATIONS/
  LET'S TALK TURKEY
PETE KANAS
KATHERINE KARABATSOS
KATHERINE KARAFOTIAS
CHRISANTHY KARIS
MIKE AND ELAINE KARUSSOS &
  SPIRIT OF LIFE, INC.
RUTH AND JAMES KOLIAS
SOPHIA KONDOLEON AND
  ELIAS TAYLOR
GUS AND SOPHIA KRIARA (IN-KIND)
MILT LAMPROS
VIRGINIA LANGUS
DORA LEE
BESSIE LEKAS
JACK AND KATHERINE LOCKIE
CHRIS AND CLEO MALETIS
ED MALETIS AND COLUMBIA
  DISTRIBUTING (IN-KIND)
KRISTI AND CHRIS MALETIS, III
NICK MALLOS (IN-KIND)
GUST MANN
GENE AND ELENI MARSCHMAN
JIM AND ANN MEHAS
HELEN MELONAS
JEANETTE AND CON MICHAS
JOY NEITLING
ELENI NICHOLSON
MARY NONUS
CLARE AND CATHERINE PANGARES

PANAGIOTIS AND ANTOINETTE
  PAPAILIOU
GEORGE AND CHRISOULA PAPAS
ARISTIDES AND BETTY PHOUTRIDES
PATRICIA AND JOHN POULOS
THEODORA RAPTOR
JENNIE REIMANN
DR. AND MRS. DEMETRIOS RIGAS
ANNA ROUSSOS
MINA ROUSSOS
ELECTRA ROYSE
DORINE AND LANCE SKORDAHL
TRACY SKORDAHL
THOMAS SHIOLAS
DAVID SLY
GENE SPATHAS
TOM AND SARAH SPATHAS
TOM STARFAS
FATHER ELIAS STEPHANOPOULOS
  MEMORIAL FUND
ZACH AND VASILIKI STOUMBOS
HELEN STRATIKOS
TERI STRATIKOS
CHRIS TSEFALAS AND
  THE PERFUME HOUSE (IN-KIND)
GEORGIA TSEFALAS
ROULA TSIRIMIAGOS
ARMA TSOUMAS
ARTEMIS VANDERVORT
ARETI VLAHAKIS
VASILIKI VLAHAKIS

*For all those who donated funds after the publication of **Flavor It Greek!**, we thank you for your generous support.

A CELEBRATION OF FOOD, FAITH & FAMILY

Glossary

arni	lamb, usually spring lamb
artoklassia	**(artoklasia)** bread breaking or blessing of five loaves. The service commemorates Christ's miracle of feeding 5,000 people. It is sweet bread that is prepared and brought to church to express gratitude for God's blessings. Along with the five loaves, a container of oil and one of wine is also included in the blessings. Names are read at the blessings for the good health for whom the prayers are being offered.
avgolemono	an egg and lemon sauce; can also be a lemon soup
bamyes	okra, used in many stews
béchamel	flour-thickened cream sauce; may contain eggs; used in pastitsio and moussakas
bergamot oil	flowery, pungent, aromatic oil used very sparingly. Sold in some pharmacy sections
bobota	corn bread; regionally found in the Peloponnesus area of Greece
calamari	**(kalamari or kalamarakia)** squid, usually small-sized are preferred
clarify	to skim the top foam from melted unsalted butter: heat the butter on low heat in a heavy saucepan; carefully skim off the foam, leaving the liquid butter. Pour the remaining liquid butter into a bowl separating the milk residue on the bottom of the bowl which should be discarded.
cumin	an herb used in powder or seed form with roast pork, sauces, or lentil dishes
coriander	an herb used in dried beans, pork and vegetable dishes.
crema	**(krema)** a custard or pudding dessert
dolmathes	stuffed leaves such as grape or cabbage wrapped around rice and herbs; sometimes meat and/or vegetables are added
faki	lentils; also lentil soup
farina	semolina; fine meal as of cereal grain
fava	broad beans; used in soups or cooked very thick and seasoned
feta	a crumbly, white cheese made from goat's milk
grabee	**(ghraybi)** a delectable Lebanese sugar cookie similar to Greek kourabiethes

halva	**(halvas)** a dessert of Turkish origin; comes from the Peloponnesus region of Greece. It is a sweet made with farina and butter
hilopites	small square egg noodles; can be boiled and served with tomato or meat sauce and grated cheese or served with lamb or beef
horiatiki	the Greek term for village; used commonly to identify "village" salad
kalamata	black marinated olives used in salads or served individually. Named for the Kalamata region of Greece
kalamidi	Greek "rolling pin" approximately 1 meter long dowel, the size of a broomstick with tapered ends
kataifi phyllo	**(Kadaifi)** a shredded phyllo used in the prepration of kataifi
kasseri	a creamy, firm cheese with a mild flavor
keftethes	**(keftethakia)** small meatballs
kefalotiri	a hard, salty cheese; grates finely and is used with pasta
kima	cooked ground meat seasoned with Greek spices and served over pasta
koliva	**(kollyva)** boiled wheat, sweetened, spiced and decorated; used for memorial services
kolokithokeftethes	zucchini fritters
koumbara(o)	the term used to describe the relationship two families have when one member of the family serves as the person in a Greek wedding who exchanges the rings and wedding crowns (stefana); also this term is used to identify the person that baptizes a child in one's family thus creating a special bond between the families
kritharaki	see *orzo*
lathera	a group of stove-top stews in which olive oil is a main flavoring
manestra	orzo; rice-shaped pasta
mayiritsa	traditional Easter soup which, when eaten, breaks the lenten fast
mastiha	mastic gum; pulverized and used in flavoring the liqueur, mastiha, as well as some sweets and breads
mavrodaphne	a sweet, rich red wine used for communion wine; also served as an aperitif or in a punch
mahlep	a spice from the kernel of the black cherry stone, ground and used to flavor sweet yeast breads

metaxa	the name brand of a Greek brandy
metrion	medium flavored; often used to describe the amount of sugar flavored added to Greek coffee; varies with personal taste
mezethes	(mezethakia) appetizers; can be either hot or cold hors d'oeuvres
moussaka	(moussakas) eggplant baked with ground meat and béchamel
mizithra	a pale yellow, semi-hard cheese with a buttery flavor usually grated for use with pasta dishes
must	grape juice intended for winemaking, not yet fermented
nouna	the Greek word for "godmother"
oregano	a dried herb used to flavor numerous dishes
orzo	rice-shaped pasta, also known as kritharaki
ouzo	a clear, licorice-flavored liqueur, turns white and cloudy when water is added
papou	the Greek word for "grandfather"
pasteli	a hard sesame candy
pastitsio	macaroni baked with ground meat and a béchamel sauce
paten	a gold or silver dish with a stand used by the priest at the altar table in the preparation of Holy Communion. The paten symbolizes the manger.
paximathia	a biscotti cookie; traditionally served at memorial coffees or luncheons
phyllo	(filo) thin pastry sheets; the basic ingredient used in preparing many syrupy sweet pastries, i.e. baklava, and savory pies, i.e. spanakopita or tiropita
pilafi	(pilaf) a rice dish flavored with herbs, to which can be added vegetables, fish, chicken or meat
pita	soft, flat bread, shaped into rounds or ovals that can be split through the center to make pockets to hold souvlakia and/or salads; a spinach or cheese-filled pie, as in spanakopita or tiropita
presvytera	the honorific term given to all wives of Greek Orthodox priests instead of "Mrs."
prosphoro	(prosphoron) bread of offering; used in the liturgy as the communion bread
psari	fish
revani	a syrup topped orange-flavored cake made with farina

retsina	a pine resin-flavored white wine
rizogalo	rice pudding
rusk	a zwieback cookie
saganaki	fried kasseri cheese
skorthalia	(skordalia) garlic sauce, prepared with potatoes or bread; can be very pungent
souvlakia	marinated pieces of meat placed on a skewer and roasted over an open fire or grill, usually lamb although pork and chicken can also be used
spanakopita	a spinach-filled pie
spanakopites	a spinach-filled pita; made individually in a triangular shape and served as appetizers
spanakorizo	a spinach and rice combination side dish
stifatho	(stifado) a seasoned onion stew made with beef or rabbit
soutzoukakia	seasoned ground meat shaped into slender sausages
sumac	a spice that comes from the sumac tree
tarama	fish roe salt-packed in jars; may be eaten on crackers or made into a thick spread (taramosalata) which may also be used as a dip. Available in specialty delicatessants.
tiropita	a pita with a feta cheese based filling; can be served as an appetizer or as a main dish
tiropites	a feta cheese based filling made as an individual triangle served as an appetizer
thiosmo	mint
tsourekia	the traditional braided Easter bread topped with sesame seeds
tzatziki	yogurt, cucumber and garlic dip
unsalted butter	sweet butter required in many of the pastry recipes
vassilopita	(vasilopita) New Year's bread (St. Basil's bread). A coin is placed in the center of the bread (wrapped in foil prior to baking); the bread is cut with each family's name being said; the person receiving the piece with the coin in it is considered to have good luck for the new year.
yiaourti	yogurt
yiayia	the Greek word for "grandmother"
youvetsi	lamb or beef cooked with orzo (manestra)
zweiback	rusk

Note: Regarding the spelling of Greek recipe titles, choices were made to guide the reader through the Greek pronounciations.

A CELEBRATION OF FOOD, FAITH & FAMILY

Order Form

Flavor It Greek! A Celebration of Food, Faith and Family

The Perfect Gift...   ☐ Gift ☐ Personal
Please send to:

NAME
_____

MAILING ADDRESS
_____

CITY / STATE / ZIP
_____

PHONE
_____

Please send _____ copies $_____
x $29.95 ea. ($38.00 in Canada)

Shipping and handling
$4.00 per book $_____

TOTAL ENCLOSED $_____

Make checks payable to:
  PHILOPTOCHOS COOKBOOK

Or charge to: ☐ VISA   ☐ MASTERCARD

Acct. No. ☐☐☐☐-☐☐☐☐-☐☐☐☐-☐☐☐☐

Expiration date: _____

_____
SIGNATURE OF CARDHOLDER

_____
ADDRESS (IF DIFFERENT THAN MAILING ADDRESS ABOVE)

_____
CITY / STATE / ZIP (IF DIFFERENT THAN MAILING ADDRESS ABOVE)

Send Order to:
  Philoptochos Society of Holy Trinity
      Greek Orthodox Church
  3131 N.E. Glisan Street
  Portland, OR 97232

Phone or Fax Orders Welcome:
  (503) 234-0468 phone
  (503) 236-8379 fax
Or visit us at our website:
  http://www.flavoritgreek.org

Books are available at special discounts when purchased in bulk for premiums and sales promotions as well as for fundraising and educational use.

All proceeds from the sale of Flavor It Greek! A Celebration of Food, Faith and Family will be returned to the community through projects sponsored by Philoptochos Society of Holy Trinity Greek Orthodox Church, Portland, Oregon.

Order Form

Flavor It Greek! A Celebration of Food, Faith and Family

The Perfect Gift...   ☐ Gift ☐ Personal
Please send to:

NAME
_____

MAILING ADDRESS
_____

CITY / STATE / ZIP
_____

PHONE
_____

Please send _____ copies $_____
x $29.95 ea. ($38.00 in Canada)

Shipping and handling
$4.00 per book $_____

TOTAL ENCLOSED $_____

Make checks payable to:
  PHILOPTOCHOS COOKBOOK

Or charge to: ☐ VISA   ☐ MASTERCARD

Acct. No. ☐☐☐☐-☐☐☐☐-☐☐☐☐-☐☐☐☐

Expiration date: _____

_____
SIGNATURE OF CARDHOLDER

_____
ADDRESS (IF DIFFERENT THAN MAILING ADDRESS ABOVE)

_____
CITY / STATE / ZIP (IF DIFFERENT THAN MAILING ADDRESS ABOVE)

Send Order to:
  Philoptochos Society of Holy Trinity
      Greek Orthodox Church
  3131 N.E. Glisan Street
  Portland, OR 97232

Phone or Fax Orders Welcome:
  (503) 234-0468 phone
  (503) 236-8379 fax
Or visit us at our website:
  http://www.flavoritgreek.org

Books are available at special discounts when purchased in bulk for premiums and sales promotions as well as for fundraising and educational use.

All proceeds from the sale of Flavor It Greek! A Celebration of Food, Faith and Family will be returned to the community through projects sponsored by Philoptochos Society of Holy Trinity Greek Orthodox Church, Portland, Oregon.